An
Oasis
in
TIME

HOW A DAY OF REST
CAN SAVE YOUR LIFE

MARILYN PAUL

RODALE.

To David and Ari

RODALE
wellness
Live happy. Be healthy. Get inspired.

Sign up today to get exclusive access to our authors, exclusive bonuses, and the most
authoritative, useful, and cutting-edge information on health, wellness, fitness, and living your
life to the fullest.

Visit us online at RodaleWellness.com

Join us at RodaleWellness.com/Join

Book design by Amy King

Library of Congress Cataloging-in-Publication Data is on file with the publisher.

ISBN 978-1-62336-662-9 hardcover

Distributed to the trade by Macmillan

2 4 6 8 10 9 7 5 3 1 hardcover

We inspire health, healing, happiness, and love in the world.

Starting with you.

Contents

Introduction: Ancient Wisdom for Modern Times......................................v

PART I: GETTING STARTED

Chapter 1: Living in Overdrive: We're Moving Too Fast 3

Chapter 2: Stopping Work: A Lively History and Energetic Debates 22

Chapter 3: What Is an Oasis in Time?..36

Chapter 4: Get Traction for Change..58

PART II: PUTTING IT INTO PRACTICE

Chapter 5: Design Your Oasis Time..79

Chapter 6: Protect and Prepare: Planning for Oasis Time 98

Chapter 7: Living Oasis Time 121

Chapter 8: Don't Let Anything Stop You.....................................141

PART III: TAKING BACK YOUR TIME

Chapter 9: Take Stock...161

Chapter 10: Strengthening Boundaries 175

Chapter 11: Navigating Your Days: Five Key Practices...................192

Chapter 12: Beyond a Haven, an Incubator..................................210

Appendix A: Quick Start for a Slow Time 223

Appendix B: Oasis Time Mini-Guide...225

Appendix C: Remember the Sabbath—A Christian View....................229

Appendix D: Additional Resources—Books 233

Appendix E: Additional Resources..239

Endnotes 241

Acknowledgments...249

Index...253

Introduction

$$\left\{\begin{array}{c}\text{ANCIENT WISDOM FOR}\\\text{MODERN TIMES}\end{array}\right\}$$

O ur passion for efficiency, effectiveness, and exertion has gone too far. We live today in a unique era of possibility and productivity; we love getting things done, but we are burning ourselves out. We stay up late trying to catch up on work, but we end up wasting time online, leaving us more behind than when we started. We use apps that promise to focus our minds and our time, but none of it really sticks. Instead of savoring our one precious life, we squander our natural vitality on endless to-dos and the stress of multitasking.

Many of us already know the value of slowing down, and we try to squeeze in a walk, a talk with a friend, or a good relaxed meal here and there. Maybe we even meditate or pray regularly—or at least think about it. But our efforts don't make a dent in the growing burden of fatigue we carry around. We have resigned ourselves to being spent and struggling to feel our natural vitality. Even when we can grab an hour or two of refreshment, our physical, emotional, and spiritual weariness soon returns.

We know we need to get off the merry-go-round, but how?

There's a way out of the constant action, pressure, and tension. It's a practice that is thousands of years old, with many different names—Shabbat, Sabbath, respite, and an oasis in time—and it is just as necessary and meaningful now as it was centuries ago. But for many, the very word *Sabbath* can bring up painful and unwanted associations—so much so that many folks reject the idea out of hand. The root of the word Sabbath just means "stop or cease." But the word has been overwhelmed by centuries of other meanings and associations.

I am writing this book to show how people can create a new type of weekly retreat, one that is so refreshing and nourishing that it changes their lives. But it may require letting go of some old perceptions. Images of restriction dominate our impressions of traditional days of rest. Who believes that they will be enriched by sitting absolutely still while being chastised in church, or by going to synagogue and listening to hours of mumbled, incomprehensible prayers? Or as a friend of mine, an Episcopal priest, described it: "a day of sitting on a couch, staring at the wall"?

Laura Ingalls Wilder's Little House series captures this distress in her descriptions of life during the pioneer days at the turn of the last century. In *Little House in the Big Woods,* the first book in the series, Wilder describes her grandfather's boyhood Sabbaths:

> *They must walk slowly and solemnly, looking straight ahead. They must not joke or laugh, or even smile. Grandpa and his two brothers walked ahead, and their father and mother walked behind them. . . . In church, Grandpa and his brothers must sit perfectly still for two long hours and listen to the sermon . . . and never for one instant take their eyes from the preacher.*[1]

If you remember what it was like to be a child, you know how hard that must have been.

In a more recent but equally painful account, popular author of *The Man Who Mistook His Wife for a Hat,* Oliver Sacks, MD, offered a beautiful and poignant description of Shabbat—the Hebrew word for Sabbath—with his family during his youth in London. He loved the closeness of his family celebration, but he could not stomach the intolerance and prejudice of the religion he experienced. Feeling deeply rejected by his family for being gay, he put Shabbat aside when he left home.

Later in his life, however, he gratefully returned to a traditional Shabbat, discovering that he could be gay and still warmly included by part of his family. "I find my thoughts, increasingly, . . . on what is meant by living a good and worthwhile life—achieving a sense of peace within oneself. I find my thoughts drifting to the Sabbath, the day of rest . . . when one can feel that one's work is done, and one may, in good conscience, rest."[2] Dr. Sacks's experience offers us a way of moving forward by taking what is best about the Sabbath and fitting it to our own lives, needs, and desires.

In the popular media, among secular writers, in the corporate world, and in churches and synagogues, people are rediscovering the benefits of taking a weekly day off for rest and renewal. This new Sabbath—which doesn't have to be based in a religious practice—is about committing time each week to remember who we really are; to reconnect with our best selves; to play, rest, reflect, and refresh; and to join with like-minded others in a time and space without action items, deadlines, and the pressure to achieve. Creating an "oasis in time," a safe haven for personal restoration, is not only the way out, but it's also the way up.

Taking back our time is a subversive act these days. It entails claiming that we are much more than producers and consumers. That we are not only about end results. That the state of our hearts and souls really matters. That we need to express our deep care for community without any haste. That we can have a good day without achieving anything other than unwinding, slowing down, connecting, and experiencing grace.

To truly reap its benefits, we need to approach our oasis with purpose. This book offers you a path to creating dedicated time each week for enjoyment, renewal, reflection, and deepening your sense of the sacred. It's hard to turn toward awe when you are racing from one thing to the next. But you can learn to put your tasks aside to protect your downtime. And you'll see how that time can renew and enrich your entire life.

Digging for Hidden Treasure

I'm a coach and organizational change consultant. I help people work together better, and lately I have been helping teams and organizations work through the pernicious costs of chronic work overload. I often recommend a full day off each weekend for all employees, but I see that many leaders in my client organizations are stumped about how to make that happen. They promote 24/7 availability. So, in part, this is a guide for them and for you.

I, myself, stumbled upon weekly rest time. I'm Jewish but wasn't particularly interested in Jewish practice. When I was in graduate school, though, I had a friend who invited me to his *havurah*—a group that had Friday night meals together. And so I was introduced, reluctantly, to this Sabbath practice of a day off a week. To my surprise, I liked it. And I knew I needed it.

Slowly I learned how to keep Shabbat. It became a reliably replenishing part of my week. As I learned how to guard this time off, I could see how much it improved my life. I was single at that time. When I was dating, I let people know that this was an essential part of my way of life. I remember one of my first phone conversations with David, my husband. He invited me to join him for a movie on a Friday night. I told him that I didn't go out on Fridays. And, I said, "If that is going to be a problem, then it's best if we don't go out." Strong words, but true. David assured me that this would not be a problem for him. But it was. Not enough of a problem to keep us from getting married; however, our views on taking a day off each week have been very different. And that was challenging for a while, but our differences led to this book. We needed to find ways to create a day off every week that we could both enjoy and both support. And, now we both deeply value our oasis in time. It gives us time for each other, for our son, and for interests we wouldn't pursue if we were on the 24/7 plan.

Our oasis time has become so rewarding that I wanted to introduce it to everyone I knew. In this book, I show you how to dig for this valuable treasure, how to brush off the dust and polish it so that it becomes a sparkling jewel, significantly enhancing your life.

We can embrace the Sabbath elements that match our own priorities and interests. We can cultivate respite in ways that work for us. We can find our own communities and our own ways to show we care. In short, the Sabbath, as people construe it now, can be a powerful resource for nurturing our souls and building a stronger sense of connectedness.

If this vision is appealing but the idea of creating an oasis in time seems overwhelming and infeasible; if you feel completely overcommitted and can't even take an evening off; or if the idea of a big change in your life generates more anxiety than relief, rest assured: There is still a path for you. You can carve out time that will enhance your productivity and effectiveness. You can start slowly and build up, you can identify a purpose and find ways to fulfill it, you can work Sabbath into your weekly life and then, if you want, you can expand it. And you can do it your way.

At its heart, the Western spiritual tradition has bequeathed us a treasure. Our Judeo-Christian-Islamic heritage tells us to stop once a week and rest, to break the pattern of the workweek and connect with what is most important. The Jewish tradition uses the Hebrew term *vayinafash*, which translates as "restore your soul," to describe what happens on the Sabbath day. This restoration improves the quality of our lives not only on that day, but also throughout the week.

DO YOU NEED THIS BOOK?

In the chapters that follow, I'll accompany you down a path toward one of the most powerful experiences you will ever have. The first step on this path is to understand the possibilities open to you if you make this change—and, equally important, the immense costs of simply continuing on as you are.

This is a book in three parts. Part I is called Getting Started. In this section, you will find everything you need to get going on your journey toward your oasis time. Chapter 1 is about the many costs of living in overdrive. Chapter 2 gives you a bit of history and background on the sources of the Sabbath, which oasis time is based on. In Chapter 3, you will learn about the five gateways to oasis time. And Chapter 4 gives you a way to get traction on creating oasis time.

Part II is called Putting It into Practice. Here you will learn how to get your oasis time up and running (or down and stopping!). Chapter 5 gives you tools to design your oasis time. Chapter 6 helps you protect it and prepare for it. Chapter 7 provides lots of stories and alternative ways to spend a day off, and Chapter 8 helps you overcome some of the obstacles you might meet along the way.

Part III, Taking Back Your Time, answers the question of how to make different choices each week so that you can take weekly time off. Chapter 9 shows you how to take stock of your current choices concerning time and how to find unseen openings. Chapter 10 shows how to strengthen your boundaries, which are essential for creating oasis time. And Chapter 11 details five basic practices that will help you get yourself, your time, and your energy under control.

Chapter 12 concludes the journey by looking at the larger picture: what oasis time can be for us and how living in oasis time can collectively lead us to a better future.

Stepping out of the relentless march once a week will call for courage and support, and I will show you how to get both. More and more people are recognizing that to have the good life, they need to stop once a week. Here is what mega-bestselling author Elizabeth Gilbert has to say about why she turns away from her beloved social media and rests each week.

> *I look forward to my weekly digital Sabbath as a way of lifting my face from my multiple screens (glorious as they are!) and drawing breath— and as a way of finding creative off-line ways to spend my time....*

Then, by Monday morning, I can return (like a stranger from a distant land) to my online life. . . . But I come back restored, and even excited to jump back into the digital world and see what I've missed. (And here's what I've noticed: I don't miss much. Also, so many of the "urgent" problems that people e-mailed me about two days earlier, somehow found a way to solve themselves during my absence from the Internet. AMAZING.)[3]

Oasis time helps you reorient to what matters most in life. It resets your inner compass so that you can remember and act on what is important. It provides time for you to rest and regain your bearings. It breaks the fatigue and burnout cycle that robs you of your zest and health. It provides time for genial, unhurried connections with others. In other words, a weekly day of rest can restore your deepest connections and communities and, in so doing, save your life.

Part I: Getting Started

1

LIVING IN OVERDRIVE

We're Moving Too Fast

We live in speeded-up times. We value hustle, big goals, and the rush of accomplishment. We love efficiency and effectiveness. Even our leisure activities can feel like boxes on a checklist. Meditate: Check. Exercise: Check. Volunteer: Check. Cook a nice meal: Check. Plan special activities with the kids or with friends: Check. We add more and more tasks to our days until our lives feel more like one long list of things that must get done than a series of deeply soul-satisfying experiences.

In his famous movie *Modern Times,* Charlie Chaplin plays his Little Tramp as a factory worker at a company whose goal is to speed up production. To that end, the company introduces the Billows Feeding Machine, which feeds lunch to the workers while they are still on the assembly line. Work never stops. The proud inventor of the machine, J. Widdecombe Billows, introduces Charlie's character to the revolving platefuls of food, the automatic food pusher, and the hydro-compressed, sterilized mouth wiper. There are three delicious courses, but poor

Charlie cannot eat fast enough, and the machine goes out of control, maniacally slapping food all over his face. Today, few of us would even consider a three-course lunch; instead, we eat nutritional power bars so we can skip lunch altogether and keep working. Is Charlie, the Little Tramp, enjoying his lunch break? Of course not. We're not enjoying ours much either.

WE ARE WORKING TOO HARD

Let me introduce you to a few people I know who are trying their hardest to live well and who feel trapped in nonstop activity.

Alan, a computer-savvy physician, went into health information systems with a strong sense of a healing mission, fully intending to contribute his unusual skill set to transforming the way medicine is delivered. But his description of an average day shows the deep impact of his team's chronic overwork.

Sleep poorly. Awaken worried about getting through day because of fatigue.

Pledge to stay cool, avoid snapping.

Arrive in time for first meeting, but without real time to organize day because meetings start earlier and earlier—eight o'clock is the new nine o'clock.

Rush from meeting to meeting—never fully prepared.

Keep trying to stay friendly, calm, avoid "anger seepage."

Rush home late, no time to clean up from day.

Many things undone, swear to do them that night. Skip exercise.

Cranky with family. Wife, kids don't think you are much fun.

Work after dinner but don't finish.

Go to bed worrying about items left unfinished. Fall asleep at 1:00 or 2:00 a.m. after taking an Ambien.

Alan sees the irony that his own health is suffering as he misses out on good times with his family and feels constantly overwhelmed and exhausted. He wants to break free from the cycles of tension he feels caught in—recently, he started meditating, which helps a bit—but most of the time, he just can't stop, even to take one weekend off. Like many people, Alan lives in a tyranny of busyness under a trance of constant action.

Alan is just one of millions of people struggling to keep up within a culture avid for productivity. The American Institute of Stress reports that job pressures are far and away the major source of tension for Americans. Job stress costs an estimated $300 billion (yes, that's billion, not million) a year in absenteeism, turnover, diminished productivity, and medical, legal, and insurance costs.[1] Ironically, ongoing stress ultimately causes people to work far less productively, thus requiring more time on the job to complete the same amount of work. Why do people put up with the stress? *When people believe that their value comes from their accomplishments, it is especially hard to stop striving for those accomplishments.*

Barbara is a lawyer for a real estate conglomerate outside of Atlanta. Like many lawyers, she tracks her time in six-minute increments. She's under constant pressure and feels that she doesn't have enough time even to track her time properly. She is constantly behind. Weekends are a blur of catching up on errands and household maintenance and squeezing in a workout and an occasional brunch with friends. Barbara deeply values her friendships and misses time connecting with herself and others. She would love to take a break of some kind, any kind, but she is too far behind to consider a vacation.

Like many Americans, Barbara feels that if she takes time off, she will put her work and her job in jeopardy. Americans have among the fewest paid days off of workers in any developed country, and what days they receive are often forfeited: In 2013, US employees failed to use 500 million vacation days—more than *$100 billion* worth of paid time.[2] Additionally, the United States is the only advanced economy that does not mandate vacation time. Twenty-five percent of full-time workers in the

United States have no paid vacation at all. Not surprisingly, 70 percent of Americans feel vacation deprived. By contrast, the Netherlands is almost as productive as the United States, yet the Dutch "work shorter hours each day, get six weeks' paid vacation, and are even given an 8% holiday bonus," according to a 2012 *Time* article.[3]

Layla is an interior designer in suburban Chicago. She chose to work from home so she could have more control over her time and more time with her kids. But it's not working out that way. Layla loves her work. Color, texture, and fabric feed her sense of vitality, and she has a special gift for helping people create a deep sense of home. But her days are a conglomeration of attending client meetings, ordering furniture, writing proposals, invoicing, and responding to urgent client requests. Her kids are in after-school care, and her weekends are packed with errands and cobbled-together playdates. When asked about the possibility of dedicated time off each week, Layla responds, "I love the idea, but that's out of the question. I just have too much to do." She's been having trouble sleeping as she runs *the everydayathon,* an apt term coined by Loyola University philosophy professor Al Gini, PhD. Self-employment, sadly, doesn't get us off the treadmill.

Layla joins the millions of us who are sleep deprived—40 percent of Americans, according to a recent Gallup poll. Good sleep is just as important to our health as exercise and good food. Researchers have found that remaining awake for 17 to 19 hours in a row leads to an impairment of cognitive abilities similar to being legally drunk.[4] Imagine what happens after days, weeks, months, and years of sleep deprivation. Yet many of us believe that we can forgo hours of sleep and pay no price.

From an early age, Nashville-based James looked at his overworked baby boomer parents and swore he was going to live a different kind of life. Now he's a musician who loves playing gigs on weekends and working with troubled teens during the week. He has a couple of interesting part-time jobs, and he makes sure he always has time for music, his true love. Yet James doesn't get a break either, for, as he told me, he never feels that he has quite earned it. He's considered practicing a type of Sabbath time, but he rarely thinks he has done enough to merit carving out real downtime. He knows he would love it, but, like his parents, oddly enough, he can't make the time to fully rest and renew his soul.

Alan, Barbara, and Layla face the same challenge in their individual ways: Our culture is obsessed with getting things done. Even James, the musician who has constructed his life to avoid being like his overworked parents, struggles to take time for himself. The social and economic pressures of work and achievement are so fierce that they even shape the experiences of those who consciously try to resist them.

We live in a world that doesn't understand the true, measureable value and benefits of downtime, and we are suffering because of it.

Do you see yourself in these stories and statistics? I do. I move too fast and do too much. I'm juggling work, motherhood, marriage, improving my health, connecting with friends, and homeschooling my son, not to mention trying to get good food on the table and maintain a livable home. I'm always striving to learn how to manage my time better and be more focused. In fact, I wrote a book about it: *It's Hard to Make a Difference When You Can't Find Your Keys.*

Fortunately, I have found this weekly release valve that saves my life. That is what this book is about. Before I describe the path to oasis time, however, I want us to understand some of the causes and effects of our nonstop lifestyle. It's worth naming the high price we pay so that we fully commit to envisioning new ways of getting our lives back.

HEALTH COSTS OF STRESS

Stress can motivate us and boost productivity in the short term, but the *chronic* stress most of us experience is toxic. Here's how costly long-term stress is to our health: According to the American Psychological Association, 75 percent of health-care costs are associated with chronic illness, and stress is a key driver of chronic illness. More than 133 million Americans— or 45 percent of the population—have at least one chronic condition, such as arthritis, asthma, cancer, heart disease, depression, or diabetes. And these are just a few examples of the many chronic illnesses that negatively affect the lives of Americans.[5]

Consider, for example, the impact of stress on one of our country's most costly chronic diseases, diabetes. According to the American Diabetes Association, "In people with diabetes, stress can alter blood glucose levels in two ways: People under stress may not take good care of themselves. They may drink more alcohol or exercise less. They may forget, or not have time, to check their glucose levels or plan good meals. Stress hormones may also alter blood glucose levels directly."[6] Some studies have suggested that unhealthy chronic stress management, such as overeating "comfort" foods, has contributed to the growing obesity epidemic. Half of us in the United States are either diabetic or prediabetic.

Stress leads to insomnia. More than 40 percent of us lie awake at night because of stress, and losing even one hour of sleep a night significantly hampers everyday performance. Stressed-out adults can lie awake for hours or turn to sleep medication for help, but sleep aids have significant side effects. Sleeping pill use and emergency room visits that result from overmedication with sleep aids are both on the rise.[7]

Stress may be linked to alcohol overuse. Excessive alcohol consumption is responsible for 88,000 deaths each year, more than half of which are due to binge drinking. About 38 million US adults report binge drinking an average of four times a month, with an average of eight drinks per binge. Most binge drinkers are not alcohol dependent, and one cause of binge drinking is reported to be "winding down" or relaxing after a stress-filled period.[8]

What is causing the stress that leads to so much illness? Workplace-related stress can be blamed for a lot of it, but other stressors include worries about money, housing costs, and family relationships. Unresolved conflict with other people is a source too. Additionally, loneliness and social disconnection are significant stressors that can lead to poor health. Researchers at the University of Pittsburgh School of Medicine found that high rates of loneliness were correlated with the occurrence of heart disease in women.[9] In contrast, *National Geographic* journalist Dan Buettner has written about scientific research into longevity in certain areas of the world where high numbers of people live into their nineties and hundreds in good physical and mental shape. Now known as Blue

Zones, these areas share one essential factor: a sense of belonging, or what Buettner calls "timeless congeniality."

The American Psychological Association reports that extreme and long-term stress can take a severe emotional toll. While people can overcome minor episodes of stress by tapping into their body's natural defenses to adapt to changing situations, excessive chronic stress can be psychologically and physically debilitating. Unlike everyday stressors, which can be managed with healthy stress management behaviors, untreated chronic stress may result in serious health conditions, including anxiety, insomnia, muscle pain, high blood pressure, and a weakened immune system, all of which contribute to diabetes and prediabetes.[10]

The $300 billion annual cost of job stress mentioned earlier doesn't capture the costs to our lives day to day and year to year. Stress makes our lives harder to live and reduces the pleasure of living. We struggle with creating deep and lasting friendships. We struggle to feed ourselves healthfully. Our enjoyment of ourselves and each other is largely diminished as we race from one activity to the next and then collapse, exhausted, at the end of the day. This is not how we want to live.

THE COSTS OF TECHNOLOGY

Digital technology is a big piece of what keeps us running. We carry our smartphones, tablets, and laptops with us wherever we go. Google Docs and Dropbox make our work accessible on any device, anytime, anywhere. E-mail, texts, and apps let us stay in constant communication with colleagues, friends, and family alike. Lifestyle apps are omnipresent, whether we use them to grab an Uber ride home from work, order takeout, or look up the schedule of the nearest yoga studio to see if we can fit a class into our day.

While technology can be a boon to productivity and enhance our lives significantly, its downside is becoming more evident. Technology is developing into a significant barrier to communication and connection even among the family members with whom we share our homes. American teenagers average almost nine hours of entertainment media use each day,[11] while adults, according to a recent Nielsen report, spend eleven hours per day on various media, including the Internet, TV, and radio. In her book *Reclaiming Conversation,* Sherry Turkle quotes a fifteen-year-old who says he would like to bring up his kid the way his parents *think* they are bringing him up. They think that they have cell phone–free dinners and that they are really there for soccer games, but that is not what this teen experiences.[12]

Rushed parents are often unaware of how hurt their kids feel when they are not available. To parents, it often seems like all kids want is more screen time. We don't realize that, in fact, our absorption in our own devices is sending a powerful message to our children. When Tanya Schevitz, a leader in the digital detox movement, talked with eighth graders about technology challenges, she thought they might discuss peer pressure on social media, or sexting. What they said instead floored her. They only wanted to talk about how hard it was to get their parents' attention. One eighth-grade boy said, "When my mom is on her phone [texting or e-mailing or on Facebook], she doesn't even talk to me. I will try to talk to her about important stuff, but she's on her phone and she doesn't even look up. It happens a lot." Another boy said, "My dad will just ignore me when I'm trying to talk to him. I don't think it is intentional. He will be on his e-mail or on Facebook, and there is just a big silence when I say something. I just get angry."[13]

I didn't think I checked my phone that much or made calls that often when I was with my son, Ari. But when he was nine, he delivered his verdict: I was a phone addict. Every time I picked up the phone, he would say, "You see, you're on the phone again." At first I brushed off his critique. Couldn't he see that I used my phone significantly less often than most people? But although that might have been true, I still used it when he was around. When he began asking for more screen time, I reluctantly started taking his feedback seriously. I wanted to model for him that making face-to-face connections is more important than digital availability; to do that, I needed to change my own phone behavior. He taught me to keep my phone down—even for brief text exchanges—so I could keep my hands and mind free to be totally present with him. I treasure the spontaneous moments of connection and humor that I would miss if I were still tethered to my phone and making excuses for it.

Face-to-face connection is vital for well-being. People thrive when they spend regular mealtimes and playtimes together, and the potential costs of missing these times are huge. Research shows that kids whose families eat meals together are more likely to succeed in school, consume healthy food, and feel self-confident. Perhaps most important, these kids are far less likely to abuse drugs and alcohol.[14] Researchers at Emory University have found that sharing family stories—something that can happen only when parents and children have windows of relaxed time together—can lead to higher self-esteem, better family functioning, greater family cohesiveness, and lower levels of anxiety in children.

The benefits are not just for kids: In her book *Wired to Connect,* about relational neuroscience, Amy Banks, MD, cites study after study that demonstrates conclusively and irrefutably that relationships help us be well and emotionally healthy.[15] We disconnect at our peril. Staying meaningfully connected with others leads to a greater sense of calm, less stress, less anxiety, greater productivity, better cardiovascular health, reduced likelihood of cancer, and fewer premature deaths from all causes. Whew! We need to find the time and attentiveness to make these essential connections happen. Moderating our use of digital technology is one essential step.

The Costs of Burnout

The combination of a stressed immune system and the overuse of technology can lead to another serious outcome: burnout. This one word is so powerful, and yet it hardly captures the deep emotional and spiritual costs of losing one's inner flame. Burnout is serious and hard to repair. Waking up without a taste for the day ahead destroys joy. We can get used to living that way—and many people do—but it leads to life as a form of despair rather than an embrace of the richness around us.

Many of us aren't savoring our lives. We may have more than enough in the way of belongings and interesting activities, yet we have a pervasive sense of emptiness, a vague dissatisfaction. Burnout diminishes our ability to savor our quality of work and our relationships. People who are chronically tired lose their gusto. At that point, life tastes like dust because we've become too exhausted to relish it.

For activists and entrepreneurs alike—indeed, for all of us—Trappist monk Thomas Merton's words describe another aspect of the most costly aspects of burnout: losing access to our inner wisdom.

> *There is a pervasive form of contemporary violence to which the idealist most easily succumbs: activism and overwork. The rush and pressure of modern life are a form, perhaps the most common form, of its innate violence. To allow oneself to be carried away by a multitude of conflicting concerns, to surrender to too many demands, to commit oneself to too many projects, to want to help everyone in everything, is to succumb to violence. The frenzy of our activism neutralizes our work for peace. It destroys our own inner capacity for peace. It destroys the fruitfulness of our own work, because it kills the root of inner wisdom which makes work fruitful.*[16]

At times, we vaguely realize the cost of our extreme achievement-oriented lifestyle, but it is even more expensive than we think. In his stunning book, *The Rest of God,* Pastor Mark Buchanan eloquently describes his costly descent into burnout.

> *I noticed at some point that the harder I worked, the less I accomplished. I was often a whirligig of motion. . . . To justify myself I would tell others that I was gripped by a magnificent obsession. I was purpose-driven. . . . The inmost places suffered most. I was losing perspective. Fissures in my character worked themselves into cracks. Some widened into ruptures.*[17]

Tony Schwartz, who is known for his breakthrough energy-based approach to time management, observed that if he wasn't being productive, he got scared.

I have spent much of my adult life struggling to believe it is accept-
able to simply, and deeply, relax. I come by this conviction honestly.
Both my parents worked obsessively. I grew up believing my value
was inextricably connected to what I accomplished—with my brain—
in every moment. If I wasn't producing something tangible, I quickly
began to feel anxious and unmoored.[18]

When Schwartz faced open, unscheduled space or time, or just one of
the simple pleasures of life, he became very uncomfortable. While he
doesn't call it burnout, he describes how he lost his taste for simple pleasures. He didn't even like walking his dogs, because he felt it was a waste
of his time. He wasn't able to relax and simply enjoy the moments that
could be enjoyable.

Leadership development consultant Dave Schrader, PhD, offers a
powerful metaphor for the way many of us feel about work and life: "The
bullet has left the gun, and we're trying to outrun it" before it hits us in the
back, Dr. Schrader says. "There is no rest, no recovery, and no useful reflection when we're running that hard."[19] It's true that we can feel energized by
having so much to do and no time to think. Yet at the end of the day, we
might sit in an exhausted stupor, feeling a trace of sadness because we've
lost the ability to relax as wholly as we work. Burnout means that we aren't
sure why we are doing what we are doing and we just don't care as much in
a world that desperately needs care and conviction.

The Benefits of Downshifting Weekly

The answer to the pressing problem of not having enough time is to
downshift for one day a week. This may sound completely paradoxical, if
not semi-insane. Am I arguing that the solution to not having enough
time is not to develop better time-management skills but to learn the
skills for taking a day off every week? Yes, that is exactly what I am saying. By routinely—one might even say religiously—taking time to rest,
relax, and savor life, we restore ourselves so that we manage our working
hours with far more gusto and heart and, often, more productivity.

Many employers are coming to realize that giving employees solid breaks is good for business. More and more companies are enforcing e-mail time-outs, vacation days, and mandatory shutdowns during holidays. PricewaterhouseCoopers is experimenting with no after-hours e-mail. Johnson & Johnson is promoting e-mail-free weekends. Not long ago, investment bank Goldman Sachs told its junior investment analysts that they had to take Saturdays off. JPMorgan Chase and ten other banks soon followed with one required weekend off a month. (Many European companies forbid e-mail use after hours.) Even though just anticipating after-hours e-mail leads to greater exhaustion, it's hard to stop checking. Some companies are going so far as to eliminate e-mail entirely—both in and out of the office. According to a 2015 BBC article, "While the no e-mail trend seems like it would be only for the most maverick of companies, it's taking root in a range of industries ... even Halton Housing Trust, a UK-based housing nonprofit [that] manages thousands of homes."[20]

Morten Primdahl, CTO of Zendesk, based in San Francisco, one of the fastest growing customer relations management companies says, "Most of the office is empty by 6:00 p.m. most days. Some people have long commutes, some work on the train, some need to pick up children; and we embrace the need for flexibility and the requirements of a modern family because of our belief in the benefits of a balanced life."[21]

We may want to create more awareness and joy in our lives, but most of us won't consider a full day off each week, or even part of a day, because we have too much to do. We fear that if we take a break, we will get further behind and lost under a mound of unfinished tasks. Much of this comes from a cultural bias for constant action and a lack of awareness of the high costs of constant work.

What we need to remember is that for millennia, many in the Western world have kept a weekly day of rest and renewal—with no catastrophic consequences. Indeed, that day off can have the opposite effect. Retired professional basketball player Tamir Goodman (aka the Jewish Jordan) credits his day of rest with being "the backbone of [his] energy and

... power throughout [his] basketball career." San Francisco Bay Area entrepreneur Noah Alper says, "There is no question in my mind that Shabbat was key to my success. It gave me the rest I needed. It would recharge me for the whole week." Senator Joseph Lieberman attributes his stamina to his Shabbat observance. He writes, "I have always been able to work harder on the six days knowing that the seventh day of rest is coming. He was even able to run for vice president while keeping a Sabbath.[22]

What does restorative time look like? Meaningful rest and renewal require more than just a break from regular activities. A full oasis in time includes *downtime, sleep time, time in reflection, connecting time,* and *playtime,* life-giving activities that are key parts of the "Healthy Mind Platter" as described by neuroscience researchers David Rock, PhD, and Daniel Siegel, MD. In fact, according to Drs. Rock and Siegel, these are *the fundamental nutrients for a healthy mind and a happy life.*[23]

This recipe for a healthy mind and happy living is identical in many ways to the activities of a Sabbath, a practice whose benefits are by no means limited to the religious. The word *Sabbath* comes from the Hebrew word that means "to stop or cease." What are we stopping? We stop working. We stop trying to get things done. We stop thinking that we are in charge. We stop prioritizing doing over being.

But there is far more depth to a Sabbath than simply stopping our routine. We don't just stop; we also *enter* an experience of timelessness. One hallmark of a Sabbath is that it is different from the regular week in activity and in tone. We enter a different world, what Rabbi Abraham Joshua Heschel famously describes as our "palace in time."

Those who have embraced the idea of a break from daily life note the different quality of this separate time. For many, the absence of technology is a key factor. In his bestselling book *Hamlet's BlackBerry,* William Powers describes his family's experiment with an Internet Sabbath.

We'd peeled our minds away from the screens where they had been stuck. We were really there with one another and nobody else and we could feel it. There was an atmospheric change in our minds, a shift to a slower, less restless, more relaxed way of thinking *[emphasis mine]. We could just be in one place, doing one particular thing and enjoy it.*[24]

New York Times food journalist Mark Bittman writes about his decision to take twenty-four hours off of his digital life each weekend: "Once I moved beyond the fear of being unavailable and what it might cost me, I experienced what, if I wasn't such a skeptic, I would call a lightness of being. *I felt connected to myself* rather than my computer."[25]

Arianna Huffington talks about a family vacation when everyone decided to put down their phones to travel with no social media contact.

> *Almost immediately, I was floored by the realization of just how much my phones had become almost physical extensions of myself—I would instinctively reach for them like phantom limbs! Unplugging meant rediscovering and savoring the moment for its own sake. Which is to say, taking in a view without tweeting it. Eating a meal without Instagramming it. Hearing my daughters say something hilarious and very shareable without sharing it. The unplugged version of myself was better able to give these things my full attention. And when I came back to the office, I was truly refreshed.*[26]

While Powers, Bittman, and Huffington found that taking a break connected them to themselves and their loved ones, bringing dedicated weekly time off into our lives can also help connect us to our planet. We are steeped in a brew of media messaging, popular culture, and entrenched habits that encourage an insatiable appetite for consumption without awareness of the environmental consequences. Time off for reflection and connection can pierce the veil of our environmental unconsciousness and deepen our awareness of how our nonstop consuming and producing creates danger for us as a species.

Indeed, entering a different world predicated upon stopping our daily habits has practical and positive consequences for the planet. Yosef Abramowitz, three-time Nobel Peace Prize nominee, notes that by taking time away from the cycle of consumption, we can see the impact we have on the planet. For example, in Israel on Yom Kippur, when a high percentage of citizens stop driving, the air quality drastically and visibly improves. Abramowitz, who is also known in Israel as Captain Sunshine for his promotion of solar energy fields, says that if we all took a day off from consuming and producing every week, we would collectively solve the problem of greenhouse gas emissions that promote global warming.

When we take regular time off, we also gain perspective on the larger world. We become less reactive and more open to connecting beyond our immediate communities. Our compassion and empathy for those in need increases.

Clearly, the benefits of weekly time off are enormous. But even though there is spiritual gold here, we will have to dig for it. A day off each week is definitely countercultural, and this treasure may take some effort to mine.

Is Weekly Time Off Possible?

A whole day of rest every week? Who has the time to actually do that? Millions of busy people, that's who—including CEOs, management consultants, secretaries, and tech people. Sabbath observers run the gamut of lives and professions and have all kinds of family pressures. My family and I are among them.

Years ago, I believed I had not a moment to spare for regular time off in my very busy life; my work, studies, and social commitments seemed to eat up twenty-*six* hours a day. I could have used eight days a week to get everything done, not six. Yet little by little, I found ways to carve out a weekly oasis in time, in part by paying close attention to my own needs and desires, and in part by returning to my Western spiritual heritage.

It took a while. As a young adult, I wasn't the least bit interested in Judaism, my family's heritage. To me, it seemed dusty and out of touch. I knew no Hebrew and wasn't interested in learning any. I started meditating at age seventeen and went to Buddhist retreats to learn a contemplative path. I fell in love with the Tibetan lineage. It offered a good set of practices to me, and it had nothing to do with the Bible.

In my twenties and thirties, I was a high-energy person who loved my nonstop days. When I went to Yale for graduate school in organizational change, I could stay up until one o'clock in the morning and get up at seven for a class or a breakfast meeting. I ran from meeting to meeting, from lunch with a friend here to a presentation there to drinks and dinner somewhere else. I loved what I was learning about creating healthier workplaces. I was high on action. Life was pressured, turbulent, chaotic, and very disorganized, but I kept moving. I would get tired—very tired— but I could always push through the fatigue.

Until one morning, to my horror, I couldn't get up. I was more than exhausted; something was really wrong. I stopped moving because I *had* to. I consulted with many doctors who had no answer for me, other than "Take a break. Get some rest." They didn't know what I had and didn't know how to treat it. After a year of seeking help, I was diagnosed with an immune deficiency disease. I understood this as a way of saying I had stretched my immune system to its limit. I couldn't live at a crazy pace anymore. I experimented with different diets, more meditation, and reducing my workaholic hours, but it still wasn't enough. I needed a complete overhaul of my life. But how?

Right around then, a friend invited me to a Shabbat dinner. I declined, actually, several times; I was still terribly ill and wasn't interested in going out to an unfamiliar setting. His persistence won out, and so one evening I struggled over to a gathering of his friends, walking slowly because my energy was limited. I remember walking into the living room and lighting candles with a group of people whom I'd never met.

I felt a sense of peace descend over the room and a collective sigh of relief—*the week was over.* We said blessings, performed some rituals, and sang totally unfamiliar songs. I didn't know how to do any of these things, yet those strangers welcomed me in and, over time, became friends. We met every month for a festive Shabbat dinner. With their support, I learned to slow down, change my life, and stop moving *on purpose*. I finally recognized that not only did I need to slow down, but I also needed to completely shift gears once a week. I needed to allow space for the ineffable to thrive in my life. I discovered that my health improved if I allowed myself a full day off to recover from the week.

Little by little, I brought this Sabbath practice into my life. First, I stopped trying to work for part of an evening, then for an evening and a morning. I learned to plan a different kind of time. The weekly time "off" was an elixir. Every week, it poured a balm of recuperation on my tired soul. I started to heal from my "incurable" illness. Over a year or two, I experienced the power of stopping my work, my rushing, and my intense focus on getting things done for a whole day every week. To my surprise, my life did not fall apart. In fact, it got so much better.

It took about a year to heal from the virus that had attacked my immune system, but I ultimately regained my health and well-being, finished my doctorate at a more moderate pace, and went on to thrive in the intense, hectic world of management consulting. By then, I had made a habit of entering Heschel's "palace in time" every week. And I never gave it up.

I drew on the well of traditional wisdom. I learned how much depth I can experience in life when I embrace and learn from my family's Jewish heritage. I learned that a Sabbath restores rhythm to my life and makes my life livable. No, actually far more than livable, for I now experience a full, lively, and connected life. Shabbat became my lifesaver, and the more I talk with others about it, the more I hear others say the same about their own rest practices.

The modern world's ambitious goals and untenable pace have made it impossible for us to regularly experience awe, wonder, well-being, and even reverence. We need a sense of timelessness, a space to breathe easily, so that we can experience ourselves and life as a gift and communicate our love. We can do oasis time in a totally life-enhancing, life-renewing way. Here in our time desert, oasis time gives us a chance for deep soul replenishment that is no mirage. What I want to do here is show how you too can take a weekly step off the treadmill and, religious or not, put this healing rhythm into your week.

When we integrate breaks into our lives, we get rhythm. When we get rhythm, we get perspective on our lives. We begin to see that there is life beyond the riveting, demanding pulsing of our workdays. We start to liberate the soul side of ourselves—the part that longs for music, song, dance, connectedness, sensuality, intimacy, and awe. We can replenish ourselves regularly. Then we go back to work with new eyes, new perspective, and new energy. Like William Powers when he returns to work after his digital oasis time, we are calmer. He writes, "We now experienced . . . two states in an intermittent rhythm, so each could be appreciated in contrast to the other. When I returned to my screen on Monday morning, I was still in a Sabbath state of mind and could do my digital business with more calm and focus."[27] You have a little bit of distance from the workaday world. And when you live in that manner, you reduce the strain and the stress of everyday life. You change your pace during your oasis in time: You change your focus, you change what you are thinking about. You slow down. You turn toward other people in order to simply be with them.

Oasis time needs to be different from your everyday routine—slower, less technologically connected, and removed from the focus on achievement. It's vital to make a plan for this time, even if your plan is to do nothing, because without our plans and switch-off rituals, we easily revert to our default pace, orientation, and habits. We need strong forces that can lift us out of our everyday patterns. We might plan to be out in nature, to be with friends, to play music, make art, jump in the mud, go river rafting; or we might plan wide-open, unscheduled time to do nothing and go with the flow. The key, however, is a plan: Without the plan and the preparation to execute it, we will revert. "Do" mode will sneak back in, and before we know it we will go back to consulting our to-do lists, checking social media, and speeding up.

There is nothing wrong with an action-oriented default mode. It's a good way of life. Except for one big thing: Many of us can't seem to stop any longer than to pause, catch our breath, wave at one another in passing, and then keep going. As a result, we miss a treasured part of life. The life of being with friends and children, creating in a slow, deliberate, relaxed (for hours) way with no checking phones and jumping up to do the next urgent thing. We need a break from all of the running, doing, and being technologically connected. Part of the problem is that in this busy mode, there is never enough: not enough success, not enough money, not enough attention. We dwell in a state of lack. Even while we are trying to attract more and better somethings into our lives, we feel that something is missing.

How do we forge oasis time? We do it with conviction, determination, and even fierceness. We do this because we need it. We do this because we know that postmodern forces will chew us up and spit us out and, if we aren't careful, we too will look just as rushed, jaded, and unhappy as everyone else on the subway or in the market.

When we commit to oasis time, we seize the rhythm of rest and recovery out of the jaws of nonstop action and live to tell the tale. We become heroes on the journey toward the well-lived life. On the way, we get help and advice from philosophers, researchers, best-selling authors, and other people on the journey. We learn to be smart about corralling the nonstop messages that try to convince us to do more, be more, and have more. We don't need any "more" right now; we need love, care, and regular oasis time to reflect on what is important.

Let's turn to Chapter 2 now to learn where this sustaining social invention comes from.

STOPPING WORK

A Lively History and Energetic Debates

M illions of people take a day off each week. They are aided by strong religious, cultural, and even political traditions that call for weekly rest based on traditional wisdom. Our challenge is to figure out how to draw on these wisdom traditions to get the rest we sorely need. If we understand traditional Sabbath wisdom, we can transform it into a contemporary practice that is shaped less by rules and more by the values we cherish and want to enact in our daily and weekly lives. Religious tradition has provided the Sabbath's structure and community for the soul. For those of us who are creating our own spiritual path, it can be useful to know what has come before so we can use it to shape what lies ahead.

HISTORY

Sabbaths come in many shapes and forms. The root of the Hebrew word *Shabbat,* which in turn gives us our English word *Sabbath,* means "to stop or cease." Stop working, stop fretting, stop thinking about the minutiae of everyday life.

Regular rest days, which are woven deep into the fabric of Western spiritual history, have been a traditional Jewish, Christian, and Muslim practice over millennia. Buddhists have a Sabbath-like practice called *uposatha,* which is based on the lunar calendar. It is a day of intensifying meditation and study for "cleansing the defiled mind." Other peoples have also built rest time into their calendars. This widespread tradition testifies to the near-universal recognition that rhythms of action and rest are highly beneficial to the human mind and heart.

Sabbath time has been around for millennia. It seems to have emerged as agrarian society developed. Among the first people to rest "weekly" were the Babylonians, who had extensive restrictions on life every seven days. However, it appears that this pattern may have emerged independently and somewhat simultaneously in Hellenistic and Egyptian cultures as well.

There is no scholarly consensus on the origins of the Jewish Sabbath. Professor Eviatar Zerubavel believes it is very possible that the Jewish Sabbath was adapted from the 7th century BCE Assyrian religious observance of "evil days," which occurred every seventh day. The Assyrian king was forbidden from participating in activities like riding chariots and eating cooked meat every 7 days in the 50-day Assyrian week. The Jews were in exile in Babylonia, part of Assyria, in the 6th century BCE.

Though it is unclear exactly when Jews began observing the Sabbath themselves, Zerubavel claims that the Jewish Sabbath tradition is responsible for the transformation of the duration and rhythm of the 7-day week as the Westernized world currently knows it.[1]

The origins of the Christian Sabbath are better known. Early Christians chose Sunday, the first day of the week according to both Jewish and astrological calendars, as their day to remember and celebrate the Resurrection of Jesus Christ, which took place on a Sunday. Sunday became known as the Lord's Day. Early Christians, who were also Jews, observed both Saturday and Sunday, but as time went on, Christians were encouraged to drop their Saturday observance, for they were commemorating something different than the Jews. The Jews remember that God rested on the seventh day and brought them out of slavery; Christians commemorate Christ rising to heaven.

When Mohammed was exploring what day Muslims should take as their day of congregation and prayer, he chose Friday, in part because Saturday and Sunday were taken and he wanted to distinguish Islam from the other monotheistic religions. Muslims observe al-Jumu'ah—a day of congregation and prayer that also serves as a break from the work world—on Friday. The Qur'an says, "O ye who believe! When the call is proclaimed to prayer on Friday, hasten earnestly to the Remembrance of Allah, and leave off business: That is best for you if ye but knew."[2] The Qur'an continues, "But when they see some bargain or some amusement, they disperse headlong to it, and leave thee standing. Say: 'The blessing from the presence of Allah is better than any amusement or bargain! And Allah is the Best to provide for all needs.'"[3] Al-Jumu'ah is thus a call to leave one's worldly business behind in order to enter sacred time and holy union with the divine once every week.

In the Arab world, the weekend is Friday and Saturday, and the first day of the work week is Sunday. Many Muslim countries consider Friday a non-workday, a holiday, or a weekend.[4] Many historians trace the origin of the 7-day week as practiced in Westernized countries to the observance of the Jewish Sabbath.[5] The Sabbath, then, grounds our very conception of the 7-day week. Though the actual day of rest or prayer differs from Judaism to Christianity to Islam, it defines the rhythm of the week in each culture.

Author and teacher Noam Zion observes:

> Whether we are religiously observant or not, weeks measure our lives in the Judeo-Christian-Muslim culture. In the West, Mondays are utterly different in psychological tone than Fridays, for this cycle has a beginning and an end like the narrative of Creation. . . . The week begins with plans, progresses ideally in stages toward execution . . . and evaluation of progress. As God notes at the end of each day, "It is good." The end is harmony, greater order, and goodness.[6]

As a time for prayer and rest, the Sabbath provides a regularly recurring counterbalance to the week of work, creating a rhythm of harmony and order in our lives. In our TGIF culture, we all have rituals, whether we realize it or not, that signify some kind of ending of the workweek; from collapsing on the couch to socializing late into the night, there's an expectation that the weekend is when the fun happens, not only a collection of errands and chores. We still expect it to feel like a reward—but not all of us take measures to protect that time to ensure that the reward truly is edifying or rejuvenating.

In the Middle Ages, sacred time was interwoven with secular time in a world infused with a sense of the divine. In poignant contrast to our current sense of time famine, people in that era experienced an abundance of time. Well-to-do people carried their *book of hours*—a book of prayers and calendars of feast days—much as we carry our own book of hours, the planner. Work time and Sabbath time were natural parts of the cycle of people's lives, unlike today, where we often approach the exploration of sacred time with extreme caution and a combination of longing and suspicion. Unlike our forebears, we have to wrest Sabbath time out of the claws of our packed calendars.[7]

Struggles over Sabbath time, rest, and work have long been part of American history. Blue laws, laws that restrict activity on the Sabbath, originated in seventeenth-century New England colonies, where the Puritans were known for their restrictive moral practices. In the nineteenth century, a Sunday Sabbath remained a significant part of the social landscape and was enforced by law. Travelers on Sunday, for example, would probably not have been compensated for an injury they suffered because it was not considered appropriate to travel on Sunday.

Some laws specified what you had to do, such as this one from 1656:

> *Every person in this Jurisdiction, according to the mind of God, shall duly resort and attend worship upon the Lord's Day at least . . . and if any person, without just cause, absent himself from the same . . . shall forfeit five shillings.*[8]

Others stated what you couldn't do:

If a man kiss his wife or a wife kiss her husband on the Lord's Day, the party at fault, shall be punished, at the discretion of the Court of Magistrates.[9]

The historical record tells us a story of a man who had been traveling for several months and was caught kissing his wife in the doorway of their home just as he returned on Sunday. He was sent to jail.[10]

Blue laws, which were common in the United States into the 1950s and 1960s, were eventually contested because of their limitations of freedom of choice on Sundays. Today, there is pressure for stores to open not only on Sundays but even on holidays such as Thanksgiving. This, of course, denies store employees their opportunities for rest, not to mention shoppers who have less motivation to put their errands on hold for a day.

Blue laws have largely fallen away in all states, aside from some restrictions on activities like selling alcohol. In Bergen County, New Jersey, however, restrictions on commercial activity are maintained by popular vote—there's no selling of clothing, lumber and building supplies, office supplies, or office equipment. Why would people in this modern age vote for commercial restrictions one day a week? Why would a group of people voluntarily restrict their freedom once a week?

Judith Shulevitz, author of *The Sabbath World*, provides one answer to this question by quoting a legal opinion of Supreme Court Justice Felix Frankfurter on a case brought to eliminate Sunday closing laws in 1961. Sunday rest, Frankfurter said, is " 'a cultural asset of importance.' It undergirds American well-being. It provides a necessary 'release from the daily grind, a preserve of mental peace, an opportunity for self-disposition.'"[11] Justice Frankfurter noted the importance of a collective day of rest and concluded that the benefits of imposing this day of rest on those who don't observe a Sunday Sabbath far outweighed the costs to those who didn't.[12]

Of course, blue laws don't affect consumers alone. They also protect employees, allowing them to have a guaranteed day off, which has been a

Getting Started

focus of the labor movement's fight to limit work hours for almost as long as there have been unions. Labor unions fought for the forty-hour work-week and eight-hour workday. Underlying the struggle for shorter work-days and workweeks was the conviction that "Higher Progress" for humans could be gained for all as workweek hours diminished and work-days shortened.

Higher Progress was a dream of uplifting the human spirit through the education of the mind for the general public, not just the elites, and making the pursuit of art and culture available to everyone. As leisure time historian and professor Benjamin Kline Hunnicutt describes it, "Throughout labor's century-long shorter hours campaign, workers were led by a vision of freedom and progress that drew heavily from existing republican expectations and millennial hopes—visions of a future in which work was reduced to a minimum and ordinary people . . . would spend the best part of their lives . . . pursuing Higher Progress."[13] Whether for religion, justice, or visionary dreams, various peoples have fought for centuries to protect a day of rest as part of the week. They recognized that realizing one's full humanity requires time and space to do some-thing other than be industrious.

THE PURPOSE OF A SABBATH

Rabbi Abraham Joshua Heschel reminds us that the reasons for a Sabbath have been debated for centuries, if not millennia. Citing a first-century CE argument, Heschel says:

> *In defense of the Sabbath, Philo, the spokesman of the Greek-speaking Jews of Alexandria, says: "On this day we are commanded to abstain from all work, not because the law inculcates slackness. . . . Its object is rather to give man relaxation from continuous and unending toil and by refreshing their bodies with a regularly calculated system of remissions to send them out renewed to their old activities. For a breathing spell enables not merely ordinary people but athletes also to collect their strength with a stronger force behind them to under-take promptly and patiently each of the tasks set before them.*[14]

This vision of the Sabbath is in the spirit of Aristotle, who taught: "We need relaxation because we cannot work continuously." Relaxation, then, is not an end; it is "for the sake of activity,"[15] for the sake of gaining strengths for new efforts. In other words, we rest so that we can work better.

However, Heschel and many others see this differently. Heschel goes on to distinguish this idea of the relationship between work and rest from the biblical idea:

> *To the biblical mind, however, labor is the means towards an end, and the Sabbath as a day of rest, as a day of abstaining from toil, is not for the purpose of recovering one's lost strength and becoming fit for the forthcoming labor.* The Sabbath is a day for the sake of life *[emphasis mine]. Man is not a beast of burden, and the Sabbath is not for the purpose of enhancing the efficiency of his work.*[16]

Heschel here brings forward one of the two main themes, rest and freedom, of the Jewish Sabbath. The first theme is based on the idea that God rested after creating for six days. We are created in the image of God, Western scriptures say, so humans rest too.

But what exactly does "rest" mean here? God certainly didn't rest for a day to garner the energy to spend another week creating.

Genesis, Chapter 2, verses 1 through 3 says:

> *The heaven and the earth were finished, and all their array.*
> *On the seventh day God finished the work that He had been doing, and he ceased on the seventh day from all the work that He had done.*
> *And God blessed the seventh day and declared it holy, because on it God ceased from all the work of creation that He had done.*[17]
> [traditional translation]

The word *ceased* in Hebrew is shavat, from which we derive the word *Shabbat* or *Sabbath*. So on the seventh day, it's time to stop. This is the kind of rest that is valuable in, of, and for itself: the kind of rest that enables us to stop doing what we are doing and find life beyond purposeful action. Thus, this idea of the holy—to God and ourselves—opens up the idea of the Sabbath as much more than just preparation for more work. Rather, it becomes the essence of life itself, that which is holy.

Exodus, Chapter 20, verses 8 through 11, states the fourth commandment.

> *Remember the Sabbath day and keep it holy.*
> *Six days you shall labor and do all your work,*
> *but the seventh day is a Sabbath of the Lord your God: you shall*
> *not do any work—you, your son or daughter, your male or female*
> *slave, or your cattle, or the stranger who is within your settlements.*
> *For in six days the Lord made heaven and earth and sea, and all*
> *that is in them, and He rested on the seventh day, therefore the Lord*
> *blessed the Sabbath day and hallowed it.*[18]

We rest in order to appreciate that life is "very good," as God declares at the end of the six days of creating. As you can see in the fourth commandment, it is written, "Remember the Sabbath Day and keep it holy." It's not "Thou shalt not work." We are commanded to *remember* to stop. The implication is that we would forget to stop—forget that we are created in the image of the Creator, forget that we are holy, forget to appreciate how "very good" it all is—if we were not specifically commanded. Note how long this passage is. It's the longest of the Ten Commandments. Also note that it is on par with "You shall not murder." It is considered that important in the ancient Hebrew tradition.

The other theme of the Jewish Sabbath is freedom. In the prayer that Jews recite at the beginning of the Sabbath meal, they thank God for taking them out of Egypt: "As first among our sacred days, it [the Sabbath] recalls the Exodus from Egypt." The biblical perspective on the Sabbath is that human beings need to be reminded regularly that they are created to be free.

Freedom to stop working for a day means that we are not slaves. If we get a day off each week, it means that whatever pharaoh or king of Egypt (or, in today's times, whatever supervisor or project deadline) we are bowing down to moves over for a day. In the place of our despotic rulers comes a day of freedom from those despots. We can enumerate the many addictions that we have and all the things that we are dependent on, but on this type of Sabbath, we get a day off. Let's take a moment to look at those dictators so that we can understand more of what a Sabbath could be.

Escape from Pharaoh: The Dictators of Our Age

Too often what keeps us running is the compulsion to produce and consume. We define ourselves by what we do and what we have. When someone asks us what we do, we name our work, our projects, or our caregiving roles. Sabbath teaches us to take one day a week off of the treadmill to restore a deeper sense of who we are. We can then carry that sense with us through the week.

The nonstop-ness of aspirations and demands on our time comes to feel like oppression. What are the relentless forces that keep us marching forward? What are the building plans that never seem to be finished? What are the duties that we are hell-bent on performing well beyond the point of exhaustion? We are called to be aware of the many ways that we feel we are not in charge of our lives.

One of the great dictators in our world is the feeling that we never quite have enough. Whatever it is—enough health, enough good looks, enough clothes, or enough friends—we are raised to feel that we are lacking. So one powerful contemporary taskmaster is the inability to be satisfied with what we have. Philip Slater points out in *The Pursuit of Loneliness* that, perhaps surprisingly, "possessions actually create scarcity. The more emotion you invest in them, the more chances for real gratification are lost—the more committed to them you get, the more deprived you feel."[19] Or, as writer and environmentalist Bill McKibben observes, "The consumer society has one great weakness, one flank unprotected. And that is that for all its superficial sugary jazzy sexy appeal, it has not done a particularly good job of making people *happy*."[20]

Oasis time is a way to counter the relentless need to consume and produce. Pope Francis drew on this perspective in his second encyclical letter, *Laudato Si: On Care for Our Common Home*, in May 2015. Here he calls on us to rest weekly:

> *[Contemplative rest] . . . prevents that unfettered greed and sense of isolation which make us seek personal gain to the detriment of all else. . . . Rest opens our eyes to the larger picture and gives us renewed sensitivity to the rights of others. . . . and sheds its light on the whole week, and motivates us to greater concern for nature and the poor.*"[21]

We are not slaves, and we do have a choice about how we live. We can overcome the compulsion to produce. We can choose to put aside the outer and inner voices that tell us that we are running behind, can't keep up, and have no time to rest. Even though our country was built on slavery, we don't have to turn ourselves and each other into commodities.

Each week, we can create a little distance from the constant pull of everyday life and turn toward the sense of blessing, sovereignty, and wisdom that is our natural heritage, our birthright. Our nation's founders viewed the pursuit of happiness—originally identified as Higher Progress—as part of that birthright which now must be for every person.[22] And we can use this deeper understanding of the Sabbath as a haven and spur for justice, freedom, equity, and stewardship to guide us toward a healthier vision of our communities, our country, our continent, and our planet.

What Is Leisure?

Life is naturally fulfilling when we aren't trying to get more or do more. So when we stop working, what do we do? This inquiry into leisure goes back to the ancient Greeks, whose idea of the best way to occupy themselves was with explorations of the good life. They had no specific word for work—the word was *ascholia*, or "not leisure."

Is a Sabbath for leisure? A question that has challenged Sabbath observers throughout the ages is what to *do* on the Sabbath. The rabbis of the Babylonian Talmud,[23] an amalgamation of ancient Jewish wisdom, share their interpretations of this conundrum:

> *Isaiah 58:13 states, "You shall call Shabbat a joy. To what does that refer?"*
>
> *Rabbi Abahu says: That verse refers to lighting candles on Shabbat.*
>
> *Rabbi Yirmiya says: That refers to a visit to the bathhouse.*
>
> *Rabbi Yochanan says: That refers to washing one's hands and feet in warm water.*
>
> *Rabbi Yitzchak of Naphcha says: That refers to a good bed with lovely bedding.*

The Sabbath becomes, in each interpretation, a space for pleasurable activities.

Another commentary on the Sabbath says the consonants of the word *Shabbat* (SHaBaT) stand for "Sleep on Shabbat is a joy" (*SHneinah shaBbat Tanug*).[24] From the earliest days of Judaism, sleep and rest have been key components of the practice of Shabbat. Note again that the primary idea here is "joy." While many people's impressions of Shabbat are negative—more about what you can't do than what you can do—this wisdom points us toward thinking about Shabbat in positive terms: thinking about what we *can* do and what will bring us joy.

Josef Pieper is a contemporary scholar and philosopher whose seminal writing, *Leisure as the Basis of Culture,* helps us understand the importance of taking time off. His conception of leisure can help with the way we think of work and joy. For Pieper, leisure is not simply the antithesis of work.

> *A break, whether for an hour or three weeks, is designed to provide a respite from work in anticipation of more work; it finds its justification in relation to work. Leisure is something entirely different. The essence of leisure is not to assure that we may function smoothly but*

rather to assure that we, embedded in our social function, are enabled to remain fully human.[25]

In other words, Pieper does not believe that the goal of leisure is to prepare for more work. Rather, leisure is intrinsic to being fully ourselves and fully open to the world.

Leisure implies an attitude of total receptivity toward, and willing immersion in, reality; an openness of the soul, through which alone may come about those great and blessed insights that no amount of mental labor can ever achieve.[26]

Pieper acknowledges that "This is a hard concept for many of us to grasp, given the hold that work has on our lives today."[27]

Americans are raised on the idea that usefulness is the foundation of all civic virtues. And it has become a more dominant value expressed by how we overschedule our families: In past decades, children were left to their own devices to play and explore; boredom was their own private experience to struggle with. Now, everyone is so overscheduled and structured that kids don't have a moment to themselves—and neither do parents. The pressure is to look and be busy, to get ahead, and to use every moment as a way to actively better ourselves.

Pieper challenges his audience to steer away from the utilitarian view of life and to start looking at our activities with the question "Is it good?" in mind, rather than "Is it useful?" The puzzle, of course, is to learn how to distinguish the two questions, because the useful is not necessarily the good. We can find value in trying to understand true leisure and true freedom.

Exercise

Try this out for yourself. As you decide what to do for your oasis time, experiment with asking "Is it good?" And if so, why?

A Contemporary Sabbath

The struggle between work and leisure lives within me. Before I found my oasis in time, I often wondered: Could I take a day off? Once? Not once a week, even, but just once? Once to wake up and not have to get right out of bed before my body has adjusted to wakefulness. Time to slowly let the sleep drift out of my limbs and let the joy of being awake get me out of bed. Time for the deep leisure that Josef Pieper refers to, the way of being that allows us to hear the voice of our inwardness. Or the quiet murmurings of the soul. The kind of time and outlook that treasures the moments of stillness, of gratitude, of receiving the blessings that are fulfilling us in every moment. It felt impossible.

We can be inspired by this history and these explorations and build a secular or religious, spiritual or practical Sabbath that responds to present-day concerns. In my explorations of an oasis in time, I found many different sets of guidelines for a contemporary Sabbath. I'm sharing one such set from Reboot, a nonprofit organization that offers the following Sabbath Manifesto originally created by Dan Rollman. Dan sat down with a small group of friends and explored whether it could be possible in our increasingly nonstop lives to have some notion of a weekly Sabbath. He and his friends did not want to work around the clock, but they had thought that the way to success was indeed working seven days a week. That pattern had begun to take its toll. So they asked the question, Could we take the centuries-old tradition and craft the guidebook for a weekly pause?

These are the ten principles of the Sabbath Manifesto that Rollman and his colleagues devised.

* Avoid technology.
* Connect with loved ones.
* Nurture your health.
* Get outside.
* Avoid commerce.

* Light candles.
* Drink wine.
* Eat bread.
* Find silence.
* Give back.

You can start with these guidelines and explore how to incorporate them into your own oasis in time.

Seven Simple Ways to Reconsider the Sabbath

It's a time:

1. To free yourself from the dictating schedule of the rest of the week.

2. To appreciate the things that are good rather than just that which is useful.

3. To marvel at the wonders of the world and experience a sense of holiness.

4. To embrace contentment rather than stoke endless need.

5. To do nothing.

6. For the arts, any kind of art, for playful creating, for letting go of the practical.

7. To enjoy, to celebrate, to connect.

Building on years of exploration, I too have tried to craft an understanding of the essence of oasis time. I discovered that guidelines weren't enough to help create an oasis in time, so I examined in depth some key elements that are essential in creating oasis time. The core is protecting and preparing, beginning and ending, unplugging, slowing down, and letting go of the focus on achieving.

3

WHAT IS AN
OASIS IN TIME?

S o if we aren't talking about a traditional Sabbath—which we aren't unless it fits your own vision—what is an oasis in time? Is it downtime? Beach time? Gardening time? Reflect-and-catch-up-on-life time? Is it sacred time? Is it a leisurely meal at a big table surrounded by family and friends? It can be all of these things and more. As you take steps to create more oasis time in your life, you will discover what it is for you.

The idea is that for one day, or maybe half a day, each week, you set aside your doing-for-the-sake-of-doing mind, your it's-never-enough mind, and your crazy nonstop trying-to-control-things mind. You enter a period of contentment and equanimity—an alternative reality of timelessness, of soul time, right in the middle of the frenzy and the perceived time desert.

When you take off your "getting things done" glasses, you soften your vision. And when you soften your vision, you can see that the world right in front of you is magnificent. You give your anxious nervous system a break. Start with an hour or two. Or start with fifteen minutes. And don't do it just once. Practice setting aside time *each week* to discover that there is another world right in front of you.

Every oasis in time provides renewal. Each one is restorative in some way. And with practice, you can experience a sense of timelessness, you can let go of that nagging feeling that there is something else to be done. You become fully absorbed in the present moment. You fully engage with the people right in front of you. You notice the clouds drifting by and the wind blowing through the trees.

When was the last time you put away your to-do list and lived in the present moment for a solid stretch of time? When was the last time you didn't check social media or e-mail for an entire day? When was the last time you ignored your screens for twenty-four hours? Most people are so tied to the grid that they can't imagine getting off of it. But it can be done. You can do it, and you will only benefit as a result.

When trying something new, it's handy to have a model. And one time-tested, incredibly effective model for pulling away from the over-work/overconsumption trap is the Sabbath. I offer here five gateways to weekly rest and renewal that come out of my own and others' experiments with Sabbath time. These are principles, not rules, and are designed to help you try out oasis practices and find the ones that are most fulfilling and achievable for you. As you start your journey to oasis time, revisit these gateways regularly to remind yourself how to stay on track. Over time, you will find it easier and easier to create a time of relaxed, connected joy and share it with others.

The Five Gateways

From years of practice and study, as well as talking to and learning from hundreds of people, I have found five gateways that will help structure your journey and shape your oasis time. Taken together, these strategies and reminders will open the way, starting us down the path that shifts us out of the world of action and into the world of renewal of the soul.

1. **Protect and prepare.** Protect your time off and guard it fiercely. Prepare and plan for it. Planning makes all the difference in creating an oasis that is truly restoring. Consider

what social time, activities, food, and spiritual connection your oasis time will include.

2. **Begin and end.** Name your starting and ending times, and stick to both as best as you can. Oasis time can come to shape your week, and it works best when it is clear and time limited. The rhythm of a regular oasis time gives you essential boundaries that help you focus at work and let go when not at work.

3. **Disconnect to connect.** Put down your digital devices. Experience life without checking for text messages, social media updates, or e-mail. Instead, connect with yourself, with others, and with your sense of what has greater meaning and is life sustaining.

4. **Slow down to savor.** Slowing your movements helps to slow your mind, and vice versa. This is key to savoring the delectable aspects of now, which is all about pleasure, enjoyment, and entering the present moment. Even a painful now can be savored for the innately fulfilling texture of a well-lived life.

5. **Let go of achieving to rest, reflect, and play.** Release the tension of going after any goal, large or small. When you do this, you let go of worries and expectations. Then you can finally rest well, reflect deeply (alone or with others), and play more freely.

Protect and Prepare

Years ago, before I discovered oasis time, I was a hard worker round the clock, or so it seemed to me. But I was incredibly inefficient. I thought I was giving work my all, all the time, but actually I was slowly running out of steam. Every week, I promised myself that the following Saturday or Sunday, I would take a real break. *Next weekend,* I told myself, *I will get organized, straighten out my priorities, go for a long run, maybe out in nature, and just get back on top of things.* But that next weekend never came. I knew darn well that I needed refreshing time off—I just didn't have a clue how to get it.

When I was on the road all week, trying to help people work together better, I would slide in from a business trip late on Friday, crawl into bed exhausted, and not move until I got out of bed or off the couch late Saturday afternoon. Although I knew that there were people who protected their weekends or evenings with strict, purposeful "no work" and "no shop" policies, I needed to figure out how to do it.

From many conversations and a lot of observation, I could see that the people who protected their time well decided in advance what was in and what was out. They weren't trying to figure it out on the fly. They protected their downtime, and they planned it. I realized that the only time I didn't work was when I was too tired to function. I never made a real commitment to creating oasis time; I always left the door open for a work opportunity to come in and pull me away from renewal: What if there was something else I really wanted to do? What if I *had* to work that weekend? What if I *wanted* to work that weekend? I never guarded time off for real restoration.

If you want to be as passionately committed to your time off as you are to working and taking action, you need to find a way to safeguard that time off, no matter what forces try to invade it. Then you prepare for it. But how do you do that?

* **Find your "big why."** Start by enumerating the reasons you need, want, and *must have* regular time off. Do this now. Set a timer for two minutes, and list every reason you can think of for committing to oasis time. Don't fret about why you can't get oasis time, simply focus on why you need it. Write down the price you pay for how you live now—frayed relationships? health issues? feeling out of sorts? Then list what you could gain—time with friends? a good night's sleep? equilibrium? (I say a lot more about your big why in Chapter 4.)

* **Say no.** In the beginning, I safeguarded my time by saying no to any off-purpose request. A lot. I said no to myself as well as to others. What helped was that the benefits were immediate—

oasis time gave me more energy, focus, and deeper contact with the sacred aspects of life, which in turn supported my determination to say no. Constantly referring to your big why helps you juggle your big and little nos.

Try this partner exercise. Give your partner a list of everything you think you have to do. Then, when he or she says, "You should . . . ," you respond by saying, "No." Go down the list. Then switch. This gives you—and your partner—the chance to practice saying no, even if the idea seems far-fetched at the beginning! This exercise is meant to be rapid fire and feels good when it gets silly. Do it in lightning rounds and have fun with it.

* **Start small.** Don't immediately take a whole day off if that commitment sounds overwhelming. I started with half an evening a week. I went to a Shabbat dinner, then came home and worked. Soon I dropped the work part, and very slowly, over years, I grew my commitment to a day a week. You could start with a specific hour once a week when you turn off your phone and take a walk with a friend, listen to a favorite piece of music, or do something else that sustains you. Then expand to an afternoon or evening. You might stop there, and that might be respite enough for you. But you might find that the oasis benefits are so powerful you want more. That desire will be your best motivator to cordon off and protect more time.

* **Make a plan.** It may be hard to know what to do with your newly free time; I struggled with this myself. I was so used to working that I had to learn to trust this nonwork time. I had to stop myself many times from doing "just a little work" to stay on top of things. Avoid that situation by planning some activities in advance to give a little structure to your hour or day.

Be intentional so that you don't fritter away your precious time oasis. Perhaps you plan to take a morning of rest; or open a book that you have been meaning to read; or, in a quiet, mindful way, finally make that big pot of soup you have wanted for a while. You might schedule afternoon childcare so you can enjoy a long-desired nap or luscious, slower sex. You might arrange to join with friends for a meal. Remember: You will always be able to think of reasons not to rest and renew, but over time, the reasons *for* renewal will increase and seem greater.

⁕ **Seek validation and reinforcement.** There is a whole world of people who are sick and tired of being on the run all the time. Talk to people about what you are trying to do. Read books, follow blogs, and listen to podcasts by folks who are talking about their oasis time and other kinds of time off (see Additional Resources on page 239). The more oasis time is on your mind, the more real it will become, and the more you'll be able to find others to join you as you seek your oasis. It's so helpful to find a buddy to explore with.

Every week, reasons not to step into your rest and renewal time will crop up. Prepare yourself to handle them. Plan to stick to your goal of creating oasis time. People exhaust themselves by doing so many things that they think will please others or even please themselves but that don't actually fill their own reservoirs even during their leisure time.

Initially, you might find that saying no to certain activities doesn't fit your idea of who you are, but if you are growing, those initial things will change. You might discover that certain television shows belong on your day of renewal, or you might learn that you lose your sense of peace and delight when you watch TV. With careful self-observation and discernment, you will find that creating your personal version of the Sabbath is worth the effort. If you are logistically and emotionally prepared for your oasis, you will have an easier time getting to it.

"Protect and prepare" is the meta-gateway, the gateway of gateways to oasis time. When I protect and prepare my oasis time, what I am really doing is protecting the time and planning and preparing for the other four gateways. This is the pivot point of happy, satisfying oasis time. Because of that, I devote a whole chapter to it in Part II.

Begin and End

When you have named a starting point for your oasis time, you won't have to squeeze your work lulls and soul time into random bits of your day, because you know your deep, expansive downtime is coming. This enables you to summon the burst of energy to finish your tasks and to get ready to enter your replenishing oasis. For me, those tasks might be writing up an interview report, creating a workshop design, or cleaning the kitchen. But whatever I am working on, I can more easily muster the energy to finish what I need to do because I know that there is a stopping point. I can go all in, because soon enough, with a great sense of relief, I will be all out.

There's always something more to do. Be aware that as your oasis start time approaches, you may not feel finished or ready to step away. Just last Friday, I was working until the very last minute. But when I finally stopped, closed my computer, and reminded myself that I would start up again in a day, I felt such a sense of liberation.

Eventually, you will get used to separating from the frenzy of your week. You will come to anticipate this moment with eagerness. But for now, name your starting time and stick with it. It may not feel like the right minute to go off-line, to stop answering the phone, to walk away from your desk or your pile of laundry. And that is the point. It won't ever feel like the right time. But you are in charge. If you're working, make notes about where you stopped on a project and where to pick up again, then walk away. Create a work shutdown ritual and make it stick.

As you end your workweek, start your oasis time with a special ritual or blessing. Rituals help us make the transition between the end of work and the start of renewal. The ritual act itself can be anything: Go for a long run, take a shower, make music, sing or play a song, put on fresh clothes, burn incense, pour yourself a great beer, or mix yourself a drink.

What's important is that you see the ritual as the end of rushing and the beginning of sanctuary.

In my family, we bring out a small prayer bowl, and our son sounds a tone. The tone is clear and pure and reminds us that we are in the present moment. The week is over. We decide to stop ruminating over sucesses, failures, disputes, and undone tasks. We light candles and say a simple blessing as we summon joy. With hugs all around, maybe a little dance, and often a lot of celebration, we greet the return of this special time that liberates us from our many obligations.

Designating an end to your oasis in time is just as important. The end provides structure. You can give your all to your renewal because you know your oasis, your breather, has a limited time frame. Within this specified amount of time, you are free to explore your connections, your inner world, and your deep sense of being.

Tiffany Shlain, filmmaker and founder of the Webby Awards, is a big proponent of oasis time ending. She is known for her advocacy of what she calls a "tech Shabbat." Her family's digital Sabbath has a starting time and an ending time. When it's over, everyone jumps right back on their screens "with so much more appreciation," Shlain says. They appreciate their time off, and then they reconnect with technology with great gusto and energy.

Blogger Sonja Haller writes about her experiments with a year of secular Sabbath experience in her blog *52 Sabbaths*. As she sums up the wisdom she gained from this experiment, she says that *an end to downtime is just as important as a beginning:* "Us worry-a-holics need an idea of when we can ease the vehicle out of idle and slam the foot down on GO! Having an end to this weekly respite time in the beginning is the only way many of us can start."[1]

As my family ends our oasis time, we look ahead to the next six days. We name our hopes and our goals for the week. We light a braided candle that creates a large, torchlike flame, and we remind ourselves to be open to whatever comes our way. Thus renewed and reconnected, we feel greater courage and energy for the joys and challenges to come. Since we end our oasis time on Saturday evenings, we often extend the sense of ease with a family movie.

Disconnect to Connect

There is a lot of talk about disconnecting from our digital devices regularly, whether it is once a week or for a designated period every day. It's more than a great idea: Executing it provides immediate benefits. When people disconnect from their screens, they can be with the people around them face-to-face, in a more connected, respectful way. They stop telling the people they are with to wait while they text or chat with someone who isn't there.

Disconnecting is very rewarding, but it does take practice. As we first begin unplugging, life can feel flat and boring. Ari told me the other day that the "graphics" of our backyard didn't measure up to the graphics of his Xbox games. He was just kidding, of course, but we are used to that online dopamine rush and so accustomed to functioning in tandem with our devices that unplugging may send us into a tailspin. *Who am I without the rest of the world?* we wonder. *How do I connect if not online?* Rather than thinking of unplugging as disconnecting from the world, think of it as reconnecting with what's most important in your life. Oasis time helps each of us devote ourselves fully to the people, activities, and pursuits that are right in front of us. Digital technology has so many benefits, and a weekly stoppage can enhance the experience.

CONNECT WITH OTHERS

People are fruitlessly trying to get the comforts of human connection through a screen. As much connecting as there is, digital media also lets people avoid themselves and others. According to a 2016 study conducted by researchers at the University of Pittsburgh, high levels of digital media use are tied to depression and anxiety.[2] Some researchers attribute these high levels of anxiety to the "compare and despair" phenomenon. We compare ourselves with other people based on their online portrayals, and it looks like everyone else is having more fun. They're posting their holiday snapshots and picture-perfect family celebrations, not their growls at their spouses, their frustrations with work, their shouts at the kids to get them out of the house in the morning. They omit the boring dates, the exhaustion on the couch, and the uninspired sex. No wonder other people's lives look better than ours.[3]

But when we spend time with real people in real life, we can connect rather than compare. Our oasis in time is the perfect opportunity to spend time with others in a slow, gentle way that enables all to be present with one another. What about a day trip to the beach or mountains, or the local park, with friends? What about going to the neighborhood playground with a group and enjoying everyone's kids? Or meeting your neighbors at the dog park? We can develop all kinds of sociable activities for our oasis time that in turn help us build the deep, connecting networks that nurture us.

Psychiatrist and author Edward Hallowell, MD, emphasizes the particular importance of this sense of connection for children. He points out that even kids who have material advantages may lack the most important advantage of all: emotional connection to people, places, and activities they love. They learn to comfort themselves with screen time rather than by playing in the yard, the street, or the woods. An emotionally connected child feels a deep sense of being part of a world that has meaning, and he or she has many people to go to for comfort and self-development. An emotionally disconnected child can act out and become depressed. Depression is now diagnosed as early as fourteen.[4] When you help a child disconnect from screens, you help him or her build much-needed human connections.

Under the direction of George Vaillant, MD, and Robert Waldinger, MD, the Harvard Grant Study's seventy-five years of research on the life satisfaction and success of Harvard men definitively illustrates the importance of connecting with others. One of the longest-running longitudinal studies on success and well-being in scientific history, the Grant Study shows that "the only thing that really matters in life are your relationships to other people." For all of the massive successes that Harvard alumni experienced, the key to their happiness was and is love and connection.

Dr. Vaillant sums up the study's results: "Happiness is love. Full stop." Far more than we realize, we need to connect with ourselves, others, and some kind of greater spiritual force or sense of meaning to experience true happiness in our lives. Dr. Waldinger amplifies this by saying socially disconnected people are "less happy, their health declines earlier in midlife, their brain functioning declines sooner, and they live shorter lives than people who are not lonely. . . . Good relationships keep us happier and healthier. Period."[5]

Connect with Something Greater—Higher Power and Deeper Meaning

Oasis time can connect us with our sense of an overarching higher power or force that dwells within and outside of us. During oasis time, you can bring the values and goals that give your life meaning into your heart and mind. Oasis time is also a good time to cultivate awe. Researcher Melanie Rudd of Stanford University and several colleagues discovered that experiencing awe decreases our sense of time scarcity and increases our generosity to others. Researchers at UC Berkeley found that awe increases our empathy and well-being and lowers our stress levels. These researchers suspect that awe is a powerful way to bring us into the present moment and shake up our view of the world, making us more open to other people and new ways of looking at things. Filmmaker Jason Silva is a big proponent of the mind-expanding benefits of awe. His film series "Shots of Awe" immerses the viewer in amazing images. "Not being in a state of awe is a way to save energy, it's easier to run on autopilot," Silva says. "It takes energy to blow your mind, but being overwhelmed [by awe] is worth it. It's what gives life its luster."[6]

Gratitude exercises are another place to start connecting with something greater. Bring to mind a few things you are thankful for. As neuroscientist Rick Hanson, PhD, says, "Our minds are Velcro for the negative and Teflon for the good." It can take effort to not only notice the good in our lives but also to allow it to touch our hearts. He recommends a practice called "taking in the good," where we notice the good in our lives and pause to deliberately feel the blessings we receive in every moment. Because any of us can feel stale, another way to jolt ourselves out of jadedness is a practice that has been used by the Stoics and the Jews: negative visualization. This entails imagining that we don't have something we really value. Rabbi Zelig Pliskin recommends taking a moment to imagine that you don't have the use of your hands. This can lead to immediate gratitude for whatever dexterity you have. Try that exercise right now. Your oasis is the perfect time to practice both taking in the good and negative visualization.[7]

Yet another way to connect with something greater than ourselves is through prayer. Prayer is the human way of acknowledging that some force beyond us shapes our lives. We shape our lives as well, of course, but there exists an ineffable mystery that is hard to fathom. Prayer comes in all forms, everything from fleeting utterances of thanks to heartfelt wishes for help. Popular writer Anne Lamott claims there are only three prayers: *Help, Thanks, Wow*, which is the title of her book on prayer. There are many ways to pray—that is, to connect with a force in life that is greater than ourselves.

Slow Down to Savor

In days of yore, travelers could move only as fast as the pace of a strong horse or the wind blowing in their sails. In other words, people were constrained by the limits of nature. With the introduction of the train and steamship, we were freed from certain natural limits and got a taste for speed. Speed has a certain pleasure. It's a feeling of power, of overcoming the laws of nature. It's a feeling of joy. We are covering ground! Yet, of course, there are risks with speed. As the pace of horseless carriages went up, for instance, so did the number of deaths on carriage roads.

The risks of physical speed are obvious to us, but we are less aware of the risks of mental speed. Once our minds start racing, it is hard to keep up. A racing mind can generate amazing ideas but also lots of problems—such as losing touch with our sensations, important sources of pleasure, and self-knowledge. Meditation and mindfulness practices have become popular because they help people slow down and become more aware of what is happening in the present moment. Slowing down means moving our bodies more slowly *and* thinking more slowly.

In her bestseller *Overwhelmed*, Brigid Schulte thinks deeply about the struggle for open, unscheduled space and time. Here she shares what she was learning about slowing down:

> *In that free and open space, when we can lose track of time and are fully present and absorbed in the moment, we become most human. We get into a state that some call "flow" or peak human experience. That can be devoting yourself to a passion, a hobby, getting lost in a book, gardening, taking a walk, sharing time with family and friends, or just feeling fully alive in the moment and doing . . . nothing.*[8]

Slowing down and experiencing open time and space refresh us, giving us renewed energy and a clearer head. We enjoy ourselves more because we aren't so frantic. We can reflect on our experience and correct our course as needed.

Being in a hurry reduces empathy. Slowing down enhances charitable action. According to the classic Princeton Theological Seminary "Good Samaritan" experiment, time pressure led even theological students to hurry past someone in need. In this study, Princeton psychology professors John Darley and Daniel Batson met with a group of 67 theological students and instructed them to give a talk in a separate building. As part of the study, some of them were told to give a talk about the parable of the Good Samaritan.

In one key aspect of the study, many of the students were told that they were late to give their talk. Most of those who were running late ignored the needs of a man (who was part of the study) who was slumped in a hallway coughing as they passed by him. Some actually stepped over him even though they were on their way to give a talk about the Good Samaritan.

As the researchers point out "Ethics [can] become a luxury as the speed of our daily lives increases." The researchers suggest that, when in a hurry, there is "a narrowing of the cognitive field." Because of that, when we move too fast, we can violate our deeply held values. Slowing down gives us a chance to think about others more broadly.[9]

My longtime friend Adam, a social justice consultant and coach, found an unusual way to slow himself down. Though he had achieved substantial professional respect in his field, he felt that he was living a life out of balance and too disconnected from important parts of himself. He had given away too much, was going too fast, and didn't know how to rein in his pace.

About five years ago, Adam returned to photography, using real film and a classic 4 x 5 large-format field camera. Every Saturday, he couldn't wait to get outside. He traveled to local lakes, hills, fields, and mountains. He loved that the equipment was cumbersome and not automatic, and that he had to slow down to set up the tripod and camera. "The economics were daunting," he recalled. "The film was really hard to get, and it could cost thirty-five dollars every time I snapped the shutter. Each shot required that I go really slowly." It took time to get the contrast, focus, framing, depth of field, and content right.

Although part of him worried about the cost, Adam was convinced that this was the currency of his inner work. Photography helped him unearth his more authentic self by focusing his attention on beauty, not just the problems of the world. What I find most remarkable is that after a few years, Adam sold his film camera and continued his photography with digital equipment. He no longer needed the slower equipment to force himself to work slowly; he had internalized the more deliberate pace and learned how to look slowly and let the landscape enter him. Now nothing can take that way of being away from him.

I believe we each have our own ways of moderating our pace. For me, I need to deliberately turn my attention to physical sensations to slow myself down. The first hours of my oasis time are often difficult, and at night I sometimes can't stop my mind from racing back to things I forgot to do or forward to things I want to remember. So I walk very slowly when I get up in the morning. I focus on making good, simple food for breakfast. Using and chopping fresh herbs and vegetables demands my attention, and as I work, I lose myself in the colors, shapes, and textures of the simple, unprocessed food.

Almost every week, this miracle occurs: When I physically stop rushing, my mind slows too. I appreciate the color of the sky and the lush foliage outside our house, which I rarely stop to enjoy otherwise. I sit in nature. I let the sun shine on me. I feel the gentle breeze on my skin and the pressure of my feet resting on the ground. I allow myself to drift. After many years of practice, I can now slow down for an entire day. During my oasis, I regain the feeling of my essential self moving at an easy, contemplative pace.

Enjoy. Savor. Relish. That should be easy, and often it is, particularly when we are savoring our favorite ice cream! But you may notice that after the first several bites, the deliciousness begins to fade and the mind goes on to other things. The vivid immediacy of the moment does not need to become dull, though. Mindfulness practice teaches us to bring our focus back to the present to discover that the ice cream is still delicious. Teachers in the Jewish tradition point out that enjoyment can be cultivated over time. They actually teach that happiness is an obligation—in the sense that returning to happiness is a basic spiritual practice that reminds us that we are created for joy.[10]

Aisha, a new mother, told me that during her oasis in time, she is able to move from highly anxious to moderately anxious. She worries a little bit less than in her day-to-day life, but even that slight reduction in stress makes a difference. During the week, her fears dominate. She worries that her daughter, Lily, didn't get enough supervised tummy time or didn't drink enough or cried too much or too little. But during oasis time, Aisha slows down. She stops trying to do it right and lets her instincts reign. Focusing on the moment, she feels a little more trust in the process of mothering. She's calmer because she is not multitasking, and she can sense her own instincts more clearly. She is able to put her worries aside for a limited time. *For the next twenty-four hours, I can be a little more peaceful,* she tells herself, and she is. "In those moments, I really enjoy Lily," she reports. "I'm calmer, and so is she. I'm so happy to be with her."

We can also learn from the Danes, who are expert in creating a feeling of sensory pleasure and connection—they call it *hygge* (pronounced "hooga") They love slowing down to create that cozy, nurturing sense of well-being and enjoy beautifying the seemingly mundane aspects of life. Some emphasize hot cocoa and coffee, delicious cakes, and a fire, but at its core, hygge is about appreciating the sense of comfortable conviviality experienced with close friends who gather frequently as their lives unfold.

As you slow down, practice turning your attention to pleasure. The more you savor, the more you can enjoy each moment.

Let Go of Achieving to Rest, Reflect, and Play

For one day a week, you can stop achieving. You can let go of your big life vision, your master plan, even your bucket list. Don't worry: You can pick them right back up when your rest period is over. The key here is to take a regular break, to find a rhythm that allows you to move back and forth between your daily drive to succeed and the oasis time that restores you. Achievement is so valued in our culture that we can be at loose ends when we aren't accomplishing something, filling in little bits of the day with *anything.* But this is your time for being, for resting, for playing, for reflecting. For just one day a week, you know that you matter simply because you exist on this planet.

To take an oasis means stopping. It means committing to setting down your to-do lists, both your actual to-do lists and the ones that pulse in your veins. My neighbor Sherry calls the one in her veins her "haunt list." This is the list of what she means to do but never quite gets to, the things she forgets to write down: the thank-yous for her wedding presents (from twelve years ago), the book she wants to write, the photos she wants to sort and place in an album. When she sits down to relax or read a novel, the haunt list appears, reminding her of all the things she hasn't done and nudging her to get moving. But for one day a week, she gives herself permission to set even her haunt list aside.

It's hard to stop when stopping seems like a waste of time, but there is so much to gain from temporarily letting go of our achievement orientation. How do you put down your to-do lists? You practice. You accept that if something has been hanging over your head for weeks, it can wait another twelve to twenty-four hours. You talk yourself out of the sense of pressure and into the present moment. You actively and sometimes forcefully turn your attention to what and who is right in front of you. You notice that you don't actually need to do something in this minute. For the time being, there is no emergency.

Elizabeth Gilbert, author of *Eat, Pray, Love,* is passionate about dialing down the achievement orientation.

> *We are the strivingest people who have ever lived. We are ambitious, time-starved, competitive, distracted. We move at full velocity, yet constantly fear we are not doing enough. Even though we live longer than any humans before us, our lives feel shorter, restless, breathless. . . .*
>
> *Dear ones, EASE UP. Pump the brakes. Take a step back. Seriously. Take two steps back. Turn off all your electronics and surrender over all your aspirations and do absolutely nothing for a spell. I know, I know—we all need to save the world. But trust me: the world will still need saving tomorrow. In the meantime, you're going to have a stroke soon (or cause a stroke in somebody else) if you don't calm the hell down.*[11]

Letting go of achieving means telling yourself that you don't have to get anything done in this moment, or the next one. You learn to ignore your inner signals that call you to take action. Productivity master Tim Ferris calls it "deloading . . . strategically taking my foot off the gas."[12] You remind yourself that pausing, slowing, and letting go of the act of creating value all have value. Yes, it's a paradox, and it is a type of spiritual discipline. We don't have to get things done all the time; we don't have to turn to task accomplishment to make ourselves feel better. In fact, if we want to bring more of ourselves to what we do, we have to be more of who we are in the first place.

One theory about workaholism is that at our core we feel we don't have value if we are not accomplishing and contributing. We experience the opposite of Rabbi Abraham Joshua Heschel's oft-quoted phrase, "Just to live is holy, just to be is a blessing." It's wonderful to contribute to the world and to make a difference, but if our urgency to do so comes out of a deep sense of lack of value, then it is hard to know when to stop trying to get more done.

What do we do if we are not trying to get something done and make our contribution, or tidy up, or be a better person? What do we do with open space and unscheduled time? We can rest, reflect, and play. We can, slowly and quietly, turn toward the joys of our existence, appreciate our friends and family, feel the unbearable lightness of our being, or gaze at the play of light and shadows on the wall. We can allow the anxiety of relaxation, and then let it go. We give the busyness a rest.

Rest

My cousin Pam, a lawyer with a lot on her plate, told me that her best vacation time is when she's able to do nothing: "People always ask me for a list of favorite activities or things to do on Martha's Vineyard because we know the island so well. But I don't have that list. They ask me, 'Well, then, what do you do when you are there?' and I always say, 'Nothing.' We do nothing. But it isn't nothing, exactly. I read a lot of books, and so does my daughter, but not to accomplish anything. We just love to read. Then we might walk on the beach. Then chat with a neighbor or two. Then perhaps we walk to the store to buy dinner. Often there is a spontaneous get-together. We know a lot of people in Menemsha, so perhaps we will grill some fish together and then watch the sun set. We have no obligations. We don't have a list of places to see or even people to visit. What happens, happens. I always feel so refreshed when we come home."

We need rest as much as we need sleep. According to Matthew Edlund, MD, author of *The Power of Rest,* we need both passive rest and active rest. Passive rest includes sleep, watching TV, and perhaps lounging on a couch or in a hammock. Active rest has four components: mental rest, social rest, spiritual rest, and physical rest. We pay lots of attention to food and exercise, but not nearly enough to rest. If we learn to direct our rest, rather than evade it, we can significantly enhance our health.

Sometimes when I sit or lie down to rest in the middle of the day, I am tempted to jump back up to take care of one last thing. I remember something else I need to do, or I feel I haven't worked hard enough. But then I guide myself back into a relaxed position. I take a few deep breaths. I remind myself that I can attend to my action steps later. Luckily, my body kicks in, and I become hungry for rest the way I crave a good meal after a long day. Relaxing may make me uncomfortable at first, but my body knows what to do.

Reflect

We tend to view reflection as a solitary activity. Draw to mind Rodin's famous statue *The Thinker:* a seated man, palm supporting his head, pondering. But here I am going to look more closely at the concept of *shared* reflection. The ancient Greeks treasured shared reflection time. Scholé describes a process of contemplation and dialogue about living a good life. The Greeks found great pleasure in conversations about what really mattered in life. Think about it: Some of the times we feel closest to others are when, together, we ponder what matters most to us and explore the quandaries we face.

The Hebrew world also saw deep discussion as the highest form of learning. Engaging in disputation over biblical passages or Talmudic texts was meant to refine the mind, heart, and soul and lead the student to greater awareness of justice, one of the key values in ancient Israel.

There is an art to thinking together, a type of deliberate dialogue where we take turns discussing challenging topics so that we can learn more, not just get our point across. We can explore all kinds of topics that help us live better; dive into the meaty, juicy questions of our lives; and get to know one another in new ways.

One of our best evenings recently was talking over dinner with other parents, while our kids played together. Joe told us that he was burned out on his high-paying, high-performing job, and he just wanted more time with his kids. We asked what was happening at work and why he wanted a change now. And instead of giving him advice about finding a new job and sharing networking contacts, we each talked about our value of good work.

We talked about the challenge of getting dedicated time with our kids when we weren't stressed out. Additionally, we each wanted to work more toward the greater good and find the time and energy to combat racism and environmental injustice in our community of Oakland. We didn't get answers that night, but we parents all understood each other more deeply and left refreshed and heartened. The act of simply stating and exploring your priorities out loud can be an extremely beneficial way of reinforcing them.

Play

According to Stuart Brown, MD, of the National Institute for Play, play is highly beneficial to our happiness. Play is essential for innovation, creativity, and joy. Here's the cool thing about play: It happens best when it's separate from the drive to perform and achieve. Google, one of the most successful tech companies, is famous for offering playtime to its employees. Management knows that people do some of their best work while fooling around.

When we play, we relax. We enjoy each other. We have no purpose but to have fun, yet in that moment of fun, something deeply human and delightful bursts forth in us, and we catch a glimpse of the uncensored self, the self that is just in the moment being human. This is the play from which brilliant creativity comes, but it occurs only when we, paradoxically, let go of outcomes. Don't *try* to access the flaring vitality that perks up when we are just playing, don't *force* the insights and joy that come with play, just let them happen. Dr. Brown has spent his life studying play. He says that:

> [o]f all the animal species, humans are the biggest players of all. We are built to play and built through play. When we play, we are engaged in the purest expression of our humanity, the truest expression of our individuality. Is it any wonder that often the times we feel most alive, those that make up our best memories, are moments of play?[13]

Achieving a flow state is a special type of play. First articulated by Mihaly Csikszentmihaly, flow emerges from a type of riveted concentration that enables us to temporarily suspend our sense of identity. This inner state is described colloquially as "being in the zone." It happens when we experience deep focus, when we are doing what we really like to do, and when there is a good balance between challenge and skill. A sense of clarity appears; often there is immediate feedback and our sense of time disappears when we are doing something difficult but doable. This type of play is so rewarding that it makes life worth living.[14]

So, when our active mind starts roving around for the next tiny action item, we let it go, reminding ourselves that "just to live is holy. Just to be is a blessing." For one day we let in the vast, infinite, tiny, immeasurable, ineffable quality of life.

It's Not Just the Rest, It's the Rhythm

That final gateway to oasis time—letting go of the focus on achievement—might just be the most important. It helps us understand that the *rhythm* of oasis time is what brings us the most value. It's not that we go to work, doing "important" stuff, and then we rest so that we can work again. It is that we live in a rhythm. The rhythm is part of our lives. We understand that we don't just breathe in; we breathe out as well. One is not better than the other; both are essential.

Jim Loehr, EdD, a top high-performance sports coach, says that "it's not that we work too hard, it's that we don't recover enough." According to Dr. Loehr, to have the strength, flexibility, and resilience to be a top performer, you *have* to rest and recover; otherwise you will burn out and become jaded. Get it? Rest as recovery is *key* to high performance. Or to put it another way, rest and recovery are keys to a good life.

If Dr. Loehr makes the case for a measured balance between activity and rest, we also need a rhythm that balances between two prevailing mind-sets. One mind-set is, "I am going to improve the world, things can get better, I can be happier. I need more of something." The other mind-set is, "Things are fine the way they are. I'm content, I'm absorbing the

Getting Started

absolute magnificence of the world right now." You can allow these mindsets to alternate. In fact, this is the ultimate in oasis time: a regular pulse between our active, busy time and our slow, restorative periods of rest, reflection, and play. After the deep rest and replenishment of just being, we go back to doing, learning, expanding, and, if we want, achieving—but an achieving that is mindful, focused, and sustainable. As we reach this rhythm and deepen each perspective, we begin to know for sure that our lives are meaningful just as they are.

These five gateways will help you access your time oasis. Try them out, see how they work for you. Look for places in your life where these gateways already exist. What has worked well for you when you tried to take a break? What has been hard? Do you find it easy to slow down but difficult to disconnect? Do you struggle to plan ahead? Do you let go of your need to accomplish something each week but find that speed still pulses in your body? In discovering what works for you, you figure out how to bring your oasis time into reality. Each step toward your oasis guides you closer to health, happiness, and deeper well-being. Let's take those steps together.

4

GET TRACTION FOR CHANGE

y now, you may be sure that you want an oasis in time and equally sure that you can't make it happen because there's just too much to do. Many people spend years dancing around oasis time. If oasis time feels like it's always just beyond your reach, if you are one of those people who has been not quite getting there for years, or if you fear you will become one of those people, this chapter offers you three ways to get traction on oasis time. The first is to create a powerful, compelling "why" for your oasis in time. The second is to turn a personal crisis into a catalyst for oasis time, as I did. The third is to be willing to face your death and let it help you ask the question, Do you really want to live the way you are living? One of these strategies may be the impetus that finally propels you into your oasis time.

My good friend Tracy is a working mom who knew early on that she wanted to dedicate part of Saturday to oasis time. But she was busy, and her boys all had different activities. Ironically, Saturday ended up being her busiest day, as she drove kids around and caught up on errands. Time went by, her kids grew up and left home, and she still hadn't made oasis time part of her regular routine. Now Tracy is on her own and nervous about dedicating part of one day a week to renewal time. She's concerned that she will feel lonely. She's aware that she fills up her time with to-dos and is not getting satisfying renewal time. She has dipped her toes into the water with a massage here and a long walk in the country there, but she needs motivation to make her oasis time a regular part of her week. Tracy is exactly the person who needs this chapter, and you might be too.

YOUR BIG WHY

When you know why you want and need oasis time, you'll be able to commit. I touched on this briefly in Chapter 3, but let's dig in further. Why do *you* want to create a rhythm of regular rest? I'm not talking about the larger cultural reasons—not the rampant levels of stress and depression in our world, not the children under pressure to perform, not the unsustainable ways we are living, though this all really matters. Instead, I am talking about you and your individual values and experiences.

When I ask people why they want to create an oasis in time, I hear so many deeply personal reasons.

* I would love one morning a week when I wake up without checking my cell phone or my e-mail.

* I'm so tired.

* I don't get enough relaxed downtime with my family. We are always on the run.

* I can't stop doing things. There is always something else to do. I don't want to do, do, do and then collapse.

* I'm burning out. I am dragging all the time and I no longer care about what I am doing.

* I never get out in nature. I mean to, but something always comes up. I even bought a kayak to force myself to get out on the river, but I still don't go. I need more time outdoors.

* We have really good friends in the next town over and we haven't gotten together for six months.

* I've started making serious mistakes at work. No one has caught them yet—I catch them—but I am scared. I'm just not at the top of my game.

* I feel like this culture is turning me into an automaton and I am losing my soul, and I will not abide by that. I struggle with the relentless onslaught of commercialism.

* I have no regular time to stop and reflect. I can't do that in minutes or even an hour. I need extended time to slow down, ease my pace, and think about what I am doing with my life.

* I am out of touch with my internal compass. It's hard to listen to the still, small voice within when I am either going a thousand miles an hour or flattened from exhaustion.

Exercise

Name all of the reasons, *your* reasons, why you want an oasis in time every week. What is motivating you to establish your oasis in time?

- How many walks in the woods have been postponed?

- How much do you wish for an experience of the sacred?

- How tired do you have to be to get to rest?

- What art or craft projects have been on the shelf for too long?

- How many visits with beloved friends or family members have gone by in a blur?

Name the costs of continuing this way. Now name the benefits of incorporating weekly oasis time.

- How would it be to follow your inner compass?

- What would it be like to feel fresh, or at least fresher, every week?

- How much longer can you afford to go at your current pace?

Translate Your Need into Your Purpose for Change

If you were setting out to build a business, be a good athlete, or learn another language, you would prepare yourself with a clear and strong intention. You can do exactly the same thing as you set out to create oasis time.

A strong, meaningful purpose for oasis time can be the motivation and pivot point for nurturing your rhythm of rest. Remind yourself of your purpose—your big why—when you're feeling pulled in too many directions and are tempted to give up on the entire endeavor. Call your strong intention to mind when you start telling yourself that you'd feel better in the long run if you skipped your oasis time just this once so you could power through your work. Drawing on your purpose will give you the direction, energy, and conviction to stay with your commitment to oasis time.

"Purpose" is a step up in meaning from "want." "I'm tired and I want to watch some TV and go to sleep" is very different from "I'm tired and I want to have a balanced life." Naming your big why entails giving yourself a meaningful goal to motivate the difficult work of carving out your oasis time.

Another way to unearth your purpose for oasis time is to notice what you value highly but can't get to when you are flat out or flattened. Maybe you are too tired to be there for your friends. Or you and your beloved just conk out at night, without the pleasure of deep soul connection or sexual intimacy. Perhaps throwing pots or going swing dancing lifts your spirit, but these activities have been edged out by fatigue, kids, or errands. Put them back on your list of things you absolutely intend to do in a spacious, life-enhancing way.

Add Up What It's Costing You

You'll become more aware of your purpose for oasis time when you acknowledge that your current way of life is costing you a lot. Adding up the costs of your nonstop life will help clarify why you want your respite.

Being depleted costs us a lot. At the very least, it prevents us from enjoying this one precious life. We often don't comprehend the overall expense of a crazed lifestyle, however, because the costs are intangibles spread out over time. Have you ever lost a promotion or a good assignment because you missed an important deadline? Have you ever felt a friendship go cold because you canceled dinner together one too many times due to exhaustion or overcommitment? Are you taking medications to ease health problems that are exacerbated by a grueling schedule? Just because everyone is paying the same price for busyness does not mean that it is healthy, or a necessary part of life, or a price you should be willing to pay. Once you clearly see the price you are paying for this nonstop lifestyle and understand that you have a way out, you can recommit to your purpose.

Increase Your Awareness

It is so easy to get caught up in the race for success, the juggling act of family, work, play, and just staying one step ahead of everything. In the busyness, we can lose track of what we are doing. We forget to ask what is truly important to us, our community, our society; we forget to connect our day-to-day actions with our larger purpose of making the world a better place. Many of us feel that we don't have one extra minute to devote to considering the needs of people who have less than we do or to reaching out to our neighbors. Perhaps at one point in your life you decided to be a community leader, yet now you are bogged down in the details of commuting to work and keeping the house in barely livable condition. When you find your oasis, your values become clearer. You experience the preciousness of time and life more keenly, and you are able to devote your energy more directly to those causes.

In *The Flame of Attention,* the Indian teacher Jiddu Krishnamurti discusses the importance of creating awareness and focus in our lives.

> *To find out what right action is we must understand the content of our consciousness. If one's consciousness is confused, uncertain, pressurized, driven from one corner to another, from one state to another, then one becomes more and more confused, uncertain and insecure; from that confusion one cannot act. . . . It is of primary importance to bring about order in ourselves; from inward order there will be outward order.*[1]

Without rest and reflection, people may quickly find themselves living a life of confusion. Oasis time can help you clarify your consciousness. Creating inner and outer respites can significantly enhance our clarity as we explore our relationship to community and society.

Shift the Fatigue Spiral toward the Renewal Cycle

For some people, their purpose arises when they acknowledge that they may be in a downward fatigue spiral, which can lead them to feel like they're sleepwalking through life. Perhaps you are one of these folks. The good news is that you can reverse the fatigue spiral once you see it in action and interrupt it by getting regular rest and sleep.

What does this downward cycle look like? Fatigue leads to mistakes

The Fatigue Cycle

Fatigue

Work More Hours

Vicious Cycle

Mistakes and
Poor Work

Time Spent
Correcting Mistakes
and Relationship
Problems

Relationship
Trouble

and poor work overall. Once mistakes and poor work develop, or we have trouble in our relationships, we end up needing to spend more time correcting our work and sorting through our relationship difficulties because we are not producing high-quality results or we're a pain to be around.

When we are tired, we lose perspective about what is important. Then we fuss about the small things and become negative. This fussing and negativity can keep us up at night, which adds to our fatigue. Sleep loss makes it difficult to maintain a cheerful, proactive frame of mind. When we are tired and stressed, we often eat poorly and skip exercise; we don't take care of ourselves.

The kicker is that we often say, as individuals or as a team, that if we can only get through this tough period, we will go back to a more balanced life. But that horizon often extends until the stressful behaviors become a normal way of life. We keep telling ourselves that we don't have time to really rest. We'll rest on vacation. Unfortunately, that is the path not just to fatigue but to burnout.

We can turn this downward spiral around with the positive renewal cycle. Regular deep renewal improves our ability to make good choices, which improves work, work relations, family relations, and perspective. We do better work because we can tap into our creativity and work with greater focus. When we rest regularly, we can enhance our connections and are able to be kind. We can keep our minds from going down a rathole of resentment, insecurity, and perfectionism. When we are rested, we are also able to take good care of ourselves, eating well, getting exercise, staying in touch with friends, and enjoying our families. Our positive energy is contagious.

THE RENEWAL CYCLE

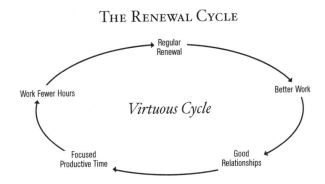

Renewing ourselves with regular oasis time helps us spiral upward. We can be more growth oriented, which means that our skills improve. We work through conflicts more easily and maintain good humor. Life improves. We feel good.

Don't measure yourself by the people who need only four or five hours of sleep. While the ordinary person requires eight hours of sleep each night to function optimally and some need more, other folks need fewer. Such hardy people often rise to the tops of organizations. Not realizing they are different, they often set a tone or pace that few others can keep, and that makes life unmanageable for other employees. And definitely don't stack yourself against the über-moms who "do it all" yet remain slim and trim in the process. We don't know what driving force lies beneath their accomplished exteriors, but it could be pain. *Hands Free Mama* author Rachel Macy Stafford's answer to the question "How do you do it all?" was "I miss out on what *really* matters in life and what I miss, I won't ever get back. How's that for a wake-up call?" She wrote a whole book about freeing herself from the "do it all" syndrome.

It takes courage to unhook from the "rapidization" of the modern world. But the courage to renew repays you many times over.

As we've seen, there are many ways to solidify your purpose for oasis time. You might:

* Focus on what you are missing or what you want.

* Determine how to activate your values for changing the world.

* Resolve to overcome your seemingly permanent sense of fatigue.

* Calculate the costs of life without oasis time.

The key is to find a big why that is clear enough and strong enough to help you when your conviction is wavering. Remember—over and over again—why you *must* create your oasis time.

WILL IT TAKE A CRISIS?

Some people need a crisis to slow down. Arianna Huffington did. She writes, "On the morning of April 6, 2007, I was lying on the floor of my home office in a pool of blood. On the way down, my head had hit the corner of my desk, cutting my eye and breaking my cheekbone." She went from doctor to doctor, trying to find out what was wrong with her. Diagnosis: She was *tired* and had fallen asleep at her desk. This humdrum discovery led her into a successful exploration of ways to value a more balanced life. Huffington is now a prime advocate for sleep and a passionate defender of the need for quality shut-eye every night.[2]

Erin Callan, the much-maligned CFO of the now defunct investment bank Lehman Brothers, was not able to stop working either. But when Lehman collapsed, she was forced into a new way of life. "Without the crisis," she says, "I may never have been strong enough to step away. Perhaps I needed what felt at the time like some of the worst experiences in my life to come to a place where I could be grateful for the life I had. I had to learn to begin to appreciate what was left."

Callan recalls how she never meant to put her friends and family last on the list. It just slowly evolved that way. "I didn't start out with the goal of devoting all of myself to my job," she says. "It crept in over time. Each year that went by, slight modifications became the new normal. First I spent a half-hour on Sunday organizing my e-mail, to-do list, and calendar to make Monday morning easier. Then I was working a few hours on Sunday, then all day. My boundaries slipped away until work was all that was left."[3]

Callan might have continued on that path were it not for the career crisis that forced her to reflect on what her life had become. She easily could have gone on to another high-powered, over-the-top job, but instead she parlayed her crisis into a life change that was more congruent with her deeply held values.

Her crisis helped her come to her senses and get back to what really mattered to her. At age fifty, she is happily married to a firefighter with whom she has a one-year-old daughter. In her memoir *Full Circle*, she says, "I was willfully distracted as I kept moving up the ladder from job to job, focused on the next rung. I was never forced to evaluate exactly where I was because I didn't pause to catch my breath to even consider it."[4] Now, she says, she has finally been able to embrace posttraumatic growth.

A less dramatic kind of inner crisis led travel writer Pico Iyer to his life change. He was in a taxi one night, hurrying home from a long day at work, when "I suddenly realized I was racing around so much that I could never catch up with my life." Iyer had the life he had always dreamed of, including a fascinating job in New York City writing about world affairs, but the reality was not satisfying.

As he put it, "I could never separate myself enough from [the demands on my time] to hear myself think or to understand if I was truly happy." And so he walked away from all this success and moved to rural Japan, where he took on fewer work demands. Once he changed his life radically, he realized that his new life gave him what he prized most—hours and days for himself—and he became the brilliant travel writer that he is today. Iyer talks eloquently about the Sabbath, recognizing that it was the time that he spent going nowhere that sustained him in difficult moments.[5]

People don't always move when faced with a crisis, however. Psycho-analyst Stephen Grosz recounts an astonishing story in his book *The Examined Life*. Marissa Panigrosso was on the ninety-eighth floor of the South Tower of the World Trade Center when the first plane hit the North Tower. The two women she was talking to didn't leave. Others didn't leave. People stood around. They ignored the fire alarm. Some went into a meeting. Marissa asked a friend, "Why is everyone standing around?" Grosz recounts how Marissa "felt the explosion as much as heard it. . . . She walked to the nearest emergency exit and left the building.

"What struck Marissa Panigrosso as odd," Grosz continues, "is in fact the rule. Research has shown that when a fire alarm rings, people do not act immediately. They talk to each other, and they try to work out what is going on. They stand around." Grosz adds, "We are vehemently faithful to our own view of the world, our story. We want to know what new story we are stepping into before we exit the old one. We don't want an exit if we don't know exactly where it is going to take us, even—or perhaps espe-cially—in an emergency. We need to be ready to change the story that we tell ourselves about our lives. That can take a lot of courage."[6] It's not just that we need a crisis to motivate us; it's that we need to be ready to hear what the crisis is telling us. This might be the key to posttraumatic growth.

My personal crisis was serious enough that I *had* to listen. My non-stop way of life led to a frightening illness, during which my energy was completely depleted. Walking across a room took concentration and resolve. I knew I had to change, but truthfully, I didn't want to. Before I got sick, I had been living a whirlwind life. I loved the sense of accom-plishment. I was never bored. I had lots of friends and nonstop meetings and power lunches. I didn't want to give up any of that. Yet I was also always behind and stressed.

When I became ill, I reluctantly started to change. When I finally (and slowly) recovered, I found that I simply could not go back to my old way of life. I had squandered my most precious physical resource, my health, and I didn't want to run myself ragged like that again. I was finally able to be honest about what was driving me and what I really wanted in life. I had been highly motivated to prove that I could succeed in a field that my parents objected to, that I could be successful my own way; but truthfully, I really wanted to savor life more slowly and live a life my soul could thrive in.

I gradually learned to trust the experience of a work/rest rhythm and to make space for renewal. I internalized the truth that turning off results in a greater possibility of turning back on. If I have one clear, strong message to share, it is this: Please don't wait to find your own time and space for rest until it becomes a dire emergency. I lost years of my life struggling to recover my energy. Take measures now that will save you from a crisis later. But if you do find yourself in a crisis, listen to what it is telling you.

What We Can Learn from Death

Writer, blogger, and tweeter David Roberts of *Grist* magazine took a year off from his overwhelming screen addiction. In an article in *Outside* magazine, he documents in detail why he reduced his dependence on technology. He is at his most eloquent describing a scene most of us recognize: playing catch with a beloved child, his son Huck:

> *[Huck and I] had settled in, and neither of us had spoken for a while. Sun dappled the grass, the air was scented with lilac, and the ball hit our gloves with reassuring thumps. I looked at Huck then, aglow in the late-afternoon light, and I felt an upwelling of sadness, so sudden and overwhelming my eyes blurred with tears. I saw with unforgiving clarity that the moment would pass; it was already passing, even as I contemplated it. Life slides by from the present to the past so fast it sometimes seems we barely get a glimpse, barely get to register anything before we're gone. Yet death is coming for all of us. Even me. Even Huck.*
>
> *And then, just as quickly, a sense of joy and profound relief. I hadn't missed it. However ephemeral the moment was, I was there, in it, fully present for it. The breeze was cool on my skin, I had nowhere else to be, and Huck was winding up.*[7]

Without a massive commitment to life balance, the push to get things done can overwhelm what we most care about. I recently went to a funeral service. On my way there, I told myself I could only give it an hour. I had work to do, but I could at least show up. When I arrived, however, I realized I had entered sacred time that cannot be rushed. I settled down to listen to stories about this treasured woman whom I had never met. I felt honored to be there and deeply renewed when I left after a few hours. I was kinder to my husband and son. I was grateful for the moments that I have left.

When we face death, we begin to treasure the most ordinary moments in life. We put packed to-do lists aside, sometimes chastened by how much importance we allow insignificant things to garner. If we make any kind of plan, it's full of moments with the people we love. Death makes us want to spend what is left of our time on earth enjoying our lives and turning toward what is most meaningful in them.

What if we could learn how to enjoy that time for one day a week? What if people could have the strength of mind and the courage to set aside one day a week for the things that are meaningful—including savoring the moment? Then life would be more satisfying, because each week they would be assured of dedicating time to what is satisfying to them. They could keep their work. Keep their to-do lists. But let go for a day a week.

Eugene O'Kelly was the CEO of KPMG, one of the biggest accounting firms in the world, when he was diagnosed with terminal brain cancer at fifty-four. He was at the top of his game, used to mastering difficult situations, and he gave this one all he had. In his extraordinary book *Chasing Daylight,* he eloquently describes how he learned to make the most of his death. He repeatedly states that he was lucky to be given ninety days, because it became instantly clear that life had to be enjoyed as explicitly and as often as possible, *right now.* And he *had* to do what was most important. He talks with regret about the ways he had neglected his beloved wife, believing that they would have time "later" to enjoy each other. He spent way too much time with people who didn't mean much to him.

At work, with constant demands on my time, I'd gotten into the habit of
meeting with certain people—good people, nice people, but nonetheless
fifth circle people. Was it necessary to have breakfast with them four
times a month? . . . Perhaps I could have found time, in the last decade,
to have had a weekday lunch with my wife more than . . . twice?[8]

His biggest message to his readers is to not wait for the clock to run out
to start making the changes to your life that you've always wanted to make.
He exhorts us to think about our own deaths: "As for those considering taking the time *someday* [italics mine] to plan their final weeks and months,
move it up." He says, "I lamented that [other people in my life] had not been
blessed as I had, with this jolt to life. They had no real motivation or clear
timeline to stop what they were so busy at, to step back, to ask what exactly
they were doing with their life. . . . Why was it so scary to ask themselves
one simple question. *Why am I doing what I am doing?*"[9]

Finally, he began to notice the sublimely perfect moments of his life,
which he hadn't noticed before.

I marveled at how many Perfect Moments I was having now. . . .
[Before] I was just too caught up in my fast-paced high-pressure life
to ever get at the sublimeness that was embedded in them.

I understood again one of the key ways into a Perfect Moment:
acceptance. The end result—the goal—of a Perfect Moment was to
taste as much of the flavor that life is constantly offering. But the
way to all that was through acceptance.[10]

Exercise

Take a moment to imagine your last weeks and months. What would you want to be
doing if you only had a few months to live, like Eugene O'Kelly? What would you be
doing? Who would you want to spend time with? Who would you *not* want to
be spending time with—your own "fifth circle" people? Look around; these might be
your last days. Whom do you need to be with? Whom do you need to tell how much
you value them? How can these realizations help you shift your life patterns?

I had my own series of perfect moments in December 2008, one of the best months of my life. It sounds odd to say this, but that time was so good because I did not know how long I had to live. It was the month between my cancer diagnosis and my prognosis. I felt so alive that month. Each morning, I woke up with such heartfelt gratitude: "I'm still here!" Each day, I couldn't believe my luck. I was still on this gorgeous planet. I was still with my crazy, amazing family. Another day. I felt so much love flowing from me and to me that I would wake up and weep with gratitude. We went to New York City for a family trip, and I was dazzled by the holiday lights. The ice-skating at Rockefeller Center was magical. I was unutterably happy that I was alive. I experienced clarity about what I wanted to change in my life. Since it was clear that my time was limited, I needed to take certain actions to shift my life immediately.

Then I received my hopeful prognosis, and the work of fighting my cancer began. Chemotherapy is the pits, and the surgery for my mastectomy lasted more than eight hours. Those two treatments slammed my energy, leaving me exhausted again. It took a year of slow, patient recovery. I experienced ongoing fatigue, and nausea was never far away. My prognosis improved. Luckily, I'm still here.

I am no longer a cancer patient, and mostly I try to push the experience away. I get better and better, and my death seems farther and farther away. I still don't know how long I have to live, but despite all I have been through, I am back to taking things for granted too often. I've wondered how to return to the raw and deeply grateful place I was living from. I have to work hard to remember those vital moments when I *knew* I was going to die.

Australian palliative care nurse Bronnie Ware has some answers to these questions. She writes about the phenomenal clarity people gain at the end of their lives. She asked her patients about any regrets they had or anything they would do differently, and she found that there were common themes. The top regret? People wished they had summoned the courage to live a life true to themselves, not the life others expected of them. Additionally, they regretted dying with so many unfulfilled dreams; they wished they hadn't worked quite so hard and had stayed more deeply connected with their friends. Only as their precious life was slipping away did they realize that they could have made different choices about their happiness. Instead, they had stayed stuck in old patterns and habits. "Fear of change had them pretending to others, and to themselves, that they were content, when deep within, they longed to laugh properly and have silliness in their life again."[11]

Exercise

Get out a piece of paper and make a list of your answers to these questions:

- If there were no consequences, what would you be doing with your time?

- What would you want to experience?

- Who would you want to be with?

- If you had all the time in the world and no demands on you, what would you do?

- How would achieving these things make you feel?

Don't set yourself up to regret, on your deathbed, not having done those things.

QUESTION YOUR BELIEFS ABOUT WORK AND REST

Our deeply held beliefs guide our actions. Unexamined beliefs, often inherited from parents and the wider culture, can lead us to places we don't want to go. Nothing can really change for us until we question our own assumptions.

Here are some common beliefs we may have to overcome: "When we rest, we rust." "I'll rest when I'm dead." "Idle hands do the devil's work." American culture is saturated with the view that rest is for sissies. A related false belief is that doing more gets more done. Doesn't that seem obviously true? But in fact, doing more can result in getting less done. If what you are doing isn't important, is trivial, is not on track, then all you are doing is wasting energy. If doing more creates problems, mistakes, and unproductive conflict, then it just creates more work rather than better results. The powerful belief that nonstop action is the path to success leads us to nonstop action. But we all know the peril of this: The hard, strategic actions get set aside in favor of swirling motion. Our busyness can keep us from true success.

Notice the hidden belief that is beautifully exemplified in the following passage from a classic of "take action" literature. Brian Tracy is one of America's top success coaches, and he perfectly articulates our fear of slowing down. In his book *No Excuses!*, he says:

> *The only real antidote for anger or worry is purposeful action in the direction of your goal—get so busy working on things that are important to you that you don't have time to think about or express negative emotions to or about anyone, for any reason.*[12]

Is this true in your experience? It's not in mine. Sometimes anger and worry indicate a need to confront a person, process a concern, or change an outlook or a situation. Doing more doesn't necessarily resolve anger or worry; sometimes it creates it. Tracy doesn't consider other effective ways to deal with worry.

Cognitive restructuring is a powerful way to observe our anxious thoughts and consciously change them. Practicing small life changes with the help of a coach can also help. Mindfulness meditation changes the brain toward greater serenity. Getting busy is not the only way to a calm mind.

The fear of open, unscheduled time is summed up by another motivational genius, Dale Carnegie, in his classic *How to Stop Worrying and Start Living*.

> *George Bernard Shaw was right. He summed it all up when he said: "The secret of being miserable is to have the leisure to bother about whether you are happy or not." So don't bother to think about it! Spit on your hands and get busy. Your blood will start circulating; your mind will start ticking—and pretty soon this whole positive upsurge of life in your body will drive worry from your mind. Get busy. Keep busy. It's the cheapest kind of medicine there is on this earth—and one of the best.*[13]

If you hold that belief, or anything like it, as many people do, it is time to take a hard look at your actions and start evaluating whether they are bringing a sense of true, fulfilling productivity to your day—or if those actions are simply busywork.

I find that my own desire for productivity gets out of hand very easily. My natural urge to accomplish something of value can overwhelm my need for rest. There is always something to get done when I'm on the lookout for something to do. Even when I'm tired, stopping does not come naturally.

We can examine these strong counterproductive messages in our culture and come up with better ones, like these.

* I work better and smarter, not harder.

* I work hard with focus toward goals that I value.

* I respect that my body and soul need rest and recuperation.

* I become skillful about understanding my worries and difficult feelings.

* Regular rest enables me to live my best life.

When Brigid Schulte realized that her life did not have to feel so pressured all the time, she started reevaluating her beliefs. She writes, "I began to question everything I assumed was true about my life. Why did I feel I never did enough work? Why did I worry that I never spent enough time with my kids? Did I really need to keep the house so tidy? Why did I feel I didn't deserve to relax until the to-do list was done?"[14]

There's a difference between accomplishment and busyness; a difference between being a whirling dervish of nervous activity and a slower-moving person who steadily accomplishes something meaningful.

Exercise

To create oasis time, you need to identify the flawed thinking that is preventing you from experiencing it. What are the items on your to-do list that you never quite get to but that keep you up at night? What "busy beliefs" do you have that keep you careening forward even when you're exhausted? What beliefs do you have about your own productivity and accomplishment, and how can you use them to shift your actions to a more productive place?

Solidifying Your Resolve

No matter how badly you want oasis time, you may notice your motivation slipping at times. Identifying your big why, listening to a crisis, and paying attention to the imminence and meaning of death can help you finally take a giant step toward oasis time. But changing our lives is still hard. We don't like it. Even if our current behavior isn't really working for us, we like the way things are more than we like moving toward something unknown.

So be prepared: Slippage on the path to oasis time is normal and to be expected. It doesn't mean you don't want to change or that you can't. You will probably look for ways to talk yourself out of this. But every single time you move in this new direction, you are laying down new neurons that are the track for your new life. It's a trace of a track at first, but the more effort you make in your new direction, the easier it will be. Remind yourself that you are on a spiritual journey. It will take time. And though it may seem that the deck is stacked against you, remind yourself that you *can* do this. Strengthen your resolve, and know that every time you experience oasis time, you are expanding your commitment to freedom.

Part II: Putting It into Practice

5

DESIGN YOUR OASIS TIME

S tart by imagining an oasis.

Imagine that you are a tired and thirsty traveler crossing the desert under a sweltering sun. You've been moving quickly, you haven't allowed yourself to stop, you haven't taken a break—you've been ignoring your need to rest. You are hot, and your face is damp with sweat. In the distance, you see an oasis, a pool surrounded by sturdy palm trees with ample fronds. It's lovely and green, a colorful sight for your sore eyes that have been scanning the desert for dangers and opportunities. The knowledge that you are on the way to respite and refreshment gives you a spark of energy. You can almost taste the cool water. You draw closer to the oasis, and you already feel better as you anticipate the pleasures of the sustenance to come.

You stop for a pitcher of water and gulp thirstily. You inhale the fragrance of the beautiful flowers and herbs. You stay there for an hour or so. You leave suffused with new energy. You get a break.

Or you stay longer, maybe half a day, maybe more. You relax in the shade. Perhaps you catch some daytime sleep before you continue. You enjoy the beautiful scene and exchange news and tips with other travelers. Rested, fed, and recharged, you and your caravan move on. You get a real respite.

You might stay even longer—a night and a full day. You arrive in the evening, tired and worn, and you bathe in the pool set aside for travelers. You put aside your sweat-stained clothes and put on something fresh and festive. Grateful to have arrived, you joyously appreciate the progress you have made on your journey. You feast that evening, joining with others to celebrate the journey with wine and song. Then you sleep a long and peaceful sleep.

You don't have to get on the road at dawn, and you luxuriate in the spaciousness of the morning. There is no packing up. No hustling the family and the camels to get going. Just some peaceful time in the desert for stories, memories, dreams, psalms, and postponed conversations with self, others, and the holy spirit, whatever you imagine that to be. You feast at midday, relishing the well-prepared food, and enjoy a long rest in the afternoon. By evening, you are fully refreshed, deeply replenished. You return to your caravan reenergized and optimistic about the journey ahead, and you find yourself making great time down your path. A whole day off. A Sabbath. You get renewed. And you know that there is another oasis on the map not too far away, where you will rest again.

The five gateways are a good starting point for thinking about your oasis time. But how do you actually design and execute your well-deserved rest? You might begin by thinking about what you will do with this time. Perhaps you imagine you will stay in bed and read or watch movies. Perhaps you will hang out with your kids or your puppy or your sweetheart. Perhaps you will go to the park. Sounds easy, right? Not so fast. It turns out that really enjoying leisure time takes some skill. So where do you start to make your oasis time real?

Sara, a top lawyer in Des Moines, was stumped by that question. She told me that her weekends were an amalgam of socializing, getting the kids to their various activities, running errands, grabbing a magazine article here and there, and trying to clean her fridge and declutter her house. She never got the replenishment she needed. Her life was out of control, and she wanted to withdraw once a week from the sense of pressure. When I mentioned oasis time, she said, "I love the idea of weekly replenishment time. I'm traveling the next two weekends, but when I get back, I want to get started. How do I make this a priority? Where do I begin? What do I do next?" She was intrigued by the idea of starting with a Friday evening, but she wondered what she would do with the time. At first, she thought she would set up playdates for her kids and just crawl into bed and sleep, but would that really be satisfying?

I remember feeling like Sara. You may feel that way too. You have a sense of your goal, but you're not sure how to get there. How do you stop working, doing, and reacting to demands? And what do you do once you've stopped? How do you craft your own version of oasis time? And how do you keep it going? Here are six steps that will help you get yourself ready to take oasis time seriously and bring it into your life.

1. Listen to unmet needs.
2. Craft support.
3. Cultivate inner strength.
4. Generate ideas.
5. Experiment.
6. Develop a practice.

Listen to Unmet Needs

It sounds obvious—listening purposefully to our own needs—but too many of us aren't paying attention (including, too often, me). Listening to our deeper unheard and unmet needs takes time and practice. We don't necessarily know what will lead us to authentic feelings of satisfaction and contentment because we have learned to override our heartfelt needs and desires.

Sometimes, when I'm out of sorts, I automatically go to the fridge to scavenge rather than patiently listen to what I really need. When I pay attention and notice how exhausted and lonely I am, I can make better choices for myself. Like everyone else, I am bombarded by media messages that suggest my deepest needs are for material things. If only I could get my body or my house to look nicer, then I would be happier . . . right? Wrong: Those aren't my deepest needs.

Practice identifying your inner wants and needs so you can recognize and affirm what nourishes your soul. Can you remember a time when you felt particularly content? Or a moment when you surprised yourself with your own happiness and satisfaction? Can you identify what made those times fulfilling?

Exercise

Start by paying more attention to small, special activities that might bring that satisfaction into your life. Do you like taking walks? Do you take pleasure in a long, hot bath? Do you enjoy reading short stories? Have you wanted to say hello to a neighbor but haven't had time? What are highlights of your life that you *don't* schedule in because you are so busy? Some of these highlights might turn out to be remarkably simple, like sitting outside on a balmy day or enjoying the beauty of a flower.

Learn to Say Yes

When I first became aware of Shabbat, I was so out of touch with my needs that I was very reluctant to attend Shabbat meals at other people's houses. I'm naturally introverted, and I would come up with every possible reason not to go: I didn't know the people; I couldn't follow what was going on; I never knew what to talk about. But a friend kept inviting me over after my repeated objections. Even though I had fervently resisted, I ended up loving it. These regular gatherings met a need that I hadn't yet been able to name—the sociability and sense of belonging found in a spiritual gathering.

Graduate student Casper ter Kuile discovered an opposite need. After connecting with people and participating in social activism during the week, he badly needed solitude and silence on the weekend. At first, his desire to have so much alone time surprised him, but he continued to find it intensely renewing. He had heard about Rabbi Abraham Joshua Heschel's book *The Sabbath* when he was a student at the Harvard Divinity School, so he tried out a Sabbath day on his own. "It felt right straight away," he told me. "I'd been looking for something like this for some time, and reading about the traditional Sabbath gave me the language and excuse to add some ritual. It was delicious!

"I am a very busy person; days are full," he explained. "I have a lot of people in my life, but I need alone time to decompress and chill out. I had a meditation practice, but it wasn't quite enough. I came across the idea of turning off my phone for the day. I use my phone as my alarm, so I decided to buy an alarm clock and put my phone elsewhere. I often spend the whole day alone, which is fabulous. I love the freedom to be bored— that's when I know that I am really unwinding. I'll have a nap or go for a walk. I'll read a lot, reading that I have wanted to do that I wouldn't read otherwise. I do it every week."

Ter Kuile came to his personal Sabbath practice by listening to his intuition. Responding to his inner promptings, he decided to try it, at least once. He discovered that he *loved* it. So find your intuitive self and listen. It will tell you what you need to do; then you say yes.

CRAFT SUPPORT

Support can be crucial to achieving your oasis, and it can come from surprising places. Sara Schley tells her story in her book about Shabbat, *Secrets of the Seventh Day.*

> *A big shift in my thinking about Shabbat came when a big-hearted neighbor I met at a local concert one Saturday night said, "Hi, you're new in town, right? Come to my house next Friday night for Shabbat."*
>
> *"I'd love to," I replied, truly delighted to be invited. "But how did you know I am Jewish?"*
>
> *"I didn't," she said. "I invite everybody!"* [1]

In the years since that first invitation, Schley's new buddy became a supporter as Schley herself became a leader in her community, inviting anyone who crossed her path to join her for Shabbat. She has guided hundreds of people toward discerning their own kind of oasis time observance.

The initial support she received from her neighbor put her on the path to supporting others. Look for glimmers of support from unlikely people. You never know who might be the crucial cheerleaders on your road to oasis time.

Seek a Community of Support

To locate your own community of support, start by looking for people who are already taking dedicated rest and renewal time for themselves. It is so helpful to have supportive allies to counter the often-intense push-back against a Sabbath. Partner with friends and family. Talk to people who you sense will say, "Great idea!" not "Sorry, I'm too busy." You might be surprised to find such people right around you. As you commit to taking a break, you may even meet a buddy with whom you can explore oasis time. This person should be interested in talking about the problems and challenges of being overwhelmed. Having a partner in any new endeavor reinforces commitment. A buddy can assist in debriefing your efforts, but it's even better to dig deep with someone who can listen to you, question you, support your understanding of what's happening, and propose different ideas. When we can't see our own needs, another person often can, and then they can help us meet them.

When it comes to finding people to buddy up with, I like the seven Cs of support, which identifies the various ways people can provide support.

* Coaching

* Collaborating

* Comforting

* Celebrating

* Cheerleading

* Challenging

* enCouraging

This model can guide us in thinking of different people who can provide different kinds of support, depending on our needs at the moment.

For coaching, we might turn to a friend who really lives oasis time. For celebrating, we might call a friend who is always up for fun. I turn to my thoughtful friend Patricia for good, reflective, even challenging talks on how our lives are going, and I can count on my neighbor Susan to encourage me to take a long walk on a perfect oasis afternoon.

Choose people who will really support you—and be sure to offer them support in return. Find the one person who will say, "Great idea, let's figure out how to do this!" Avoid the person who says, "I can't imagine taking a day off each week—I need eight days a week, not six." Watch out for shaming or sabotage, and don't let anyone talk you out of your oasis time practice.

And don't forget to consider a regular support group for creating your oasis time. Dr. Dean Ornish found that, for his patients recovering from heart disease, a key success factor was active participation in a support group. Group support provided unexpected breakthroughs and sustaining love. Reversing heart disease is considered almost impossible, just like carving out oasis time. Group support might be the lever that helps to move your world.[2]

Once you start looking, you will be pleasantly surprised by the number of friends and acquaintances who will want to be a part of the journey. As life design experts and Stanford professors Bill Burnett and Dave Evans say, "Designers believe in radical collaboration because true genius is a collaborative process. We design our lives in collaboration and connection with others because *we* is always stronger than *I*—it's as simple as that."[3]

Step Outside Your Comfort Zone

Don't limit yourself to people you already know. Go outside your comfort zone. Tweet about what you are doing or put a note on Facebook or Instagram. Set up an oasis time meet-up group. Above all, keep telling people what you are doing and invite them along. Sure, they might turn you down, but someone else may be eager to join in.

You might also consider group support. When Drs. Mark Hyman, Mehmet Oz, and Daniel Amen got together to help people at California's Saddleback Church lose weight through the Daniel Plan, they found that being part of a group was far more important to participants than following any particular diet. Using the motto "Better Together," church members tracked their progress and helped each other along.

In the first year, fifteen thousand church members formed groups and lost a total of two hundred and fifty thousand pounds. You could follow their lead by forming a group of friends or fellow congregants and making a shared commitment to practicing oasis time—maybe read this book and do the exercises together.

You can find support in resources as well as people. Keep a pile of inspirational books by your bed or reading chair. Fill your Kindle with readings by others on this oasis path. Watch Tiffany Shlain's video *Technology Shabbat,* where she talks about unplugging one day a week. "I feel so much more grounded and balanced. . . . I feel like a better mother, wife, and person," she reports. "Every week it's like a valve of pressure releases from the bombardment of interesting facts, articles, and tidbits I consume daily as I travel on this inforocket of discovery, procrastination, productivity, and then, eventually, overload."[4]

If you immerse yourself in the idea of oasis time, it will make it that much easier to find fellow travelers.

CULTIVATE INNER STRENGTH

What obstacles come to mind when you think about adopting oasis time? The kids have too many activities? You should really be exercising? You're way behind on personal e-mail? You've just got to clean the house? You could be using the time to get ahead at work? Trust me: You will always find an excuse to delay. But if you shift your inner narrative from "I can take a break when I've crossed everything off my list" to "Taking an extended break is the next thing on my list," you will be amazed at how those excuses can fade into the background.

How do you shift that narrative? Take the same driven energy you mobilize to get things done and use it to mobilize yourself to stop doing. Cultivate the strength to say no to a culture maniacal for action. *Grit* is the popular term for tenacity and perseverance. Your grit is what keeps you going when the going gets tough. We all have grit, not just the special gritty people. By cultivating your can-do attitude and your tenacity—traits you already possess—and applying them to creating your oasis time, you will be on your way toward incorporating into your life the rhythm of rest you need and want.

Believe That You Can Do This

To succeed in this endeavor, you must adopt the powerful belief that taking regular time off each week will give you greater control over your life. Know that resting is countercultural and that you have it in you to foment your own revolution against the status quo. Believe that you *can* change—your habits, your mind-set, your behavior.

Self-efficacy is a term often used to describe the skill that underlies the success of people who make significant changes in their lives. It is your belief in your ability to achieve your goals. Not surprisingly, it is a term associated with entrepreneurs, people who bring their innovative visions into reality, which is exactly what you are doing in your personal life.

Use your can-do attitude to help you stop doing, like Benyamin Lichtenstein, PhD, associate professor of entrepreneurship and management at University of Massachusetts, Boston. "I wanted Shabbat so badly, but every time I got close to candle lighting, the world crowded in and said, 'Go, go, go!'" he recalls. "There was always something clamoring for me to deal with. Always. It felt impossible to close up shop at a reasonable hour on Friday evening. I was going to have to snatch quiet time out of the jaws of constant action. My absolute commitment to high achievement was the lion that roared at me as I tried to settle down and rest. I finally realized that I needed to summon that exact same quality in the service of a completely different goal. I took my single-minded focus and my ability to shut out distractions and applied it to achieving my goal of rest and reflection each week."[5]

Your commitment is a kind of faith. Believe that the direction you are headed in is right. Have you ever climbed a steep mountain trail? Have you sought a handhold, found it, and hung on? Then found the next toe-hold and pushed yourself up just a little farther? Sometimes you can see the top of the trail, but sometimes you can't. The climb can be thrilling, but also arduous. Still, you keep going.

Remember how you accomplished the things in your life you're proud of. You believed in yourself, which enabled you to commit, dedicate, and focus on your goals. Bring to mind the dedication that it took to overcome obstacle after obstacle. Now this time, commit, dedicate, and focus on achieving the goal of oasis time, and it will be yours.

Cultivate Tenacity

In his *New York Times* bestseller *Hamlet's BlackBerry,* William Powers describes how he and his wife were at a loss about how to have more family time. They both worked long hours, and too many of their weekends were spent with their backs to each other, staring at their computers. Powers and his wife were well aware of the gains offered by the digital world, but as parents, they were concerned about the losses. They heard about the concept of a digital Sabbath and knew they were ready to try it.

They made a commitment to try weekend-long digital Sabbaths for a month. The first weekend was disorienting and difficult. Yet they stuck with it because they had said it was what they wanted to do, even though no one else was doing it and some good friends questioned their choice. Within the family, there were tears and frustration. "Our son was ten," Powers says. "He couldn't understand. For him, the digitally disconnected house felt like an alien planet." The family wanted to determine the movie schedule at their local cinema, but they couldn't go on the Internet to do so. When their son lay sobbing on the floor, Powers learned that he had no idea that there were alternative forms of information. Their child was surprised that there were movie listings in the newspaper.

Although that first month was challenging, each member of the family realized that he or she felt really good by midday on Sunday. As

Powers puts it, "Our family was being healed from something that pulled us apart from each other. After the first several months, we all found that we were looking forward to our weekends." After about three more months, it started to feel normal. "And now we can't live without it," says Powers.[6]

Remember, *it was harder before it got easier.* It took tenacity to figure out how to work around the surface inconveniences and make their oasis stick. When things got difficult, Powers and his family reminded themselves over and over again why they started this experiment. They had been lonely even when together. They had spent too much time with their backs to each other. They wanted to connect more deeply as a family. It was their unshakable faith in their decision that got them through the rough beginnings.

Is calling on courage and determination a little too dramatic for creating oasis time? No. In our nonstop world, stopping before life stops you can take every ounce of conviction you've got. Even if it seems that all is lost and it's impossible to extract your oasis time from your beckoning to-do list, don't give up. It took me more than a year to carve out significant oasis time each week. Resting weekly was a daunting change completely at odds with my ferocious commitment to action. Yet now, like William Powers, I would never give it up.

Generate Ideas

What could you do that would replenish your energy and refresh your perspective? I'm not asking you to add more things to the to-do list you never manage to complete. Instead, I suggest that you brainstorm what could enable you to recover your resilience, your elasticity, and your brave heart so you can meet the needs and fulfill the desires you identified in step 1 (Listen to your unmet needs). What kind of experience would enable you to tune in to aspects of the world that are not available to you when you are running around with your cell phone in hand, checking texts, Facebook, and e-mail?

What Can You Do for Your Oasis Time?

- Drink tea slowly.
- Go for a walk in the park.
- Shoot some hoops.
- Nothing—lots of nothing.
- Go to a movie.
- Get out on a bike.
- Play with your cat.

- Borrow a dog to take for a walk.
- Sleep late.
- Sing.
- Reread your favorite book.
- Build something with papier-mâché.
- Plant tomatoes.
- Cook.

Your feelings are as important as your activities. Brainstorm how you would like to feel during your oasis time.

* Relaxed

* Silly

* Inspired

* Openhearted

* Conked out

* Amazed

* Content

Be creative with your ideas for what to do and how to be. Just throw out ideas. Don't edit. Have fun. And stay away from what kills the brainstorming process: being judgmental, trying to implement, mocking or making fun, and disqualifying ideas.

List Your Ingredients for "Joy and Meaning"

Brené Brown, PhD, LMSW—known for her work on vulnerability and strength—and her husband, Steve, asked themselves a question that led to significant changes in how they live their lives. They asked, "When things are going really well in our family, what does it look like?" This is her list of "our ingredients for joy and meaning" from *The Gifts of Imperfection*.

* Sleep
* Working out
* Healthy food
* Cooking
* Time off
* Weekends away
* Going to church
* Being present with the kids
* Sense of control over our money
* Meaningful work that doesn't consume us
* Time to piddle
* Time with family and close friends
* Time just to hang out [7]

Brené and Steve contrasted their "joy and meaning" list with the "dream" list that had been the foundation of many of their weekly choices. "Everything on this [dream] list was an accomplishment or an acquisition—a house with more bedrooms, a trip here, personal salary goals, professional endeavors, and so forth. Everything required that we make more money and spend more money."

Ironically, trying to attain those things was exactly what kept them from their "joy and meaning" experiences. It became clear that if they tried too hard to live out their "dream" goals, they wouldn't have time for joy and meaning. Alternatively, when they focused on incorporating their "joy and meaning" list into their lives in the present, they would be living the dream they really wanted.

Brené acknowledges that making the shift was challenging: "Embracing our 'joy and meaning' list has not been easy. There are days when it makes perfect sense and then there are days when I get sucked into believing how much better everything would feel if we just had a really great guest room or a better kitchen or if I got to . . . write an article for that popular magazine."[8] But she has stayed committed to joy and meaning, because it has brought such benefit to her family's life.

When you find the ideas that make your oasis time come alive and meet your needs, you too will find yourself experiencing more joy and meaning in your present.

EXPERIMENT

As you make your plan for your oasis, don't expect or demand a totally magical, completely flawless execution of every little detail. The truth is that perfectionism isn't just the enemy of the good; it can be the enemy of any action at all. Design thinkers are into "rapid prototyping." This basically means to keep trying out your new ideas the best that you can and then learn what works.

For one afternoon or weekend, what if you skip the perfectionism? Instead, pick one idea and try it out. You might say to yourself, "Hmm, I think I want to put on fresh clothes and have a quiet dinner with a friend, and I won't go on my computer after dinner." Or, "I'm going to take my dog for a long walk in a different neighborhood."

These small moves can be a kind of oasis time when they take place in the context of unplugging, savoring, letting go of achievement, and allowing things to just be. They can ease you toward a realistic larger vision that is right for you. At the end of the experience, ask yourself: "How was that? Did that feel like my oasis? Did it feel like enough? Did it feel too busy?" If it worked, do it again. Maybe do that one thing for another week, or several more weeks, or add something else. Or perhaps you didn't get enough downtime. So the next Saturday or Sunday, try something different. Tell yourself, "I wasn't ready to host a big lunch with friends, so next week, I am going to plan three hours of downtime and then a walk in the woods."

Find Middle Ground

My husband, David, and I came from very different places with respect to our shared oasis time. I wanted a strictly observant twenty-five-hour traditional Jewish Sabbath. He didn't want to do that. His idea of a great Saturday was to lie in bed with the paper, have a late breakfast, do errands in a leisurely way, maybe meet up with a friend, and then play a game of tennis. In the beginning, we didn't know how to experiment with possibilities to find what resonated with us as a family. Over the years and after many conversations, some of them seemingly hopeless, we were able to bring in a little creativity. In fact, that's partly the genesis of this book, because our experiments led us to a very different oasis time than what either of us originally had in mind.

One thing that helped us in the journey toward middle ground was recognizing that we could divide the time into different activities and experiences. Since Friday night and Saturday return every week, we didn't have to get it "right" every time; we could take turns exploring our heartfelt desires. We experimented with excursions in nature, beach time, all kinds of social gatherings, synagogue, and lots of reading time. We found ways of alternating what we each love and find renewing. We learned to accept each other's preferences and build a family oasis time that is truly replenishing.

Once our son, Ari, came along, we recognized our need for weekly downtime as a couple and engaged a sitter or set up playdates as soon as he grew out of taking afternoon naps. Even though we are now many years into a committed practice of oasis time, we continue to try out different activities, different conversation topics, and different kinds of play.

Experiment by Replacing Rules with Discernment

Meaningful oasis time is about paying attention to the impact of your choices on your soul. If you find strict rules useful to implementing this practice, that's great. In a way, rules make things easier. But if you don't like regimentation, you can take a discerning approach instead: Think about your actions and how they affect you.

My friend Amy is on her own journey to oasis time. She told me that one Saturday, she felt compelled to clean out her storage unit and bring a lot of its contents to Goodwill. She wanted to get rid of that stuff and also open up space in her garage. Still, in her mind, it was clear that this was not oasis time; it was a chore, or work. This experience helped her realize that the weekend has two days and she could designate one for chores and the other for her oasis. In general, she scheduled whatever plans worked out on whatever day, without thinking about protecting her extended rest. Now she has shifted her practice to ensure that she has the true oasis time she needs on the same weekend day every week.

Another friend, Ayelet, also had a notion that Friday night was supposed to be a traditional Jewish Sabbath with a white tablecloth, roast chicken, and traditional songs, but what she really wanted was pizza and movies. According to the traditions she had been raised in, having pizza would mean she was observing Shabbat "wrong," so she ended up not doing anything special at all on Friday nights. But what if she decided pizza was okay? She could pick up the best pizza in town and serve it with a flourish. She could choose a great movie instead of mindlessly channel surfing. Such experiments would give Ayelet a chance to rethink her complicated relationship with her ancestors and their traditions. She could take what elements she finds nourishing and leave the rest.

Creating your own oasis in time need not be an elaborate process. It's not about applying a fixed solution for a common problem. It's about identifying your own small steps and taking them. It's a process of planting a seed, cultivating the seedling, and harvesting the fruit. You may go down blind alleys and back out again, and that's okay. You can learn as much from what seems to go poorly as from what goes well.

Adopt the belief that you can't fail. Don't say, "Well, I tried that and it didn't work, so forget it." Instead say, "Hmm, that was interesting. That rest was helpful, but it was hard to put my phone down. I didn't get pleasure from checking my text messages, but I was very satisfied with our quiet family moments playing in the backyard. I think I want to prioritize putting my phone away when I am with my children." Keep your tone gentle, exploratory, and curious. Even if you start off saying, "This was a complete failure. I'll never be able to do a digital detox. I'm an addict," let your discouragement shift and lift, then try again.

Eventually, you will gain clarity. In her book, *Sabbath in the Suburbs,* MaryAnn McKibben-Dana describes what her family learned from their oasis time experiments:

> *Celebrate your successes. Notice the experiences that go well so you can return to them. After a month of Sabbath successes and failures, we are learning what brings us delight. We love listening to music. Cuddling with our kids. Singing together. Playing with blocks. Cooking and baking. Riding bicycles. Being together, out in the fresh air.*[9]

Keep learning about the experiences that bring *you* delight. Develop a list of renewing activities, including hanging around and "doing nothing," so you can augment and refer to a repertoire as you develop future oasis time. Your experiments will slowly yield knowledge about how you want to live your oasis time, and then you can practice with intention.

DEVELOP A PRACTICE

Having a practice means you commit to oasis time through thick and thin. If you take a break for a week, you return the following week. If you drop oasis time for a month, you come back on week five. Little by little, this beautiful practice becomes part of your life. It becomes a touchstone.

Build Your Oasis "Muscles"

We can learn how to develop an oasis practice from how we have embraced other new routines. Many people have experienced how yoga can significantly change the way they move, think, and feel. The more they practice yoga, the more its principles seep into their way of living.

It's a slow process, and it takes time to develop a comfort level with the movements, breathing, and mental practice, but eventually yoga becomes second nature. So too with your oasis time. Understand that it is a discipline, and you'll build up the strength for it slowly. Just as you might not do a headstand on your first day of yoga practice, so too you might not take a whole day off on your first day of oasis time. You try a taste of it, then you keep going.

Cultivate What Could Be

As the years went by and my oasis practice solidified, I grew less perfectionistic. I graduated from perfectionism to a view that allowed for one mistake: "Mess up once, you are learning, mess up twice, you are stupid." That was a little progress. Slowly, I learned to value the profound messiness of real life. I could even mess up three or four times! Still, for years, all I wanted to do was "get it right." And so I went through many iterations of trying to get Shabbat right. I now know we don't get it "right." Rather, we learn to experience an openness that is unfamiliar in our non-stop, success-oriented world. Failure-proof yourself by embracing the mistakes. Know that the wreckage of failed oases—when you feel worse rather than better afterward—are part of the journey to your ongoing practice.

My friend Amy reflects on how she grew her oasis practice.

> I always liked the story about how Michelangelo worked. When creating a sculpture, he would carve away everything that was not the sculpture. As I created my oasis time, I tried to carve away the activities that were not part of it. I experimented on Saturdays. One week I didn't wear a watch. One week I didn't drive. One week I didn't use money. I explored taking away what isn't oasislike for me and then cultivating what it could be.

Like Amy, we can all carve away what doesn't work for us, cultivate what could be, and make it so.

When I started observing Shabbat, I had no idea what I was doing. Every time I took action toward my oasis in time, I felt like I was headed in the right direction. But it was a bit like the children's game Warmer, Cooler. I would try something. Getting warm. I began to copy people. Getting warmer. I tried out something else. Getting cooler. As I learned from others and experimented on my own, I started to feel that I was creating a valuable practice in my life.

Luckily, I had a few encouraging people as guides who were less interested in making sure that I got it "right" and more interested in encouraging my initial feeble efforts to rest. I didn't really know how to rest in the beginning, I didn't know how to prepare for rest, I didn't know how to host people, I didn't know how to attend Shabbat gatherings. I didn't realize that skills were involved. I kept looking at other people and feeling inadequate. They seemed to know what they were doing, and I definitely did not.

I persisted through many feelings of ignorance and inadequacy because I knew I needed what oasis time had to offer and I couldn't see how I would get it any other way. I had a strong meditation practice, but I needed more luxurious downtime to recover my joy in life. I didn't mind failure in my attempts to carve out oasis time. I was willing to keep trying and keep building the skills that I needed to make this work. Protecting the time and learning to plan were key.

6

{ # PROTECT AND PREPARE }

Planning for Oasis Time

S ay you are planning a vacation, maybe your annual getaway. You spend time looking at Web sites, talking to friends, maybe even picking up a guidebook or two at the local library. It finally comes down to a rustic sojourn in the Poconos or a beach week in Mexico. After weighing the options, you choose Mexico. Would your next step be to walk out the door?

Of course not. You know that's not enough: You need plane tickets, a passport, a hotel or campground reservation, books to read, sunscreen, and perhaps a new bathing suit. Without at least a little planning, your vacation is unlikely to be either restful or renewing. (Imagine having to spend your precious Mexico time shopping for that bathing suit rather than heading straight into the ocean.) Even though oasis time is like a mini-vacation, many people don't prepare adequately for it—and are then surprised and upset when their time of rest and renewal isn't actually either restful or renewing. It may feel like one more thing on the to-do list, but the minutes invested in preparing for oasis time will be repaid ten times over in the quality of your experience.

My friend Paula told me about a beautiful Sunday morning in early May when she needed a real respite. She decided to ride her bike down the Minuteman Bikeway outside Boston. It's a lovely tree-lined rail-trail, safe from cars and pleasantly flat. The bike path was full of friendly bikers, walkers, and families enjoying the spring lusciousness.

And yet she was unable to enjoy that precious moment because she had not consciously set it up as an oasis in time for herself. With no transition to downtime and no specific declaration that she was off the clock, she could not stop herself from puzzling through a trying situation at work. She was angry because her boss would not stand up to his boss and tell her that her people were overworked to the point of diminishing returns.

Paula was so caught up in this conflict that on a balmy, sunny day in May, the kind of day that New Englanders await with longing all winter, her bike ride became just one more place to experience the pain and stress of her powerlessness to influence a difficult work situation. She didn't have the tools to let go of work and turn her break into an oasis.

Travelers often think they are moving toward an oasis, only to find it is a mirage. They approach what they thought would be a place of genuine renewal—swaying palms, cool water—and find nothing, just more of their time desert. You don't want that. You want the real thing, the genuine oasis that will refresh you and enhance your life. You don't want to chase renewal and end up empty and even more tired and dispirited. This is why planning and preparing are so important.

Plan the Gateways to Oasis Time

You know how to plan; you do it all the time. It's vital to make a plan for oasis time, even if you plan to do *nothing*; without your plans and switch-off rituals, you will revert to your default pace, orientation, and habits. You need to invoke strong forces that lift you out of your everyday patterns of speed and technology use. The details of the plan are up to each of us, but what is essential is the plan itself, for without the plan and the preparation, we will revert to our to-do lists, to our overreliance on social media, and to the unsustainable fast pace.

Planning doesn't have to take a lot of time and effort, and yet planning is the foundation of successful oasis time.

Make Time for Planning

Planning and preparing are among my least favorite activities. I like to launch into life. I love the feeling of lunging forward into the thick of things; I only remember later, sometimes quite painfully, that for most activities preparation is the *key* to success. I forget too that a tiny bit of planning can make a huge difference. So, bowing reluctantly to reality, I have trained myself to build in a few minutes of oasis time planning each day to make sure that when my oasis time arrives, I have some plans for social activities, food, and rest. Otherwise, I risk a day that is too unstructured or too lonely or that snuck up on me and I'm just not ready.

So, for oasis time, it's best to put into place ways to:

* Begin and end

* Disconnect

* Connect

* Slow down

* Savor

* Let go of achieving

* Rest, reflect, and play

I have many tips for you in this chapter. It's a lot to absorb in one reading. Consider this chapter to be your guide when you are ready to plan.

Plan to Begin and End

To protect your oasis time, guard its boundaries. Clearly identify your beginning and ending times, because both are important. You could say you're going to rest next Saturday from ten in the morning to midnight, or that you won't look at your phone for the first two hours you are awake, or that this Sunday you'll spend the whole afternoon, from one to five o'clock, out in nature. Clear beginnings and endings enable you to protect time that otherwise could get frittered away. They also assuage the panic you might feel about all the things on your other to-do lists, because you know exactly when your oasis time will end and when you'll be able to get back to them.

Suzanne, mother of two boys ages five and eight and head of HR at her firm, decided to plan her oasis time around a yoga class that she had been meaning to attend for months. She made a plan with a friend so that she wouldn't bail at the last minute, as she often did. Her oasis time would start when she left the house for yoga class and would end when she reentered her house after having tea with her friend.

She put down her phone, told her husband he was in charge of the kids, stopped thinking about work, and left for class, allowing plenty of time to drive slowly and savor the moment. She entered the class with no other goal than to be there. No fitness goal, nothing to accomplish, no being the best, no looking at others to see how she ranked. She just wanted to be there.

"It was amazing, it changed my whole weekend," Suzanne recalls. "I was suddenly struck with how much I had been living in my head to frantically get everything done. It had been months and months since I'd had time to move my body. At the end of the session, I could feel my body again; I felt at one with my body and mind. It felt like living." The experiment totaled four hours one Saturday morning. It was doable, and she was determined to do it again. Now she does it regularly.

Suzanne cues herself for oasis time when she puts on her yoga gear and picks up her yoga mat. She ends it when she returns to her family. But she has found that its effects linger, for now that she brings her refreshed spirit back to her family, she can include them in the feeling of an oasis in time. Her oasis time has changed her whole weekend. She is truly happy to be back with her family, not just dragging herself along. And she finds that she no longer jumps right into errands after her respite but enjoys relaxed family time—and thus her oasis expands.

Rituals for Beginning and Ending

Let's use the power of ritual to enhance the sense of a special, even sacred time. Ritual helps us distinguish one type of time from another. Ritual designates the boundary. Rituals engage several senses: smell, taste, sight, sound, or movement. And rituals often draw on the four elements: fire, water, air, and earth. Whether you are stopping for an hour or a day, begin your oasis time with a ritual to shut down work and move into rest. Some of us need to start with practical steps that definitively end work.

For many of us, the most important thing is to switch out of our work mind-set. To do this:

* Take your attention away from the rushing in your mind by focusing on an image, singing a song, or calling to mind a person you find restful.

* Decide that you don't have to achieve anything in the next time period. You are "off the clock."

* Scent the air with perfume or incense.

* Do a mini-visualization. Think of the things that you have to do, and one by one, imagine placing each thing away in a box, drawer, or cabinet. You might visualize locking them up and putting the key in a safe place where you will be able to find it when your oasis time is over. You are done for now.

Physical movement can be a decisive entry into oasis time. You could:

* Note your physical experience. Any tightness? Loosen your jaw. Feel your feet on the ground. Wiggle your toes. Settle down.

* Press a few pressure points on your face and neck. Press gently right below your nose, at the edge of your nostrils, and at the bridge of your nose. Take a deep breath.

Putting It into Practice

* Take a two-minute walk in silence.

* Sit outside and feel the sun and air on your skin. Look up at the sky. Listen for birdsong.

* Take a deep breath and note three things that you appreciate about yourself.

* If you are stressed or angry with someone, leave that person's presence if possible, take a fast walk, punch a pillow, or even jump up and down.

* Look into the eyes of the person you are with. Mentally note three things that you appreciate about him or her.

You could also light a candle, sound a tone, burn incense, play a special piece of music, take a shower, change clothes, move into a different room—or do all of these. What matters is that you do something, but that something is up to you. If you do the same ritual every week, you will cue your body and soul to slow down and calm down. You will automatically move into oasis mode cued by your regular ritual. Once we light candles at our house, my breathing slows down and I can feel myself relaxing, even though only a few minutes earlier, I was scrambling to get things done.

You should also design a ritual that lets you know you are ending your renewal/rest/reflection time and heading back to your action/achievement/ass-kicking time. Make sure you stop when you said you were going to stop. If you keep going with your renewal time beyond your designated end, you might not trust yourself to begin next time. Here are a few possible rituals to bring your oasis time to an end.

* Put on your favorite power song.

* Dance.

* Make music.

* Light a candle or blow out a candle.

* Pull your phone out of its sleeping bag and uncover your computer with a flourish.

* Identify an important goal for the week and say it out loud.

* Choose a character trait that you want to develop.

If you share the end of oasis time with others, perhaps name something that you are each looking forward to. Plan to return to your life of action and accomplishment by setting an intention for the time ahead. In my family, we end our oasis time on Saturday nights by lighting a braided candle; it lets off extra light that represents hope and courage for a good week. We often sing a song and dance our way into our week ahead.

Set Up Your Begin and End Times and Cues

Ask yourself the following questions as you prepare the boundaries that will establish and protect your time. Write down your responses and commit to yourself.

* What time will my oasis time begin? What time will it end?

* How will my oasis time begin? What cues will I use to signal my start?

* How will it end? What cues will I use to signal the end?

* Do I need to set up an out-of-office message? Whom should I remind that I won't be available?

PREPARE TO DISCONNECT

We need to plan for both effective disconnecting and effective connecting. Planning ahead enables it all to happen more easily.

Planning to Unplug

Think ahead about the things you want to do that you might normally use your smartphone for. Then, look for alternatives.

* How will you tell time?

* How will you get directions?

* How will you figure out where to eat? Or whether the activity you are interested in is taking place?

* How will you connect with the friend that you are meeting?

It's hard to imagine, but in the early 2000s, none of us owned smartphones. Now we can't live without them. Except that we *can* live without them for a day each week. It takes planning ahead, though.

Find alternatives to your technology. If you usually check the time on your phone, pull out a watch or make sure there is a clock nearby. If you read on your tablet but can't resist a peek at the Internet, equip yourself in advance with books, magazines, or newspapers for your reading time so that you stay off your tablet altogether. If you use your smartphone to control your music system, find an alternative. Pull out an old tape deck or create a playlist that can play quietly throughout your oasis. That way, you won't be tempted to start texting.

An old friend of mine, Deirdre, told me that as a single woman alone, she couldn't be unplugged for any amount of time. She felt too detached from the world when she was home by herself without her phone or e-mail. But she was willing to look for events to join, so she found an "unplugged" party and stayed for hours, having the best time. People handed over their phones to the host when they walked in the door. "I had more conversations that evening than I had during years of going out to bars," Deidre said. "You just start to talk with people."

* Put down your phone, or even hide it. Don't pick it up for your oasis time, no matter how pressing something seems. Make sure that you have plans for telling time, getting directions, making connections, and searching the web.

* Close your computer. Cover it, if you want. Slowly step away. Grab a pen or pencil if you need to make notes.

* Close the door to your office, whether you work in a big office building or at home. Cover your computer if your workspace is in your bedroom or living room.

Inform others about your unplugging. Dan Rollman, founder of the Sabbath Manifesto, suggests that you let your network of family and friends know you won't be available by phone. Give them the time frame during which you will be out of phone contact; otherwise you may get some unpleasant blowback about your unavailability. If you don't want to turn off your phone, consider putting it on vibrate and consciously choosing the few things you will use it for.

Plan to Connect

Deep connection with others is one of the things we crave, one of the things that keeps us going, and one of the things that, ironically, our technology prevents, even with all that e-mail, texting, and social media.

Start to think about whom you would like to spend time with. Maybe make a list. Include people who might be out of your life now. How would you like to connect with them? Is face-to-face time possible? Perhaps a long catch-up call?

Think about bringing people together. Take the lead and invite people to your home to celebrate your oasis with you. Many people don't have comfortable, easy gathering time in their lives. For some of us, inviting others can be intimidating. We risk rejection: What if they say no? We risk embarrassment: What if they don't understand what we are doing? But we can take a chance on creating opportunities for deep enjoyment of a meal, a conversation, perhaps singing together or taking a group walk, and there is little that is more rewarding.

Overcome some of the sense of risk by starting with people you are closer to, but don't be intimidated about approaching people who simply seem to have a great vibe. If you make a plan that is easy to execute, and you focus on enjoying the company of others, you will create an experience of calm and relaxation that everyone enjoys.

My friend Marcia started inviting family friends, of all backgrounds, for Friday-night dinner every week. Anyone her family liked was fine. These end-of-week evenings were no-tech zones. Adults left their phones in a basket at the door and the kids weren't allowed to have phones or tablets or to listen to music with earbuds. Her kids grumbled at first, but later her son reported, "You tricked me into having fun." She said that for her family, it would be easier to have a family movie, but "this is Shabbat for us. We have challah and candles and we mark the end of the week. It's time to be together—it's our downtime."

Once you have your list of people to invite, share this book with them so they get a sense of what you are trying to create. Inviting people well in advance has been my weakness, and I neglect it to my detriment, because people make their plans far in advance. But when I plan ahead, friends often make the time to be with us.

Over time, you may find oasis time buddies who can join you regularly. When she was in her midtwenties, Rabbi Jessica Minnen was invited to come one night to a dinner sponsored by a group of families that met monthly to celebrate Shabbat. What started as a one-night invitation became a monthly Friday-night potluck. The families that gathered became close over the years; in fact, even though some of the children are grown now, they still love to get together.

For many of us, disconnecting to connect becomes one of the central pleasures of oasis time, the result of both the freedom from our technology and the bonds we grow with others. But it takes strategizing to make it happen.

Plan to Slow Down and Savor

There are so many ways to slow down and savor. Slowing down entails paying attention to your mind and body. Think about low-tech activities that can help you slow down. Lying down? Listening to music? A slow-paced mindful walk? Mindful eating? Name your special ways of bringing yourself to a halt, or at least to a slow trot.

Put out your favorite loose, comfortable clothes. Put out a book that you have been meaning to read. Or set yourself up to do a few slow stretching exercises. Maybe you have a pair of soft socks that help you feel cozy. Designate your oasis time chair or corner of the couch. If the weather is good, find your outdoor spot. Alternatively, play music that will quiet you down. Or make music. And then open yourself to hanging around *doing nothing.* Sometimes doing nothing with a friend is deeply satisfying. Do nothing slowly on a beach, in a park, or at a café.

You can find so much wonderful guidance on mindful living that here I am going to focus on one of the most loving and healing ways to slow down and savor: bringing people together to share meals in a relaxed way.

Hosting Meals

In this section, I'll talk about arranging shared meals so that you can make eating together a central part of your oasis time. You might read this chapter and say to yourself, "I can't take time off and get a wonderful dinner on the table. Who has time for that?" But as you learn the amazing benefits of shared meals—intellectual, social, spiritual, and emotional—you might decide that there are lots of benefits for a little bit of planning ahead.

PLANNING MEALS IN ADVANCE

I find it hard to plan ahead, even though I know our special dinner is coming. Planning in advance means just a little bit of thinking ahead about dinner when I am in the thick of a busy week. I have three regular menus for Friday night meal: roasted chicken with roasted vegetables, Bolognese sauce with noodles and a big salad, and baked salmon with sautéed vegetables. While I would love to create more imaginative dinners, I rarely have the time or the mental bandwidth to plan, shop, and cook something new.

> *It's Wednesday morning. I have a packed day and when I'm in "do mode," all I want is to tackle my burgeoning to-do list. The last thing I want to think about is dinner on Friday night, and I can't imagine I'll have time to cook this week.*
>
> *But even as I grouse to myself, I know enough to stop and consider my tried-and-true Friday-night dinner menus. Now that I think about it, I can pick up the ingredients for a Bolognese sauce tonight while Ari is at the skate park. If Ari and David will chop the*

vegetables for the sauce this evening, then I can put it in a slow-cooker tomorrow night, and let it simmer until morning. Then all I'll need to do on Friday night before candle lighting is boil the noodles and prepare a big salad.

Set a reminder in your calendar to think ahead about oasis time meal planning. It makes a big difference for a relaxing respite.

Special but Easy Food

Good food comes in all shapes and sizes. Diane is Episcopalian, and she loves her comfortable, simple Sunday lunches. She has four kids, and her idea of a wonderful Sunday feast is to lay out a spread of sliced turkey, sliced ham, and sliced roast beef. In summer, she makes a few large salads, and in wintertime, she makes a big, easy soup—or she buys prepared salads and an array of the terrific soups from the prepared-foods section of the supermarket. This little bit of prep helps her relax and really enjoy her family gathering with no fussing about food.

I can prep our Friday-night meal in an hour. I serve roasted chicken a lot. I get the chicken ready to roast by slathering it with olive oil mixed with turmeric, salt, and pepper, then throwing on some fresh herbs—sage, oregano, thyme, or rosemary. When I put the chicken in the oven, I add one baking sheet full of cauliflower florets, plus another one full of mushrooms and sweet potatoes cut into fries (and tossed with olive oil and salt). I do this so frequently that it has become easy but always special and always so good.

Janette Hillis-Jaffe, author of *Everyday Healing,* eats a plant-based diet. Her Shabbat lunches are filled with splendid salads and her specialty, homemade sushi. Her boys love it, and although it can seem complicated to a non–sushi maker, she has learned to roll sushi right before lunch, even while talking to friends who have gathered in her kitchen. Before Shabbat, she also makes a terrific olive tapenade in minutes, throwing the ingredients into a food processor and swirling it into a delicious dip. Delicious can be easy *and* special.

Fresh Herbs Make Food Festive

Herbs help us slow down and savor. Their pungent aromas are powerful enough to bring us into the present moment. We need to use every trick we can think of to stop the speeding locomotive (ourselves) in its tracks. Herbs can be part of the myriad ways to step away from the sense of urgency, reconnect with earthiness, and put our minds at ease.

Fresh herbs are simple, delicious, and easy to grow. They transform an ordinary meal into a savory delight. Put sprigs of mint in your lemonade. Drop fresh thyme into your tea. Crush garlic with basil to make pesto. Use your hands, activate your sense of smell, and let the sensual nature of cooking with herbs lead you to a deeper sense of contentment.

Prepare Food with Others

For my family, shared food prep made all the difference in getting good, easy, tasty food on the table. We needed to have a heart-to-heart conversation about meal prep and helping with food chopping. When I was the only one engaged in food prep, I occasionally defaulted to some kind of takeout food, which is okay, but not what I really wanted. David and Ari both agreed that things had to change and that we would try different strategies until we were all (meaning me) happier with the way meals were prepared and dinner was served.

So we put a change into practice. It turned out that Ari (age 8 at the time) loved chopped vegetables, and he chopped like a champ. Some of that was like a baseball champ, tossing the celery and batting at it with his knife. But he got all the celery chopped, collected the pieces (many of which had fallen on the floor in his enthusiasm and thus needed to be rinsed), and added them to the vegetable sauté. Then he vigorously chopped a red pepper. Meanwhile, I chopped the onion, broccoli, and sweet potato. David did all of the dishes.

Another way to share in building a meal is through potlucks. If you're nervous, ask a friend to help you organize. Tell people that you are trying to organize a special meal, and ask people to make or bring something that evokes a celebratory feeling. I went to one oasis potluck where everyone brought take-out food, but they brought lovely dishes to serve it in, so it still felt special.

Make Cleanup a Cooperative Effort

Hosting need not mean doing all the dishes. Today, that's not going to fly. We can develop a different kind of communal understanding that when we share meals together, we share cleanup because we are all tired.

There are nice ways to let people know you could use a hand. As everyone sits down together and you welcome people to your table or circle, you can warmly greet them and say, "And we would love help with cleanup at the end of the meal." If it is a large gathering, enlist a friend to remind people to help with cleanup. If your guests don't volunteer, ask them directly. It's easier if you make specific requests. "Jorge, can you put this food back into this container? Audrey, can you rinse the plates and put them in the dishwasher? Jamal, would you please bring everything from the table into the kitchen? Addy, would you take this large trash bag and toss in all of the paper goods?"

Sometimes it's not easy to ask reluctant cleaner-uppers, but if you keep asking nicely, you will feel much better at the end of the evening when you aren't spending an hour cleaning up after everyone has gone home.

SOME THOUGHTS ABOUT BEING A GRACIOUS OASIS TIME GUEST

* If you can, show up on time, and if not, give your host advanced warning that you are running late.

* Contribute delicious food or drink or another gift. Even if you are super busy, don't show up empty-handed.

* When you arrive, give yourself a chance to relax and feel the peace. Leave your worries at the door. Oasis time is for developing a sense of serenity and rejuvenation.

* Be a kind and enthusiastic helper both with serving and cleaning up. Offer to set the table or clear it; and you will be an unforgettable guest if you help wash the dishes.

* Show interest in everyone at the gathering. If the host has children, make sure to acknowledge their presence and speak with them.

* Pitch in with good conversation, do your best to avoid work talk, and use your excellent conversational skills including listening well.

* If the hosts propose special conversation topics or singing, join in with good will. Even if you feel awkward, this might be a good opportunity to expand your range.

* Of course, say a big thank-you when you leave, and send a follow-up text, e-mail, or letter of thanks afterward. This little kindness is a huge boost to hosts. As Erin Bried, author of *How to Build a Fire,* says "Show your host your gratitude twice." This is a great way to be sure to be invited back.[1]

A Few Words about Tidying Up for Guests

Tidying up for guests is a nice thing to do, but don't let a messy home keep you from hosting. First of all, let go of any ideas of perfection. Then, if you want, use hosting as a way to get yourself to clean house. It's nice for the guests, and for you too. But if you can't clean up, do a twenty-minute "swoop" (that's a technical term) and collect stray items into grocery bags or large plastic bins so the place looks uncluttered. I used to put stray objects in my bathtub and draw the shower curtain before guests arrived. You won't find that tip in *House Beautiful,* but it's a good one.

Even if you don't want to be compulsively tidy, cleaning up can work wonders for clearing your mind and heart. When you clear your space of excess items, you have a chance to experience your own being. The word *clutter* derives from the word *clot.* Clutter clots our space. Chögyam Trungpa, a Tibetan Buddhist teacher, says, "The attitude of sacredness towards your environment will bring *drala* [magic]. You may live in a dirt hut with no floor and only one window, but if you regard that space as sacred, if you care for it with your heart and mind, then it will be a palace."[2] You want to feel like you live in a palace, not a dumping ground.

From this perspective, mindful organizing could be as valuable a spiritual practice as meditation.

Clearing Up for Your Oasis Time

I am sympathetic to the antipathy to "decluttering." As I learned how to get more organized (see my book *It's Hard to Make a Difference When You Can't Find Your Keys*), I learned how to create a more spacious feeling in my home and my life. Here are a few tips for bringing in the open, spacious feeling of *drala*, or magic.

- First, know why you are clearing up: Clearing space relaxes the mind, creates space for hosting, lets you breathe, and decreases stress. As you create space, you honor your need for clarity and emptiness. You are creating a clearing for you and your friends to show up.

- Second, keep your goals simple. Perhaps you clear excess belongings from one room or you just free the chairs and sofa. Or clear off the dining table and one kitchen counter.

- Third, know that clearing your space is a worthwhile activity. Through cleaning up, you show respect for yourself and others, you value the things that you have, and you allow yourself to rest in the physical world.

- Fourth, let things go. The more we deal with belongings, the more we realize we just don't need so much stuff. That's a good thing. If you don't have room for everything you own, find ways to let go. When you have too much, less really is more.

When your space is ready, you can welcome yourself, and then your guests, into it to enjoy your connecting time.

PREPARE TO LET GO OF ACHIEVING

How do we let go of achieving? How do we create a little distance from that often-consuming drive that makes us feel like we need to possess more and do more, and like we have more to prove? Start by reframing what success means for you. Many of us measure our worth by what we accomplish— what we've made, what we've crossed off the list, what we've produced. But during your oasis time, you have a chance to reframe your mode as a human, as someone who lives to live, rather than a machine. Know that your pounding sense of scarcity can be seen as an illusion. We can cultivate an assurance that we have and are enough—at least for one day a week.

One way to reframe is to think of yourself as a soul rather than a performer. There is far more to us than our ability to produce, but many of us have internalized the myth that achievement gives us value.

One thing you can do is write down ten ways in which you are worthy that have nothing to do with what you accomplish. Why would you still be worthy of life and love even if you never accomplished another thing?

Your oasis is a good time to practice gratitude, mindfulness, and self-compassion. As you begin your oasis time, or even in the middle of it, you may notice yourself thinking of all the things you could be accomplishing. When this happens, say "Stop!" out loud or to yourself. Then turn your attention to something beautiful, something restful, or a prayer. Letting go of achieving includes lowering your expectations for the moment and allowing what is present to unfold. Letting go of controlling the outcome means relaxing your intense ideas of how things should be.

You can carry this attitude through the day. Actively seek out and notice moments of pleasure: a beautiful sight, a smile, the slight breeze on your skin, the taste of fresh fruit, the feel of fabric on your skin, a feeling of contentment. Be on the lookout for those moments instead of looking out for tasks to be done or e-mails or text messages to be sent.

Does accepting the present moment and letting go of control make you anxious? Does relaxing and going with the flow make you hyperventilate? Welcome to the club! Bring your attention to your tension. Notice your shortness of breath. Journal for a few minutes about what it's like to settle down and rest in the moment. Bring mindful self-compassion to your breathing. Your body does know how to relax; you just have to let it.

I often have trouble settling down for our oasis time. Even if I can relax a bit with friends on Friday night, by Saturday morning my mind is often up and running again with all kinds of things to do, even though I know that I am not going to do them. Sometimes I write them down, and sometimes I just remind myself that it is okay to let it all go. Sometimes, amazingly, I fall back to sleep.

Some Tools for Letting Go of Achieving

- Remind yourself that you are a soul, not a performer.

- Write down ten ways you are worthy of life and love that don't have to do with achieving. This is your list of how worthy you are even when not producing or caretaking.

- Practice mindful self-compassion.

- Journal. This is an excellent way to expose challenges we are facing with performing rather than being.

PLAN FOR REST, PLAY, AND REFLECTION

Once we are less achievement-oriented, we can turn toward the present moment. And here, it does make sense to think ahead a bit about what you will do with yourself. I suggest planning for rest, reflection time, and play. I'm going to focus most of my suggestions on shared reflection because there is so much to learn about this topic. But first, a few thoughts about planning for rest and play.

Rest

What is restful for you? Earlier I mentioned active rest and passive rest, so think about what enables you to feel refreshed. The body has an amazing capacity for refreshment. There is a certain effortlessness to rest, a sense that you can finally let go of trying and can focus on enjoying. Is reading restful? Watching a movie? Make your list of restful activities. Could your list include gardening? Knitting? Sitting on a park bench?

Locate a restful space for yourself. Clear a chair by the window or take a blanket to a nearby park. Straighten the sheets so that you can rest in bed in the middle of the day.

Play

We need play. We need goof-around time. We need to feel free without fearing judgment from others. This is what play can do. We simply feel much better when we can enjoy activities in a free and non-goal-oriented way. Dance without worrying what other people think, sing or make music for the love of it, or just play games, indoors or out. Planning ahead for play means thinking ahead. Yes, it seems like a contradiction in terms because we think of play as spontaneous. But go ahead, think of some games to play, plan a mini–dance party, bring out the musical instruments, or build a pillow fort. If you are at a loss for how to be playful, plan to borrow (babysit for) a little kid or a frisky animal if you don't have one of your own!

Reflection Together

Having meaningful conversations can be one powerful and satisfying way to be together and deepen our understanding of life. Good conversation helps us make meaning of our world. It also can lead to wise action. A good conversation engages all parts of the self. You can explore topics from the intellect, but remember to speak from the heart and listen from the soul.

There is a world full of engaging topics. It helps to select topics in advance and provide a little background information. You might pick out a passage from a book or the newspaper. Here is a compelling one from Lynne Twist, author of *The Soul of Money*.

> *No matter who we are or what our circumstances, we swim in conversation about what there isn't enough of. For me and for many of us, our first waking thought of the day is "I didn't get enough sleep." The next one is "I don't have enough time."... We don't have enough exercise. We don't have enough work. We don't have enough profits. We don't have enough power. We don't have enough wilderness....We are not thin enough, we're not smart enough....The mantra of not enough carries the day and becomes a kind of default setting for our thinking.*[3]

Do you think her observations are accurate? In your opinion, is there another more powerful way to think? How could we experience a sense of enoughness for one day a week?

Or discuss what it takes to create significant social change. Here is a passage from the Reverend Dr. Martin Luther King:

> *Power properly understood in nothing but the ability to achieve purpose. It is the strength required to bring about social, political and economic change....Now we've got to get this right. What is needed is a realization that power without love is reckless and abusive, and love without power is sentimental and anemic. Power at its best is love implementing the demands of justice and justice at its best is power correcting everything that stands against love.*[4]

Do you agree with him? How do you access the power to bring about social justice?

You could also explore questions that have preoccupied thoughtful people for centuries, such as:

* What is friendship? How can we be good friends to each other?

* What did you learn from your parents that you would like to pass on to your children?

* How do we respond to people in need—both the people near us and those farther away?

* What is freedom? How do different groups in our society experience freedom?

Or you could start by telling the group something you recently learned and asking, "What do you think?" Ask other people who are joining you at the table to bring a topic to discuss or a compelling question that they would like to explore with others. Dr. Orit Kent, a researcher in conversation and learning at Brandeis University, emphasizes how valuable these conversations are for connecting more deeply.

> *When we enter a reflective conversation, we try to develop our ideas and understandings in relationship with others. We seek to attune to each other. We might try out more inquiry, asking different questions,*

stating our views with more openness, being willing to consider dif-
ferent angles, and being willing to refrain from having the answers.
All of these approaches lead to a more fulfilling exchange.[5]

Help yourself and those around the table develop conversational skills. You might even say, "Let's experiment with a different type of conversation." Some of the basic skills include:

1. Paying attention and listening with care
2. Talking slowly
3. Taking turns
4. Making eye contact
5. Being respectful of different opinions
6. Building on another person's thoughts

Kids need to learn these skills, but we have all noticed adults (including, sometimes, ourselves) who could use a conversational refresher, too.

You can tell family stories, too. Kids who know their family's history, even a difficult history, are more resilient than children who know little about their family's background. In fact, researchers found that it is important to tell stories about difficulties and how the family overcame them.[6]

In his book *In the Absence of the Sacred,* American philosopher and activist Jerry Mander relays a testimonial by Cindy Gilday of the Dené Nation about the impact of stories on children and families. She says stories were part of what kept her people close.

> *When I was a kid we were told the same stories over and over again, then we'd ask for them to be told one more time. Every mother and grandmother would be into it. And everyone would tell the story slightly different. We wanted those stories so much we'd scheme so that maybe we could hear some story for the thousandth time.*[7]

Family stories can be a way to engage children in group conversation. Once they have been persuaded to let go of their digital devices, children often love to listen to adults discuss interesting topics. Children can learn a lot by being encouraged to participate. Even more important is to create space for teenagers to express themselves and be heard as full members of the conversation.

Parenting expert Ronit Ziv-Kreger, PhD, relates that "Engaging children in conversation is often more about listening than it is about talking. With that, children love stories—not only family stories but also stories from their tradition." Each tradition holds a treasure chest of wisdom and wonderful stories.[8] You may need to think about stories that you want to tell in advance. Take time for your memories to surface or talk to elders in your family about their stories.

We have found that avoiding conversations about work, school, chores, and errands is invaluable for preserving the sense of peace and harmony. It forces us to talk about other things. If David or I bring up one of these topics in the middle of our oasis time, we interrupt ourselves by remembering, "This is not an oasis conversation."

It's helpful to let people know in advance that you will try to avoid work talk. One night we had some acquaintances over for dinner on a Friday night. We all introduced ourselves and of course we talked about work as a way of learning about each other. Then one of them said, "And you guys would be the perfect people to help me name my new business. Here are a couple of my ideas. What do you think? Shall we brainstorm?"

Well, no. But we actually didn't say anything so we went along with it. We were feeling more awkward and uncomfortable until he asked us a bit about the dinner rituals that we had shared and we brought up the concept of no talking about work. He loved the idea and said, "But why didn't you tell me at first that this was a 'no work zone'?" So now we let people know beforehand that we avoid work talk at our oasis-time table.

Sherry Turkle writes in *Reclaiming Conversation* that it is through face-to-face conversation, with all its pleasures and difficulties, that we learn to keep growing and learning.[9] This can be a vital part of your oasis time.

MAKE A HABIT OF PREPARATION

In this chapter, I have introduced you to many ways that you can think ahead about your oasis time, but they boil down to making a habit of asking yourself every week what you can do to prepare for the four other gateways.

* *Begin and end:*
    * How long will my oasis time be? How will I start it? How will I end it?

* *Disconnect to connect:*
    * What do I need to plan ahead for so I can unplug? Travel? Meeting up with friends? Reading material? Music?
    * With whom will we connect? When and how?

* *Slow down to savor:*
    * Have I planned enough "nothing" time?
    * What is the simplest food that I can purchase or prepare?
    * Do I want to host? If so, how?

* *Let go of achieving to rest, reflect, and play:*
    * How will I get myself to take real downtime? How will I keep myself there? What is restful for me?
    * What's one really fun or deeply soulful activity that I would like to make sure happens, and what do I need to do to pave the way for it?
    * How can I create one reflective conversation during oasis time?

To keep myself in the preparation habit, I've put my preparation guidelines in my smartphone and set reminders so I don't forget to think about how we are going to create a terrific day of rest, play, and reflection. You might set up preparation time in your online calendar or datebook or attach a reminder note to your fridge with a magnet whose picture reminds you of the value of rest—perhaps a beautiful mountain or a lake, a delectable apple or beautiful flowers, or maybe even a photograph of some of your favorite people. Or you might not need any kind of reminder, because preparation has become an ingrained habit. When that happens, you will truly be living oasis time—as we will see in the next chapter.

7

LIVING OASIS TIME

You may be wondering what your oasis time will actually be like. Here's the thing: It looks different for everyone. There are so many ways to live oasis time. As you continue to craft yours, it can be helpful to learn what other people do. We need lots of different images of ongoing, committed free time, playtime, and sacred time that are a *regular* part of people's lives. Models are inspirations for learning. They show us how it can be done but don't force us to do it any particular way. We can choose to emulate or ignore a model, adopt it wholesale, or pick and choose from its elements: The choice is up to us.

When oasis time works, it meets our needs and sends us back into our busy lives renewed and recommitted to our fundamental values. To make this happen, each of us needs to answer certain basic questions in our own ways: How can we learn to find deep satisfaction in oasis time? How can we use the gateways in our own way? What is the journey toward oasis time like?

In this chapter, I will explore these questions through sharing stories I have collected over the years as I've become more and more interested in oasis time. I'll also talk further about my family's oasis time. Every person I speak to about oasis time tells a unique story. And each person finds a way to genuine soul refreshment and recovery of his or her zest for life. You can do this too.

Remembering What Really Matters

Shasta Nelson, one of America's go-to experts on the subject of women's friendships, and her husband, Greg, a speaker and corporate coach, protect 24 hours a week for their oasis in time even though (or because) they are on the go all week. There is no doubt that they could fill up all seven days each week if they didn't intentionally choose otherwise. So they carve out Friday night and Saturday day for activities of renewal, including things like nature, relationships, service, spiritual practices, and yummy food. Both grew up in a strict Seventh-Day Adventist tradition, but they let go of the stringent rules and chose instead to practice the essence.

As Shasta explains:

> We have guiding values instead of rules. We step away from work, chores, housecleaning, errands, TV shows, e-mails, the stuff of all the rest of the week, and away from anything to do with building our work identity and reputation in order to leave time for what fuels us. It's funny how scary that might feel at first, and then what an amazing freedom and relief ends up taking its place!
>
> For one day, I am enough, I have enough. I don't need to buy more, do more, or be more. I tend to be an achiever, so it's a big gift to remember on a day of not "earning" or "producing" that I don't have to achieve to be loved or valuable. On Sabbath, I rest from what the world says makes me important and try to plug back into what I know is important.
>
> I love the Sabbath. I love having a restful day, I love lighting candles on Friday; it's so peaceful, it would be ridiculous to not do it. The main thing is to turn toward gratitude and connection no matter how challenging our week has been. Friday night is for family and friends, and our hope is that anyone who walks in feels peace and enjoys the food and the laughter.

On Saturday mornings, we go to a favorite café to sit, drink coffee, eat delicious croissants, and talk about our lives and what we are learning. It's a sacred conversation where we dive deeply into the big things in life.

On Saturday afternoons, we often go for long walks or hikes or share a meal with friends. I love those long, lingering times at the table. We could sit there for hours, laughing and sharing, talking, and basking in each other's company. The important thing to me is having love in our lives. So many people say to me, "I just don't have time to take time off," and I say, "If you are thinking that thought, it's a sign that you need it."

Sabbath to me is about reconnecting to love: love for myself, love for others, love for this world, and love for God. Way too much of life is fear-based, and I relish having one day that grounds me back in my highest values.[1]

A REAL DAY OFF

My cousin Ronny Perlman lives in Tel Aviv and is a retired therapist, activist, and involved grandmother who takes Saturdays completely for herself and her friends. Even though she is supposedly "retired," her weeks are full with helping with her grandchildren, volunteering at a clinic, and her peace activism. She was a refugee from Czechoslovakia and escaped her former country with nothing. Ronny says:

Sometimes I spend the late Friday afternoons as Shabbat comes in—even in godless Tel Aviv (!)—listening to chamber music CDs. For me, religion is about spirituality. I used to live in Jerusalem, and the air, the quietness, the special soft golden light of Friday pre-Shabbat Jerusalem is a Jewishly hued spiritual moment for me.

Some Saturdays I lie in bed all day. I am a grandmother now and retired, but my weeks are chock-full of grandchildren, political meetings, friendship time, and just taking care of myself—working out, taking walks, and doing yoga. But on Saturday morning, when I wake up, I turn over, sometimes go back to sleep, sometimes daydream.

Sometimes I lie there and count my blessings. I'm grateful I escaped my former country. I left on the spur of the moment, with nothing. I landed here in Israel and built a good life.

Saturdays offer me unheard-of luxuries. I make a great cup of coffee and I read my novel intensely. Maybe a friend will join me for a fabulous lunch. I love to cook. And then, in the afternoon, I sit on my westward-facing porch and absorb the rays of the sun. Also I'm an avid hiker, so some Saturday mornings you will find me up early and hiking with my hiking group. This for me is adoration of Mother Nature. By evening, I am rested, I am full of another world. Maybe I'll take a long bath. And then, soul refreshed, I am ready to reenter my very busy life.

And just so you know, I am vehemently against the political, nationalistic, and racist interpretation of Judaism/religion. I do believe we can make the world a much better place. I want my grandchildren to know what true peace is. So I go back to my peace work.[2]

An Island in the Storm

Environmental and social justice advocate Odin Zackman is a highly effective change agent who takes oasis time in the middle of the week. Odin has a demanding job supporting other social justice and environmental activists. He works from a home office, so he is on the road often, including a fair amount of airline travel. But the hardest part of his job is to be fully present, with others, to the social justice challenges and environmental threats that overwhelm many and are denied by some. Odin says:

My life is so intense, if I didn't protect my midweek time off, I would be useless. I am really into sustainability, and I had to learn to sustain myself, so I schedule time off each week. I got the idea of taking a Wednesday sabbatical from a memoir called The Diamond Cutter. *The author was a very successful businessman, a self-made man, and he found benefit from what he called a "Circle Day" of rest and renewal right in the middle of the week. For a Circle Day, you are creating a metaphorical circle around you and you are clearing it out. I take mine every Wednesday. If I am traveling and have to be away midweek, I still take off that block of time, but I move it some-where else in the week. I can do anything I want on that day. It is so nice to know that in the middle of the week, I have that island.*

That midweek break for me is so critical. I'm an advocate for change at the core of the way we live our lives. We all have to con-sume less. Me too, of course. I always remind myself of the Angeles Arrien perspective that change happens at nature's pace, in the slow lane. One of my favorite quotes is from Krishnamurti: "In the trans-formation of the self is the transformation of the world." I'm very eager to support positive change in the world, and there is always more to do. If I don't take real breaks, I end up feeling squeezed and pressured all the time.

If things get tough with a client, I let things be tough, and I still take my break. We have become acculturated to wanting to address things immediately, to salve people's pain immediately, to come to closure immediately. But if things are going badly, it is a chance to pause, and we can let it just sit; sometimes letting it sit can help.

If you don't keep your eye on the compass, you will end up where you don't want to be. Time off enables you to put your eye on the com-pass. We have to stay on track for the long haul. I see taking regular time off as a practice, so I don't get down on myself if it's not perfect. It's not about perfection, it's about perspective.

I could fill every minute of every day. It's hard not to do that. I have a little bit of FOMO [fear of missing out]. I try to be ruthless about creating the space for slowness in renewal. I ask myself ques-tions such as: Am I really applying myself in the way that I would like to apply myself in the world? I have to take time to sit with the challenges. If I didn't take time off, I wouldn't be able to reflect on those questions. And that is what really gives my life meaning and sustains me.[3]

An Artistic Oasis in Time

My friend Brigid is a busy Boston architect who organizes her oasis time around painting, an activity that sustains her. Her oasis time is usually on Saturday or Sunday, and it has a set of routines that help bring her to that place of sustenance. She says:

I always painted when I was younger. In later years, I had to come to the discipline of it. It is a necessary part of my life now, part of what makes my life good. Living without painting just wasn't working for me. It reminded me of a quote I ran across [the Gospel of Thomas, verse 70]: "If you bring forth what is within you, it will save you; if you do not bring forth what is within you, it will destroy you." Strong, yes, but I could relate to that. It is physically painful for me to stop in the middle of my painting, and I had to learn to schedule hours for my painting so I didn't have to stop before I was finished. I couldn't "squeeze it in." When I do paint, it benefits everything else I'm doing in my life.

When I wake up, I am looking forward to painting. I am careful about getting distracted—I don't spend any part of the morning emptying the basement or decluttering or doing errands. I need to protect my fresh, open quality of mind. I definitely don't get on my computer, and there is no texting, no calls. When I start painting, I put on my special apron. It makes me feel as if I am in professional gear. And then I go somewhere different to paint: I go to a room at the top of our house. It is a different place, not the kitchen, the living room, or the bedroom.

I go through a whole range of feelings on my painting day. At first there is anticipation. Then it's, "What the hell am I doing here?" And then that settles down into a period during which I get very absorbed. It used to be that I would feel sort of bipolar—first I feel great, then I feel horrible. Now I know I can go through these intense swings, and they don't throw me off balance. I'm in some kind of a zone. At the end of my painting time, I feel satisfaction. I love having made something. I feel strong. I feel in my own skin. It's a coming back to myself, and I am happy.[4]

A Taste of Heaven

Jeffrey, a graduate student in Berkeley, California, is in his late twenties. He is Quaker, and when he married a Catholic woman, they combined their Quaker and Catholic practices. He is self-employed right now, which gives his life a slightly chaotic quality. Some weeks are very busy; some are full of errands, catching up with reading that he has to do for graduate school, and then some open time. But he has his Sabbath every week. He discovered his Sabbath during a very difficult period in his family. Jeffrey says:

My younger brother's appendix burst while he was attending an out-of-state university. He got an infection in the hospital. It was almost lethal partly because they gave him the wrong drugs. My mother and I were the only people who could go to be with him because he was far away. He was so sick, and all these friends and family members were calling me day and night, asking, "How is he doing? What can I do?" It had been incredibly exhausting. I was so overwhelmed, but I didn't know how to stop.

One of my closest mentors had come across the subject of Sabbath through reading Rabbi Heschel's book and was drawn to it. He suggested that I try turning off my phone for a day, and my response was, "What if someone needs me?"

I just want to point out here that if you cannot put your phone down, you might be thinking that you are the one holding everything together, but you are not. There is a force beyond us that is. I am not the center of the world and not the salvation of everyone. I had to stop thinking—at least for one day—that if I don't put in the effort, then nothing good will happen. So I learned to turn off my phone. And I learned to stop being so available. And I learned to go back to a proper relationship with God. God is God and Jeffrey is not God.

*Take a bite of Sabbath, and you will know if you like it. For me,
it was a taste of heaven. It cultivates a very positive feeling. When I
started this practice, I was single, but I would have peaceful time
with my roommate. He was also into Sabbath time. We would unplug
our phones and walk through the local bird sanctuary. Then we
would have a really nice Sunday lunch. After lunch, we would go outside, play games, and have a lot of fun. We had an excuse to treat
ourselves and get nice beers and excellent food. We didn't shop. We
didn't work.*

*Sabbath becomes a wonderful form of resistance. You have this
life-giving way of resisting the overwhelming pressures to just keep
doing things.*

*When I got married, I wondered how I could get my wife inter-
ested in this. So I would make her a wonderful breakfast of eggs and
sausage, and then we would walk to a nice coffee shop (she loves
good coffee). There we could look back on our week with delight. The
first week we tried it, it went great; she could see how true and how
beautiful it is.*

*We're reminded that after six days of Creation, God leans back
and says, "Damn, that was good!" And I look back at specific things
and say, "I like how that turned out." It's so good to say, "That was
good." Crazy how good it feels when I am content.*[5]

Food and Community

In talking to people about their oasis time, I heard many wonderful stories of food and community. I want to highlight a few of them here, focusing on both the weekly events some families have developed and the
insights and connections that can emerge over food.

Shared Brunch

For my friend Betsy, Saturday morning is a time to sleep in after a long
week and then gather with family and friends. She gets up late and reads

the paper while her husband meditates and prays. By eleven a.m., she puts out a spread of fruits and pastries. Their friends know that they can drop in to talk about news, catch up with each other, and enjoy each other's company without scheduling in advance. They get to know each other as well. No one has to make a phone call or send a text to find each other; they will be at Betsy and Menachem's either this Saturday or next Saturday. An easy intimacy grows. Children get to know each other. Months turn into years. The beloved faces now have more lines on them. They are sharing their lives over savory pastries and coffee.

Potluck Lunch

Jerusalem-based rabbi Susan Silverman, author of *Casting Lots* and comedian Sarah Silverman's sister, invites friends, acquaintances, and even people she has not yet met to a buffet lunch with her family of seven every Saturday. Most Saturdays, between fifteen and twenty-five people arrive for lunch, but that's no problem. She sets up a large table and puts out plenty of food, some that she or her family prepared, some brought home from the local markets, and some brought by guests.

Susan and her husband, Yossi Abramowitz, host this gathering every week. Before they start the meal, Susan asks each person to introduce themselves and, if they would like, offer a thought. They serve the meal buffet-style because she often invites so many people for Saturday lunch that she loses track, and thus she often has no idea who is coming for lunch. In her busy life of social activism and mothering five children, she would never give up this weekly meal and gathering. Since people always brought food, and it always worked out, she decided to stop worrying about how many places to set at the table.

Ample Dessert

My friend Sara Schley, whom I mentioned earlier, has an abundant attitude toward dessert during her family's time oasis. One Friday night, friends had brought a chocolate cake, a pumpkin pie, an apple strudel, and a bunch of cookies to their festive Friday evening meal. Her son Sam, who had eaten nothing but bread and butter for dinner, piled his plate high with one serving of each. Sara says:

> A mother looked at me sideways. "You're going to let him eat all that sugar???" "Here's how it goes in my house," I said, paraphrasing the holy text, "Six days thou shalt discipline and mold thy children with all thy might, but the seventh day is the Sabbath and thou shalt give it a rest." I get one day free of disciplining them. It's totally liberating. For all of us. As is the practice of letting go of my entire to-do list. Atlas will have to hold the world up by himself for the next twenty-five hours while I'm gone.[6]

Sara's kids love their Friday-night rituals. There is some deep safety in the consistency of the ritual. No matter what craziness is going on during the week, they can count on lighting candles and feasting together on Friday night. The official start of their oasis time is at sundown (more or less); they put on some rocking music for the occasion and dance and sing. The purpose of all this is to literally change their vibration so they can open to a deeper level of renewal and healing.

OUR OASIS TIME

My husband, David, and I have many differences. I am more attracted to some of the structures and teachings of a traditional Jewish Sabbath; he prefers hanging out and maybe playing a game of tennis. As I have mentioned before, we found that we do better as a family when we find our way together, allowing for our differences. The traditional rhythm of Shabbat shapes our Friday nights and Saturdays, but we use that rhythm to create our own unique oasis time, always with good food and good friends, and always completely off the economic grid. We use no money during our oasis time.

The Storm before the Calm

For me, oasis time starts with the storm before the calm. On Friday afternoons, I always have so much left to do. My ticker-tape mind is enumerating

Putting It into Practice

every last task on my list: "I just didn't get enough done today. I didn't even get to the most important thing. What last thing can I get to? I have to finish this note. And wait, there is a phone call that I still haven't made." Often I'm working hard on a project, and I am finally making headway. Sometimes I don't want to stop for oasis time; I can't imagine stopping. In fact, I think, "Today, I'll just go a little over. I'll keep working. I have so much to do."

But as the afternoon moves on, I start putting things away and creating order anyway. Sometimes I say to myself, "If I am obsessed, I can come back to this," and then I never do. I do my shutdown. I list what I have left to do, making notes for Sunday morning, and then I put away the list. I put my prepared chicken in the oven to roast with sweet potatoes and chopped cauliflower. Then I run through the house doing my decluttering aerobics. This is when I put on my running shoes and good music and, running as fast as I can, put away the detritus of an active week. Twenty to thirty minutes usually does it, and I am sweating by the end.

Then all three of us start the final unplugging. Ari gets off his screen and into nicer clothes. We unplug our phones and put them in drawers, out of sight except for the occasional use of GPS or text communication with a sitter or friend. I often shower and find a fresh outfit. David puts on a festive shirt. We put away a few more things and check on the food we have already cooked or purchased. Finally, but always at the right time, we are ready.

Emptying Our Pockets

I love the traditional Jewish teaching about the emptying of pockets before Shabbat: Whatever we have collected during the week, we let it go.

I don't have pockets, but I do have a backpack and a briefcase. So I translate this teaching to my life. We can let go of *all* the stuff we are carrying around from the week: e-mails we didn't respond to, unreturned phone calls, receipts lurking in our handbags and briefcases, threads of arguments we didn't have time to finish, grudges, hurts, and slights.

I empty my "pockets" of the keys and small notes, but I also do my very best to tone down my arguments and fusses, release my fears, and ease my disappointments. With empty pockets, we can enter the present moment free of the weight of our entanglements.

And then, I'm done for the next twenty-five or so hours. I'll be back to goals and lists soon enough. By then, the urgency around many of the items will have faded. I won't need to take action on some of the things that were so hot when I closed up shop.

Beginning—Off the Clock and Off the Hook

We start our oasis by gathering in the dining room to celebrate—we are off the clock and off the hook! No obligations for the next twenty-five hours. We each take a deep breath and consciously turn our thoughts to the present moment with people we love. Then we light candles. As we light them, we use our hands to "bring" the light toward us—"splashing" the light over our bodies and souls.

Then we close our eyes as we chant a traditional Hebrew blessing over the candles. Opening our eyes, we are in our oasis in time. We have created a wedge of space between our monkey minds and our spacious souls. We welcome this sense of spaciousness by greeting each person with a hug and a kiss.

In gratitude for these moments of quieting down, we sing a song welcoming the angels, sometimes simultaneously marching around the table with tambourines, rattles, and other handheld instruments. We are still in entering mode, and we need all the waking up and tuning in that we can get. Like climbing up a ladder or crossing a bridge, these rituals help us move to another place, step by step.

Evenings

I love gathering at the table. We've dressed up a bit. We have created a wonderful meal. We begin the process of unwinding and settling into oasis. We are often reeling from the week on Friday nights. Sometimes it takes every ounce of energy to stop whirling around and just *stop*. We have to be fierce about letting go of the next thing to do that is still clamoring for our attention. We close our screens, put away our phones, and change into something fresh, something with a little flair. We then gather in the dining room for candle lighting and there we *are*. It's time to catch our breath and just stop trying to get anything done. At that point, we often welcome guests or head out the door to see friends. Some nights, it's the pleasure of simply settling down.

Unwinding As We Let Go of Achieving

Long ago, on a visit to a nature sanctuary in Costa Rica, David and I were sitting on a porch after dinner when we noticed a flock of turkey vultures settling down for the night. The birds were arrayed along five or six branches of the tall tree across from us. The birds each found a spot and, with a little bit of flapping, settled. And then one bird flew up to perch in a new spot. This launched a great deal of reshuffling, flapping, and new settling. Then quiet. Soon another bird found a new perch, and the whole flock reshuffled. We watched, entranced.

After about an hour of this, silence reigned among the turkey vultures. Being enthralled by this spectacle had settled David and me down, and we headed to bed in a peaceful state and slept deeply. But we had noticed that the birds were just like us, flapping and settling, flapping again, shifting position, and then settling down. I think about those vultures often as I try to settle into my oasis time.

Late-Night Snack

Late one Friday evening, I serve myself a small snack of a beautiful red beet. I want to focus and eat with awareness. Yet I can't keep my eyes from straying over to the article on mindful eating that just happens to be right in front of me. Yes, right here it is written, "Don't multitask." Multitasking fatigues the brain and keeps you from savoring the moment.

Another bite of the beet. Mmm, delicious—but what does it say here about savoring? "Focus on the pleasure of the moment," the article continues. "Let yourself slow down. Look at the food. If you read and eat, it diminishes the pleasure of eating." But my rushing, hurrying, helter-skelter mind can't stop. I *want* to read and eat at the same time.

It says here that this professor has done thirty years of research on savoring the moment. More knowledge. More beet. I notice that I am actually thinking that I don't have time to just focus on the food. But for a moment, I try it. I put the article away. I notice my breath. The antics in my brain slow just enough to really observe. Then I slow down even more. My body is relaxing. I reluctantly, slowly, and then gratefully turn toward a wonderful small meal before bed. Luscious red beet. A little oil and salt. Quiet.

Mornings

The oasis commitment to remain off our screens opens us up to many new pleasures and ways of connecting. Savoring, enjoying, appreciating all can lead to greater happiness. This day off is about relishing the moment, returning ourselves to contentment, and opening to awe.

Waking Up with Awareness and Gratitude

I often start the day by enjoying the sweet warmth of my sheets. I don't need to bolt out of bed. In the past, when I did have to jump out of bed to care for our young son, I would bring him back to bed with us and together we would enjoy the quiet pleasure of waking up slowly. Last week, when Ari woke up, he took a book along with him for our Shabbat morning snuggle. After a few minutes, he said, "What can I do?" which I took to mean that he was bored and wanted screen time. I was slow to answer. We looked at the shadows on the wall. We pretended we were on a trip to Japan. We imagined walking the streets of Tokyo. Ari told me what he was learning about Japan in school. He settled down. Soon he was engrossed in his book again, unmoving when I called him to breakfast.

When I notice my brain conjuring rushing thoughts about work or action, I take a long, deep breath and turn toward pleasure. I feel the texture of the fabric on my body. I pause to look out the window and enjoy the beauty of the palm tree. I take a longer breath. Breath is the cleanser because it moves us from fight-or-flight mode to calm-and-receptive mode. With each breath, I too settle down a little more.

Awakening slowly and relishing the moment even briefly sends waves of pleasure hormones known as endorphins through our bodies, setting the stage for a day of enjoyment. It's not easy to have a day of sensual pleasure for us speedniks. I do enjoy speeding along, but I notice that when I am in a hurry, my mind is blinded to the pleasures right in front of me. It's hard to be happy and rushed at the same time. Savoring my first awake moments sets the tone for a day of joy.

I often read passages from different books, like this one from Thich Nhat Hanh's *Savor*. He writes, "Please ask yourself, 'What nourishes joy in me? What nourishes joy in others? Do I nourish the joy in myself and in others enough? Do I appreciate the many reasons for joy that are already in my life? Or have I been living in forgetfulness, taking many things for granted?' If you have good eyesight, appreciate it, even though it is easy to forget what a gift this is."[7] It helps me remember to appreciate the gifts I have, including my glasses. My eyesight is poor, but my glasses are great.

Family Reading

After breakfast, we might go to our synagogue or head out to the redwood parks nearby. But often we keep reading, enjoying that sweet, full, companionable silence that descends upon us, sharing from our books or reading aloud from the newspaper.

One morning, eight-year-old Ari was reading a book called *It Can't Be True,* full of amazing facts about the world. He was very excited to share some of the things he was learning. "Mom, Dad," he called out. "How many months does it take for an elephant baby to be born?" We had no idea. "Twenty-two months!" We all went back to reading peacefully, enjoying the peace, because life isn't always this way.

A few minutes later: "Mom, Dad, this is amazing! Tell me how many Empire State Buildings does it take to match an Egyptian pyramid in weight." David answered, "I don't know, one, maybe, four." Ari was exultant. He had stumped his dad. "It takes sixteen!" A conversation ensued about how to figure out how much a pyramid weighs—and the Empire State Building too, for that matter.

Every few minutes, Ari piped up with another amazing fact. And since we were not trying to get anything done, David and I were relaxed, open, and interested in listening to Ari's news about the incredible world we live in.

Letting Go of Work Temptations

One Saturday, I woke up churning with ideas and energy for this book. I wanted to get up and get on my computer and write. I wanted to charge ahead. My brain was full of ideas, and all I wanted to do was work. This is not an unfamiliar state for me. I often feel best when I am working and creating. I have never liked resting, and I don't like clearing up when my work is done. Work itself is my sweet spot.

Over the years, though, I have come to learn that as much as I ground myself in work, I *must* take breaks, and sorry to say, that means I have to clean up and rest. Otherwise, I run myself into the ground. Yet there I was on Shabbat, full of ardor to get working.

That was a choice point for me—not such a hard choice now, but still a real one. It reminded me of the days back when I was learning to keep and protect my oasis time. The choice to rest is easier for me now, and even though I was sorely tempted to open my computer and type up a few notes (my deadline was looming), I didn't do it.

Once I made my choice, I wrote down a couple of thoughts, then put them away. I began to relax again. The idea of working slipped away, and I got ready to head out to a gathering that I was eager to participate in. As I did on that Saturday, sometimes I have to choose my oasis in time again. That choice gets easier and easier until it is not a choice any longer.

Afternoon

Stories around the Table

One day at lunch, we were meandering between family stories. David told the story of a letter his aunt wrote about a Passover dinner in 1932 in the Hague and how, seventy years later, he discovered that a new friend's father was at that very same dinner and in fact he and his new friend were distantly related cousins.

I discover that I never told my dear friend of thirty years how my father had won a coveted scholarship to Yale and then had to leave, alone, at midnight, desolate and ashamed, because at that time, in the early 1940s, Yale had no Jewish community and no kosher food. He went home to Buffalo and finished college at the University at Buffalo. I discover to my surprise that her mother had the exact same story: She left Skidmore to return to her familiar neighborhood in Chelsea, Massachusetts.

Without our oasis meal, there is no time for this slow unwinding of family history. We don't have time for the long pauses, for allowing the conversation to unfold and take unknown directions. As we relax, the quality of our listening deepens. We ask different questions. We wonder how it is that our parents left their homes under such difficult conditions. We discover commonalities we hadn't realized we had.

We go beyond discussing television shows and movies. We go beyond catching up with each other's lives. We ask the children questions and discover they have points of view and opinions we don't know about. We are now in the land of discovery. Elie Wiesel once said, "God made man because He loves stories." And now, old stories are being told in new ways. Our children haven't heard some of these stories. We are enriching our worlds with stories; we look at one another with new eyes and deeper understanding.

Outdoor Time

The three of us—David, four-year-old Ari, and me—were home together one Saturday afternoon. After a few rounds of boccie ball, we drifted slowly toward the sandbox in the deep shade under the maple trees. I started to pick out the leaves and sticks from the sand. Soon Ari was shaping the sand. Amazingly, for the next two hours, my normally highly active child and I played quietly and peacefully. Ari was building a castle. I was making sand balls to decorate the castle. We were comfortably cool in the luscious shade of the trees on this hot, hot day. When we became suddenly, achingly thirsty, it was time for a cool glass of minty lemonade.

Another time, several years later, we had planned a swim with another family, which was good, because we had a tough start to a day that later turned into a bit of heaven. I needed that, since I had been having a *hard* time.

I had had setbacks at work, and I had lost a lot of sleep over a painful confrontation with a good friend. A change of scenery helped. Being out in nature helped. Being with trusted friends helped. Sometimes resting and playing during my oasis time is the only way out of the thicket of misery which I can get trapped in. It doesn't matter how much I try to focus on the good and tell myself everything is okay. My old habits of worrying and ruminating and resenting still come back. What I really need at those moments is outdoor time, rest, and playtime. Luckily, we build our oasis time to make sure that happens regularly.

Ending

We all need to return to our busy lives. The key is to do so consciously, to mark the end of our oasis time with the same awareness with which we begin it. In our case, we use the traditional Jewish ritual of *Havdalah* to end our oasis time and start a new week.

Havdalah means "to make a distinction." The core message of this ritual is that we signal the end of our nonwork time and that we will go into the week with trust. We enter our week heartened and renewed for the challenges that await us. Darkness falls, and we light a special braided candle. We relish the fragrance of pungent herbs, raise the flare, and let it light our way into the week.

OASIS DAYS LEAD TO UNEXPECTED OASIS MOMENTS

One of the wonderful benefits of practicing oasis time weekly is that we can more readily use the same principles to create nourishing breaks during the week. One Tuesday afternoon, I decided to walk along the waterfront by the Berkeley Marina before I picked up Ari from school.

Even though the stunning San Francisco Bay was not far from our house, I rarely went to the waterfront because it meant passing by Interstate 80, which was often plagued with traffic slowdowns. As I got out of the car, I noticed the heavy, dense sky and the gray, choppy waves. I started to walk out the long jetty. My mind was racing. *Do I have enough*

time to be here? What about the phone call I need to return? Can I put my
phone down and stop texting?

With each step, I became more aware that the wind was picking up. I
slowed down to savor the force of the blowing wind. My thoughts scattered
into the air, and my focus shifted from my ruminations to what was right in
front of me. I saw the blue-gray water stretching toward the low, brooding
hills on the opposite shore. There was an odd, stark, leftover jetty that
stretched out uselessly. What was it, so many years ago? Now it was nothing. Lines of Percy Bysshe Shelley's poetry, learned in childhood, came to
mind, and I recalled the ancient wasted statue of a pharaoh:

My name is Ozymandias, King of Kings;

Look on my Works, ye Mighty, and despair!

Nothing beside remains. Round the decay

Of that colossal Wreck . . .[8]

The lone and level sea stretched over to Marin County. For a moment,
I longed hopelessly for the epic, the vast, a sense of awe of the mighty and
the powerful. And then, surprisingly, awe itself crept up and swelled into
a moment of amazement and gratitude. The allure of my crackpot mind
had been crushed for the moment, and in its place arose a moment of
unforced receptive silence. I walked back to the car, quiet and humble.

In his book *Sacred Time and the Search for Meaning,* professor Gary
Eberle says: "Many believe there is only one way to celebrate the Sabbath,
but in truth there are infinite ways, for the experience of sacred time is
the experience of being itself and cannot be limited by historic forms. . . .
The important thing is to stop, be receptive and find the fine balance
point between tradition and innovation."[9]

Your oasis time can unfold as you choose. You may take it on
Wednesday or on Saturday. You may paint for a few hours or relax at
home for an entire day. At the beginning, you can slowly unwind or start

with a ritual. In the middle, you can connect with others or really relax. At the end of your oasis time, you can wait patiently for what comes next or appreciate your time out of time—or both. Whatever you choose to do, however you spend your time, you reenter the world a little more peacefully and with a little more perspective than when you left it.

CHAPTER

8

{ DON'T LET ANYTHING STOP YOU }

L et's acknowledge the powerful forces that can keep us from our oasis time goals. In this chapter, we will look at three of them. The need for rest, renewal, and connection is built into our bodies, but we have learned to override our rest signals time after time. It's essential that we understand the obstacles that stand between ourselves and the rest that we need—physically and spiritually— so that we can commit to overcoming them: work as an addiction, being out of touch with our own nature, and our immunity to change.

WORK AS AN ADDICTION

Would I call myself a workaholic? Not really, but it sure was hard for me to stop working and doing. What's tricky here is that we may not recognize ourselves as workaholics because the addiction has a large cultural component. Our Western culture values work over almost everything else and views crazy overcommitment patterns very positively. However, there is a big difference between being a hard worker and being a workaholic. Hard workers are people who love what they do but know that the value of their lives extends beyond work; they have a robust existence doing and enjoying non-work-related activities. In contrast, workaholics invest everything in work and have all of their personal value bound up in it. They prioritize work-related activities above all else, and they don't leave room in life for any other kind of enrichment or meaning. If workaholics renew themselves at all, it is a temporary fix designed to enable them to work again. That was me. For many years, I could not voluntarily stop working to play, enjoy, and rest. Yet, I still would not have thought of myself as a workaholic.

We get a lot of reinforcement for being hard workers. It's considered a sign of moral superiority to work long and hard. I actually heard someone say, "You're a workaholic? That's a good addiction to have!" We are admired for our workaholic behaviors. However, although most workaholics are materially successful, they are more likely to be unhappy about their work–life balance. According to Ray Williams, a psychologist who specializes in workaholism, "They neglect their health to the point of devastating results and ignore their friends and family. They avoid going on vacation so they don't have to miss work. And even if they do go on vacation, they aren't fully present because their mind is still on work."[1]

But *was* I a workaholic? When I stepped back to examine my big assumptions, I found that I demonstrated many of the workaholic traits described above. I hadn't thought of myself as an addict, yet I could not stop working. When I squeezed in lunches, breakfasts, and walks with other people, my attention was on getting back to work as soon as I could. Even during those precious social moments, I felt an internal pressure to focus on work, often interrupting conversations to make notes about projects and plans.

This focus on work was a way of avoiding my fear that perhaps I did not have value in other areas of my life. I partly worked so hard to avoid my fears of being unappreciated and unseen. I didn't realize that my pace of work was creating distance between myself and the people and experiences that I valued in other areas of my life; my behavior led to the isolation that I feared.

As I started on my own journey into oasis time and taking weekly breaks, I found invaluable support from twelve-step programs such as Workaholics Anonymous. Being in a recovery program helped me see how work was an escape from my anxiety—in my case, anxiety about feeling valued by others. And it's not just full-time workers who can become workaholics. Anyone can be a workaholic: stay-at-home parents, students, artists, part-timers, self-employed people, even out-of-work people.

The pace of our lives has continued to increase. For some people, the drive to accomplish, to compete, or to be the best has taken over every minute. In the moments when we want to be connecting with others, we also might be aware that we wish we were completing tasks instead. When we're with close friends or our children, even watching a movie, we might be telling ourselves, "Oh, I wish I had gotten that task done. When am I going to get to it? And how will I remember it?" Slowly our capacity for savoring the moment diminishes, until each moment is invaded by the unending quest to accomplish. We are mesmerized by taking action. Digital connectedness only adds to the possibility of staying "at work" constantly.

Workaholics Anonymous offers a powerful set of tools for coming to our senses and restoring our ability to rest and to play.[2] Here are some of my favorite tools (from their Web site, workaholics-anonymous.org, which is filled with more excellent information), followed by my comments in italics.

* **Underscheduling.** We allow more time than we think we need for a task or trip, allowing a comfortable margin to accommodate the unexpected.

    What feels like underscheduling is actually a much more realistic way to allow time for what I need to do.

* **Playing.** We schedule time for play, refusing to let ourselves work nonstop. We do not make our play into a work project. Workaholics have found that having fun and relaxing are essential tools in our recovery from workaholism. Play and fun help us to live in the present moment, rather than driving ourselves for hoped-for fulfillment in some faraway future time.

Last Shabbat, I was running around the house with Ari, and all of a sudden I realized I was playing. I decided to check off the "play-time" box. Play: Check. I watched myself turn a delightful moment with my treasured child into another overachiever accomplishment. Was I playful enough to get the deep benefits of play? Oy!

* **Accepting.** We accept the outcomes of our endeavors, whatever the results, whatever the timing. We know that impatience, rushing, and insisting on perfect results only slows down our recovery. We are gentle with our efforts, accepting what is happening in the moment, and letting go of our desire to control outcomes.

    I acknowledge that rushing and pushing are my ways to escape my anxieties about failing and being rejected.

* **Asking.** We admit our weaknesses and mistakes. We realize we don't have to do everything ourselves, and we ask our Higher Power and others for help.

    Even though I feel vulnerable when I ask for help, I have learned to humbly admit that I just can't do everything on my own.

* **Balancing.** We balance our involvement in work with our efforts to rest *before* we get tired. To remind ourselves, we check our level of energy before proceeding to our next activity. We do not get "wound up" in our work, so we don't have to unwind.

    This is why I started keeping Shabbat. I love the feeling of getting to rest before I become exhausted, and I like keeping my energy more in balance. I hate exhausting myself. It's like falling into a deep pit with no handholds to get out.

* **Nurturing.** We nurture our bodies with healthy eating, exercise, and rest. We nurture our minds by looking for positive aspects in every encounter. We nurture our spirits by surrounding ourselves with beauty, harmony, and tranquility. We recognize we are neither what we do nor what we feel. We foster our sense of self-worth and self-respect.

*This approach calms me and moves me toward serenity. Oasis
time is an extension of that; it's a time when I nurture myself with
the blessings of rest, good food, and loving companionship.*

Workaholics Anonymous recommends meditation as a key part of healing from workaholism. Sitting quietly takes practice, but little by little we can let go of the chatter in our minds and interrupt the nonstop bursts of thoughts about what to do next. We start to notice that much of the time, we are ricocheting from demand to demand and that what we call thinking is actually random bits of inner dialogue. When we observe our brain activity, we redirect ourselves to the present moment and begin paying attention to breath or body sensations. It's the practice of noticing our thoughts and then returning to present-moment awareness that allows our brains to change. Slowly we train ourselves to experience some inner quiet and peace as we develop the patience to slow down and sit quietly.

The norm in our society is to overbook and not leave enough time to do things well. But we feel and do better when we approach the world as a craftsman or artist who takes her time to do her work well, not hustle on to the next thing. This is what "abstinence" for a workaholic means. Workaholics Anonymous sums up the experience.

*For many workaholics, abstinence means far more than relief from
compulsive working on a physical level. It also means an attitude
that comes as a result of surrendering to something greater than ourselves. Abstinence means not only freedom from compulsive working
but also freedom from compulsive thinking and worrying. Each of us
is free to determine our own way of being abstinent according to personal needs and preferences.*

Oasis time is an outstanding way to expose and confront our workaholism—and the underlying fears it masks—in constructive ways every week. As I learned how to take breaks, I learned that my life was richer for them. Rather than discover that I had no meaning or impact outside of my work, I began to connect on a deeper level with the people and things that mattered to me. Moving toward oasis time can be seen as a path to growth that offers a concrete way to put the Workaholic Anonymous tools into practice.

Being Out of Touch with Our Own Nature

The second powerful force against oasis time has to do with how disconnected we are from our own natural rhythms and from the sense of well-being provided by time in nature. We're so used to pushing and rushing that when we take our day off, tuning in to our bodies' needs can feel awkward and unfamiliar.

We are disconnected from *our* nature and from nature itself, which is a source of healing and wisdom. How is it that we do not know *viscerally* that we need regular rest? How can we keep shunting the people we care about to one side or another? How can we not know instinctively that time in nature restores our balance and well-being? How can we not follow so much of the excellent advice on mitigating stress? Why do we need so much advice in the first place?

We are alienated from our bodies in a deep way. Our muscles are overly tight. We've gotten so accustomed to being tired that we think fatigue is a normal part of adulthood, even when our kids can sleep through the night or if we have no kids at all. What if we weren't pushing our bodies around? What if we fully inhabited our bodies?

Sonja Haller, the blogger who explored fifty-two Sabbaths, describes how she learned to manage her migraines by listening to her body. She remembers being asked what symptoms she noticed before a migraine. "I could not think of any," she writes. "Now ten years later, it's plain my body gave several signs before a headache would hit. For example: frequent yawning, squinting at light, cravings for coffee or chocolate, and a foggy brain. Knowing these today is why I experience very few headaches anymore. But the reason I never noticed these things was because I was disconnected from my body."

Taking weekly oasis time reconnected Haller to her body. "The gentle nudges and knocks of my wise body had to become a firework for me to pay attention. Over the weeks of my 52 Sabbaths Experiment, my body has reemerged as the compass it was designed to be. She sends butterfly flutters at things my soul wants more of—yes to sunrise walks. . . . She sends electrical currents up my spine when an idea is worth pursuing. But, too, she sends choking sensations at the failure to take action of a soul desire. She sends belly dread when I'm preparing to do some people-pleasing activity."[3]

Haller's migraines make her reconnection with her body particularly important, but even those of us who suffer from ordinary aches, pains, and exhaustion can gain much by listening to, appreciating, and reviving our bodies once we enter the regular rhythm of rest and connection. We often ignore our bodies' signals, but in doing so, we miss something important: the art of being whole. And this diminishes a key intelligence about our lives. But when we consciously refresh our bodies, we go beyond the false impression that body and mind are separate in the first place.

In his book *Intelligence in the Flesh,* Guy Claxton draws on current research that demonstrates conclusively that intelligence is not located only in the brain, but rather is distributed throughout the body. In fact, Claxton tells us, we don't *have* bodies, we *are* bodies. We aren't a clunky piece of meat that has to be governed by the wise intellect; that is a dated idea. The more accurate view is that we are a finely tuned, exquisitely designed whole creature in which all the parts are synchronized. We lose our intelligence if we ignore or separate out our physical being. Claxton says, "I am smart precisely because I am a body. I don't own it or inhabit it; from it I arise."

This has profound implications for how we think and especially for what "thought" really is. In addition to thoughts running through our heads, it turns out that we think with our gut as well. We also have sensations we call intuition; this is when our entire body is thinking with us and for us. We separate our mind from our body at our peril. The increasing popularity of mindfulness practices reflects our desire to reconnect our physical, emotional, and psychological bodies.

Breath is one of the ways that we can connect to the physical self that we inhabit. We can breathe deeply and pause for a moment as we take in the deep refreshment of air. As we exhale, our brains calm down, our cortisol decreases, and tension drains out. After we release the sense of exhaustion, a refreshing calm can arise. We then bring this refreshment into our next moment, our next day, our entire workweek. This is a way of using our physical bodies to set the tone for our full selves.

Oasis time provides a recurrent setting in which we can renew ourselves. For several hours each week, we stop taking constructive action, we forgo competition, we put down the computer, we release the tension in our faces and bodies, and we settle into the comfort of self-acceptance and appreciation of what we have.

You can spend part of the oasis day focusing on your core self. Explore these questions as the day unfolds.

* What's in my heart today?

* What small murmurings call for attention?

* What body signals do I notice, now that I am slowing down? What are they trying to tell me?

* What am I dreaming about?

* What are my soul's desires?

You can't answer those questions when you are on the run. You don't have access to those depths when you are in "do" mode and rapidly checking things off your list. When you move fast, a different part of your brain kicks in and your executive function is in charge. Not your heart, not your soul, not your intuition. Oasis time is time to allow for connection with your inner life. Holding these questions in your heart gives life richness and meaning.

Time in nature also helps us reconnect to the spaciousness of our own souls. It offers open-ended experiences that encourage awe and wonder. Richard Louv, author of *Last Child in the Woods,* notes that painful symptoms such as "tunneled senses, and feelings of isolation and containment" can develop in people when they are away from nature too long. By contrast, he cites extensive research demonstrating that, for young people, time in nature leads to calm, reduces anxiety and ADHD, and leads to a sense of connection with others. Time in nature gives children opportunities to enjoy and develop each one of their senses, engage in free play and make their own meaning, develop divergent thinking and creativity, and, ultimately, experience reverence and mystery.[4]

Jesse Sachs, outdoor educator in Oakland, California, has ample examples of this positive reconnection for young people. He brings teenage boys into the wilderness. Each boy has a solo experience for a night and a day. For some of the boys, it's the first time they have sat alone, still and quiet, for that length of time.

Sachs says it's astonishing to hear the wisdom that bubbles up effortlessly from the boys when they return and share their experiences around a campfire. They come back with brilliant dreams, deep wisdom, and, almost to a boy, immense gratitude for their parents, even though some have had a rough time with them. Sachs told me, "I feel it too. I feel immense gratitude and a poignant sense of loss about how many years have gone by when I have not been expressing gratitude to my parents."[5]

The boys come to appreciate the amount of work it takes to feed and clothe and house them, to educate and love them. "One boy in particular stands out in my memory," Sachs recalls. "This kid told us how his dad had gotten an amazing job and wanted to move the family. The boy said, 'I've been so angry with my dad, and I told him I won't go. I couldn't understand how my dad could take me from my school, my friends, and my comforts. And while I was away on the solo, I was thinking about how much he has done for me. I'm so grateful to him. I want him to have his thing now, I want him to take this job, I'm going home without that fight in me.'" That boy had his own realization. It came from being alone in his body, on the earth and under the sky.

We don't have to go deep into nature to connect with a sense of awe and appreciation. You don't have to trek in a faraway forest; you can stroll your neighborhood, go to a park, find a twig or a leaf to examine carefully. You can simply pluck herbs from your garden.

Mindfulness teacher Mirabai Bush describes the way she taught this process to a group of somewhat reluctant college students. Giving each student a leaf, she told them that their assignment for the next five minutes was simply to focus on the leaf: Study it, bring awareness to it, let go of distractions, and allow their energy to center on the leaf.

She wanted to show them how it was possible to cultivate a sense of awe for something as simple as a leaf. After the exercise, the room was silent for a while. And then a football player sitting in the back row raised his hand. To Bush, he seemed like the person most resistant to "making himself vulnerable in any way. He said, 'Can I say something?' I said, 'Definitely.' He said, 'I love my leaf.' Then they all started to talk about what it was like to really look and look and look."[6] Paying attention to nature around us awakens love.

The Reverend Dr. Kirk Byron Jones, author of *Addicted to Hurry*, offers this exercise, drawing on the teaching of theologian Howard Thurman.

> *Sit down at a park bench or on the ground. Wait for a moment of stillness. You're not doing anything, not praying—just sitting, paying attention to what drops in your spirit. You are just being. The soul whispers what we need to hear. Develop an ear for the sounds of your soul. You don't conjure the words; they arrive on their own. Then you begin to hear what you can hear. The exact words that you need to hear will arise. Listen for the voice of the genuine inside you. If you can't hear that inner guiding voice, you will always be on the ends of strings that other people pull.*[7]

OUR IMMUNITY TO CHANGE

The late William Perry Jr., a therapist and Harvard professor, used to say, "Whenever someone comes to me for help, I listen very hard and ask myself, 'What does this person really want—and what will they do to keep from getting it?'" This keenly observant statement appears at the beginning of Robert Kegan and Lisa Laskow Lahey's business bestseller *How the Way We Talk Can Change the Way We Work*,[8] and it zeroes in on a puzzling feature of human life: Even though we may want to change, we often sabotage our efforts to do so.

Kegan and Lahey call this our "immunity to change," and it shows up especially when we want something very badly. We know the change we want would be great for us, yet something internal conspires to keep us from the experiences we so dearly desire—almost like a flock of contrary gremlins. In this case, we want significant weekly time off, yet we always find something else to do. Kegan and Lahey call those gremlins "competing commitments." Competing commitments can seriously block our way, regardless of our internal desire to shift. But we can't simply push our way through them to change. Instead, we have to discern them and then disarm them.

We can detect a competing commitment when we say we want one thing but we keep doing another. We want a peaceful evening with our family, but we keep spending time on screens and business calls. We want to get fit, but we keep postponing our yoga class or run. We want to experience oasis time each week, but we keep saying yes to work that isn't essential. We want to change, but we can't, and we don't know exactly what is holding us back. We are up against these hidden but powerful commitments, which now compete with our new goal. Because they are unknown to us and pervasive, they make it almost impossible to take the necessary steps toward creating the change we want, oasis time.

According to Kegan and Lahey, we can become more aware of these barriers to change, especially when they play out in common behaviors that go against the changes we say we are committed to making. When we look more deeply into what is getting in the way of change, we can identify the compelling competing story, make better choices about what we really want, and pursue our dreams more successfully.[9]

Immunity to change initially hampered MaryAnn McKibben-Dana

as she and her family brought oasis time into their lives. MaryAnn wrote the insightful journal of her family's year of Sabbath observance called *Sabbath in the Suburbs,* which I mentioned in Chapter 5. They chose Saturday for their family Sabbath time because McKibben-Dana worked on Sundays. Midway through the book, she reflects on the challenges they faced, saying, "I am mystified that six full months into the Sabbath experiment, I still fight the impulse to work around the house. . . . It isn't my commitment to Sabbath that stops me from doing this stuff. It's the lack of proper tools. The work still calls to me on the Sabbath. Even after half a year."

She identifies the instincts that are competing with her new commitment to stop and let things be.

> *It's complicated. The fact that we anticipate the arrival of each Saturday with the giddy relief of kids at Christmas suggests that there's something right about it. But the impulse to tidy, to beautify, to make everything all better is always there. And that is what this year has been about: a commitment to something simple but not easy. A resolution to stop changing things. To stop controlling the chaos for one blasted, blessed day.*[10]

Her struggle is familiar. Her commitment to stop busyness conflicts with her commitment to control her home environment. It is only over time that she is able to relax that struggle, let go of that need to control, and learn to enjoy her Sabbath more deeply.

How might this apply to your creating an oasis in time? Let's say you decide to experiment with keeping oasis time for the next four weeks. Say you have decided to take a good chunk of time off—perhaps Friday evening or all of Sunday morning. You are strongly committed to your plan, but somehow over each of the next four weeks, something comes up and gets in the way. One time, perhaps, a friend calls with a last-minute request for help. The next time, you start checking e-mail; two hours later, you realize you've missed most of your oasis time. The following Friday night, you get home ready to unwind, then realize you forgot to get food for dinner. Or you wake up Sunday morning, check your phone automatically, and set off on e-mail and errands without even thinking about it. The fourth week, on your way to your oasis time, you get an urgent text that requires immediate attention. Week after week. What is going on here?

Lisa Lahey explains that this type of inadvertent self-sabotage is the essence of immunity to change. Lahey emphasizes that there are very good reasons why people don't change. For instance, we prefer to stay with what's familiar, even if it is painful.

So the first thing, she says right off, is to stop badgering yourself about your inability to take time off. Self-criticism won't help you explore your competing commitment. Remember, the competing commitment is hidden to you, and you will have to investigate to reveal it. Think of yourself as a detective. Assume that something valid is going on and you have not yet figured out what it is. Now investigate with care.

How to Unearth Your Competing Commitment

Perhaps one of your core motivations for oasis time is experiencing refreshing relaxation time. Start by being honest with yourself about your current situation. Maybe you've told yourself many times, "I am committed to bringing more relaxation and unscheduled time into my life. I value friends and family, and I want more time at ease with them." But then you don't make it happen. You find yourself doing just one more thing for work, or you "have" to get some errands done, or you decide to clean your apartment before you can relax. Perhaps you get drawn into Facebook, and you imagine you have more of a social life than you actually do. The end result is you don't make time for the relaxation and renewal that you claim you want.

Be as honest as you can about your role in the situation. Describe your situation with no shame: just the facts. Describe what you do that impedes your goals and what you are doing (or not doing) that gets in the way of your oasis time. Forgetting to make plans is as much a factor as deciding to do errands. Recognize that those behaviors are serving an important purpose and that only when you recognize why they are there will you be able to change them.

At this point, when you can't get oasis time going, you have to answer these key questions:

> What else am I committed to?
>
> What explains these seemingly contradictory actions?

Thinking as a detective, you recognize that you are being driven by something else. What is that something else? If you inquire deeply, some fascinating details arise. Perhaps you are also committed to being the "always on" person at work, or to making sure everything is done right or your way. Perhaps you hate to say no when someone makes a last-minute request. Or you may think that if you aren't responding to e-mail within the hour, you will be seen as a slacker. Perhaps you fear that you could lose something precious if you walk away from work for your oasis time. In other words, moving toward your oasis time places something profound at risk.

As a result of your detective work, you might find yourself saying, "I am committed to oasis time, but I am also committed to being available to my work colleagues at all times." Or, "I am committed to being on top of any work situation." Or, "I am committed to making sure that my home is orderly," like MaryAnn McKibben-Dana. Don't criticize or judge yourself. These are all valid commitments based on your life experience. Many of them are also embedded in our larger culture, which competes with our desire for a sociable oasis time. Once you identify and accept the competing commitments, your next step is to explore why they have such a hold on you.

Examine Your Big Assumption

Our lives are governed by deep, often unexamined assumptions. Here are examples of common, persuasive "big assumptions" that stop us from getting the weekly rest and renewal that we want and need.

* I assume that I must be available 24/7 in order to keep my job.

* I assume that I must constantly deliver to be of value.

* My value depends on my doing and accomplishing.

* I will never be good enough for anybody.

* I will not be loved or cared for just as I am, with all my flaws.

These assumptions, tucked away deep in our subconscious, influence our daily behavior. They can keep us in constant performance mode even when intellectually and physically we know we need to take a break.

Once you expose a big assumption, try to explore how accurate it really is. For example, if one of your big assumptions is, "If I don't go 100 percent, I will be seen as a slacker," try performing at 90 percent one day. If that works, take another baby step and be more discerning about how you expend your energy.

Look for situations where you don't need to go all out and can give a little less while still succeeding. When you create a draft of a report that is going to be reviewed and changed by other people, don't obsessively perfect it on your own before sharing it; you know that others are going to weigh in, so give yourself a chance to receive constructive feedback first. That might turn out to be a better—and less time-intensive—way to proceed, rather than setting yourself up for frustration because you worked so hard and then had to revise the project to incorporate what others requested.

We don't know whether our big assumptions are true until we test them. One way to test them is to look for disconfirming data. Look actively: Are other people taking actions that you believe you can't? Are you holding yourself to a standard that's out of step with what others are looking for? Is it possible that your assumption might not be true?

You can test your assumptions by changing your behavior and observing the results. If you fear being rejected, you can start by asking a new acquaintance to go out for coffee. If that action is liberating, you might try again with others, knowing that you are testing an assumption that may not be correct. Eventually, you might throw the dinner party you've been dreaming about for years. As we test a big assumption, we can see other, smaller assumptions more clearly and address them too. Ultimately, we become much better at making choices that meet our deeper needs.

In his book *Busting Your Corporate Idol,* Greg Marcus, PhD, recounts how his assumptions of what was required for success were all wrong. He worked ninety hours a week to complete a project that had impossible deadlines. This went on for a *year.* Then the project flopped, possibly because he tried too hard. He did keep his job, but at that point he was exhausted. He cut his hours back to seventy a week. To his astonishment, no one seemed to notice the change. So he cut back again, to sixty hours a week. Again, no comment—and the quality of his work actually improved. He was surprised to discover that his own assumptions were driving him to work such long hours, even more than the culture of his firm.

In another case, a manager I worked with was dying to attend her son's soccer games, but she felt uncomfortable asking for permission to leave early on Thursdays. One day she did leave at three thirty and got to watch her son's game, which was wonderful. She was still able to get her work done in time, and no one said a word about her early departure from the office. So she tried it again. Again, fine. Her assumption was completely unfounded. She felt happier in her work environment once she realized it allowed her to participate in an important family moment. This won't be true for everyone every time, but it is worth taking a small risk to discover the truth.

Often, when people run these experiments, they not only realize that the worst-case scenario is not going to occur, but they also reap benefits they never imagined. The worry about taking risks starts to dissipate not because there will never be complications or conflicts, but because the problems seem more surmountable in the face of the larger benefits.

Kegan and Lahey have developed a four-column exercise for examining competing commitments and deeper assumptions:[11]

1. I am committed to the value or importance of . . .	2. What I'm doing or not doing that may prevent my commitment from being fully realized	3. I may also be committed to . . .	4. Assumptions that ground my competing commitment
I am committed to living my life well. I want to have downtime every week. I want to work effectively, and I want to have time for my family and friends.	I overcommit myself. I take on too many projects. I find it hard to say no. I book too many activities on the weekends.	I might also be committed to being seen as the go-to, do-it-all person, the essential one. I am committed to people knowing they can count on me at work.	Work is my primary area of success. I am only valuable when I am being productive.

Once you see your competing commitments and big assumptions more clearly, you will be in a position to decide how to work with them. First you determine how important your column 1 is to you. You can then develop a number of ways to change your assumptions. You do this not by stating the opposite assumptions; rather, you determine how willing you are to risk real change. Then, actively seek out data that contradict the big but false assumption. Be creative. Take more actions that test your big assumption. Experiment with naming the ways in which you are valuable when you are not working and not getting things done, for example. By doing this, you may break through your stumbling block and into a world of experimentation and discussion that will open you up to yourself and move you toward your oasis time.

Testing and exploring your big assumptions can be very helpful; you are no longer at the mercy of unconscious competing commitments. Now, you can make more of a conscious choice about what you really want.

You can overcome obstacles to oasis time. Take the attitude that nothing can keep you from your rhythm of rest each week. Not your workaholism, not your alienation from self or nature, and not your immunity to change. You can triumph over all of these obstacles and bring yourself to a life where you actively and successful balance different kinds of time and different aspects of yourself.

Part III: Taking Back Your Time

CHAPTER
9

{ TAKE STOCK }

You want weekly time off, and yet you may be absolutely certain there's no "extra" time in your schedule. But is that really true? It's worth examining how you actually spend your time. In this chapter, we'll take a penetrating look at how you spend your time, your energy, *and your* thinking power.

We'll start by asking a few questions: Are you on top of your game? Do you know how to detect your energy and time leaks? You might be going a mile a minute and feel that every minute is accounted for, but research shows that most people don't have a good handle on what they do with their time. It's hard to get where you want to go if you don't know where you are, so it's worth assessing what is happening to those minutes, hours, and days.

In *What the Most Successful People Do on the Weekend,* time management master Laura Vanderkam points out that the most successful folks don't work all weekend but instead take serious time off. A study conducted by the makers of DeskTime software, which tracks employees' time use, discovered that the most productive people also take regular breaks throughout the day.[1] They work and rest in rhythm: The highest-performing 10 percent work for fifty-two minutes and then take a seventeen-minute break. Bestselling author Tom Rath boils this down to what he calls the 45–15 model in his book *Eat, Move, Sleep:* Work for forty-five minutes, rest for fifteen. It sounds wrong, doesn't it? But it is a path to far greater effectiveness.

Why aren't we taking frequent and long breaks when it is clear that they increase our productivity and well-being? And how do we find—or more accurately, create—the time for these breaks?

You have taken the first step by reading this book and committing to creating this time. It's also valuable to believe, as Rath points out, that being committed to establishing a rhythm of work and rest is essential *before* trying to "find" the time. Be willing to get very curious and open-minded about looking at your time, because there may be more of it available for rest and reflection than you think.

The next step is to look closely at how you spend your time: What do you actually do? Then, reflect on what you have learned and try to experience your actions as a series of choices. That's challenging because it means moving from a reactive to a proactive orientation toward time use. Then choose to make small changes and slowly create the habits that will give you the time and energy you need to live the life you want. In short:

1. Believe in the value of rest and make a commitment to it weekly.
2. Take stock—learn how you spend your time.
3. Experience your actions as choices. Be proactive.
4. Create new small habits of thought and action.

You've been developing your commitment to weekly time off as you've been reading this book. That is step one. If your commitment feels wobbly, keep going. These next steps can reinforce your commitment to weekly rest. And now let's take stock.

Take Stock—Learn How You Spend Your Time

When we first think about creating our oases in time, many of us become paralyzed. We can't imagine squeezing another minute out of our hectic lives, even if it's for a positive thing like rest, play, or spiritual nourishment. A crucial step in creating refreshing downtime is scrutinizing how we spend our time now. What the heck are we doing all day?

Brigid Schulte, author of *Overwhelmed*, first explored her plaguing sense of always having too much to do by tracking what she did each day. She kept a journal of every single thing that she did, and then she turned it in for analysis. John Robinson, time researcher and analyst, reviewed her schedule and told her she had twenty-eight hours a week of leisure. "Absurd!" she thought.

But when she questioned the findings, she learned that Robinson defined "leisure" in his own terms, which included things like listening to NPR while she struggled to get out of bed one morning or waiting for a tow truck to come and move her immobilized car when she was stranded one day. Her so-called leisure time came in tiny bits and pieces, what Schulte called "leisure confetti." She certainly didn't experience those twenty-eight hours of leisure confetti as true leisure, but by starting to observe herself in action, she began to learn more about what was actually happening in her life.

She realized that in trying to do everything, she ended up with a sense of nothing. Her life was a blur because she wasn't focusing on any one thing. Instead, she was multitasking, rushing from one activity to the next, not allowing for transition time but instead squeezing in family time and staying up late to make cupcakes. She was tired, running behind, and not able to recognize when an activity was her choice or when her time was her own.[2]

Many of us spend our days in such a blur that we have no real connection to what we are doing or why we are doing it. But it's impossible to make new choices without understanding our current choices.

So let's give it a shot. It is time to launch a modest inquiry into how you use your time. The idea is to get to know what you do all day, to examine your current reality, bringing as much open-minded curiosity and compassion to your inquiry as possible.

Four Tools for Learning How You Spend Your Time

Start by committing to tracking your time for a day. The tools below offer a few different ways to do this. Don't worry about trying to create a perfectly accurate record; simply doing this exercise is eye-opening. I always learn something from tracking my time.

What's most important is that you be honest about what you're doing during the day and that you keep an open mind. For example, I recently learned that I don't spend nearly as much time with David and Ari on weekday evenings as I thought I did. It wasn't a comfortable discovery, but it helped me make some needed changes to both my expectations and my behavior.

So look over these four tools for time tracking and choose one or two you would like to try.

1. Track Every Fifteen Minutes

> ## *Exercise*
>
> - Create a place for your tracking notes: Get a small notebook, open a new page in your smartphone Notes app, or open a new file on your computer.
> - Set a timer for fifteen minutes.
> - When the timer goes off, make a quick note of what you are doing. Keep it simple.
> - Set the timer again. And again.
> - Keep tracking for several hours or a full day.

That's it! This fifteen-minute check is a quick and easy way to see what you are up to. The key is to keep going. It can be illuminating to discover how far off track you can get in just a few minutes—or how much you can accomplish. I recently completed this exercise and discovered that it took me fifteen minutes to refill my coffee one morning. Fifteen minutes?! Why? Because I wasn't just making my coffee; I also treated myself to a couple of articles in the *New York Times* without realizing that I was actually grabbing a little break time.

We all have our ways to sneak in breaks, but are those sneaky breaks refreshing? Pay attention to how you get your breaks and whether they renew your energy. Are you appreciating that you're on a break, or are you moving through it so quickly that you don't enjoy it? I'm a print addict, so I have to be vigilant about not absentmindedly reading any print publication in sight. It's often my mode of procrastinating rather than a truly restorative break—and yet it saps time that I could be using for a real break.

Are you on task? Checking to see what you are doing every 15 minutes can be a wake-up call.

2. Track Your Activities As They Unfold

For this tracking approach, use one of the many time-tracking apps like Hours or ATracker. Or simply take out a piece of lined paper and get started.

Exercise

- On your grid, write down the name of your activity and its starting time.
- When you're done, make a quick note of when you ended that activity.
- Then write down the name and starting time of your next activity.

When I use a time tracker app, I also set my timer for 15-minute intervals, because I often forget about the app. Putting these two methods of tracking my time together gives me good information.

This can be a challenge if you are often interrupted, but the result can be illuminating.

3. Use the Hourly Check-In

In his book *18 Minutes,* management consultant and top *Harvard Business Review* blogger Peter Bregman talks about using the hourly check-in method. You set a timer to go off every hour. Then you stop what you're doing to spend a minute checking your to-do list, reviewing the last hour's work, and quickly re-sorting your priorities.

This rapid self-scan can keep you at the top of your game all day.

4. LIST ALL COMMITMENTS—LARGE AND SMALL

If you can't conceive of tracking your time during the day, try this approach. Make a list of your current time commitments and look for ways to reduce them. Write down every single thing you can think of that you are doing throughout the day—including everything from ordering takeout to carpooling to scrolling through social media. Then look for ways to cut back the list.

Pulitzer Prize–winning journalist Katherine Ellison details this process in her masterful book *Buzz*. Ellison describes how she was telling Jean, her psychiatrist sister-in-law and phone support buddy, how overloaded she was. Finally, Jean said, "Write down your list"—everything Ellison had to do. She came up with about twenty items she calls "chronophages," or time-eaters. These include taking care of her two boys, writing, holding three part-time consulting jobs, spending time with her parents, staying fit with running and tennis, dropping off meals at the homeless shelter, and much more. "Just looking at those twenty items makes me feel exhausted," she writes. "How did I ever convince myself I could carry them all without screwing up in some major way?" Yet as she went through her list, looking to eliminate items, she delivered some hard news to herself. "Hey, come to think of it, everything is in the *can't eliminate* category."

Over time, however, things shifted. Some changes happened by attrition, like when certain client work ended. She also eased up on her perfectionism, which can be a huge time sink if it manifests as reviewing the same material over and over. She finally quit the parent-teacher group that she didn't get anything out of but didn't want to embarrass herself by leaving. She also eliminated many of those tiny time-eaters, the ones we often think don't count—like forwarding e-mail chain letters, funny cat videos, and highly recommended Facebook entries—but which can take up to more than an hour a day. Ellison's "heightened sensitivity to chronophages" helped her get better at fending them off.[3]

Exercise

- Write down everything that you have committed to doing.

- Go through the list and cross off the lower-priority commitments.

This is part of the process. When you look more carefully at what is on your plate, you recognize that you are the one who has put some of (or many of) those things there. By taking a deep look at what she was doing and recognizing her limits, Ellison was able to start doing less, which opened up the family time she had been wanting, including more time together on weekends and a festive family dinner on Friday nights.

Each of these tools offers you ways to explore whether you are on track—or off. I don't find it easy to track my time, but it's always worth it. This morning, for example, I woke from my Internet trance at a blog post far, far away from what I had been looking for. You might find yourself playing games, reading the news, or keeping up with favorite blogs.

For some people, off-track time might involve social distractions or mindless eating. These little off-track journeys are often our ways of sneaking in breaks because we need them. But we take those breaks unconsciously. Researchers keep telling us that high productivity does not mean being glued to our desks; it means taking *good* breaks that refresh us. But we often don't know what those are. So part of your inquiry is to explore how you take breaks now in order to think about how you could take better breaks.

Take Stock of How You Focus . . . and Lose Focus

It's also very important to take stock of your patterns of focusing. Studies show that we lose our focus a lot! This is due to both internal and external interruptions. The good news is that a few adjustments in three areas can improve your concentration: your work environment, your physical state, and interruptions.

As you take stock, look at how your work environment is set up. First of all, make sure your environment is conducive to focusing on your work.

* Are you physically comfortable?

* Is the noise level right for you? I myself concentrate quite well in a relatively noisy environment, but while I like the noise, you might not. If noise distracts you, try wearing noise-reduction headphones or playing low-key music.

* Dehydration can make it hard to focus. Do you have a system to encourage yourself to drink water?

* What concentration tools do you use? Have you tried using the Focus (full-screen) view available on some versions of Microsoft Word or downloading the Freedom program to block out all other screens?

* What kind of breaks do you take? How often?

Second, assess your physical state. Taking care of your physical needs helps with concentration.

* When are you physically at your best?

* What are you eating and when?

* What lifts your energy? What depletes you?

* What energizes you and gives you joy?

Third, learn how your interruptions happen. Observe yourself, but don't criticize, especially if a lot of your interruptions are self-generated.

* When are you interrupted?

* Who is interrupting you?

* How do you interrupt yourself?

* What happens when you receive social media notifications?

* How do you respond to the different interruptions?

As you learn more about what helps you focus, your productivity will improve. In sum, if we look carefully and compassionately at the choices we are currently making, and if we can recognize them as choices, then we have some influence over what we are doing. And then we can move, even if slowly, toward the big choice we want to make, which is more oasis time. Remember Brigid Schulte and her leisure confetti? She reports that she has become much more intentional about taking real, replenishing breaks. She and her family are enjoying life more *and* are highly productive.

EXPERIENCE YOUR ACTIONS AS CHOICES: BE PROACTIVE

To make new choices, you need to acknowledge what is really happening with your time and proactively choose to do something about it. I've had people throw up their hands at this point. "Forget it," they'll say. "I can't step off this treadmill." At first it all seems unworkable, as it did for Kathy Ellison. But remember, she made significant changes and so can you.

So stick with it. There may be some wiggle room in there. You might be so sure you know what the problem is—too much to do—that you don't take the time or gain the perspective to inquire more deeply.

We can't change many circumstances of our lives. But we can change our minds. We don't have to be imprisoned by our crushing sense of too much to do. Neurologist and psychiatrist Viktor Frankl, who was imprisoned in a death camp by the Nazis, points to the possibility of freedom in even the most oppressive of circumstances when he says, "Between stimulus and response there is a space. In that space is our power to choose our response. In our response lies our growth and our freedom." The exploration of freedom is serious and complicated, and it requires great honesty with the self.

We must teach ourselves to find the space in our circumstances. Even when the experience of choice feels elusive, we can dig deeper to locate where we do experience choice. Think of the times when you or a colleague or loved one became too sick to work. One day, life was full of compelling urgencies, none of which could be put aside; the next day, those "urgent" demands were completely on hold. And guess what? The world did not fall apart because you could not respond to them.

When we are agents in our own lives, and we get more clarity about what is happening in our own lives, and we see our own contribution to things as they are, then we can take more responsibility for making things different. And the earth will still spin on its axis, and what needs to get done will still get done—perhaps even better and with less stress. Here are some questions that I ask myself from time to time.

* Where does the pressure to do so much come from?

* How am I contributing to my sense of being overwhelmed?

* Am I making things harder for myself in some ways?

This very morning, I was working myself into a snit about how I don't get enough help with food preparation from my family. (You can see this is an issue.) I was getting ready to make a major exasperated, put-upon complaint: "I'm the one under the gun! I have deadlines to meet! I can't be preparing all the meals and work the way I need to right now."

However, before I launched salvo number one, I managed to ask myself the all-important question, How am I contributing to this? The answer was clear: I don't ask for help. I like the feeling of being in charge of meals. I love to cook. So I headed a fight off at the pass by saying to David, "Can you make dinner this evening?" "Sure

thing," was his answer. And yes, we do need to rethink some roles, but
it will be easier when we aren't angry at each other.

Part of becoming a stronger agent in your own life also includes deciding what addictions you will give up. Think, for instance, about those little addictions we all turn to. Think of my news addiction; or someone's gaming, shopping, or Facebook addiction; or pretty much everybody's addiction to blaming other people for being jerks. Even our need for approval can be seen as an addiction. Giving them up may feel hard, even impossible, but there are significant gains, in our experience of being proactive, to be reaped—huge gains, in fact—when we do.

Those yummy little addictive escapes might not be getting you the real satisfaction you crave, because they take up precious time that could be better used for truly replenishing rest and renewal. We really do want a more satisfying life, and backing away from our cozy addictions is one step in that direction. They can run our lives, when really we want our purpose, our deep connections, and our values to be guiding us.

When you become more proactive, it's easier to take responsibility for your life. You can clear up grudges and blame—you don't have time for them. Then you can start asking the deeper questions: What are you here for? What are your strengths? What really matters to you? Even if it is tiny, it is what matters to you. Take that as a clue. That is your passion. Your passion will fuel your energy. And you will see your life start to change.

If you watch your mind in action, you might find that you, like most people, obsess over small choices, worry about what people think of you, complain about how someone is bugging you, grouse about the unfairness of a situation, and occasionally freak out about climate change, only to ignore it again. But none of this is really making choices.

Often we add on tasks and commitments because we can't distinguish what's important. But more often than we realize, it's because we don't want to deal with the important things. Perhaps we don't feel we have the mental energy for the big tasks. Perhaps we don't know what to do. Perhaps we are simply overwhelmed. And we hope, maybe, that at least we can get that good feeling of checking something, anything, off the list. We can always find something to do other than what we must. But the resulting feeling of impotence is costly, with overwork and burnout among the highest costs.

We have more power than we think. We are effective at creating pressure. As we begin to notice how we create some of this pressure, we can see the consequences of our actions more clearly. We begin to discover, through close observation, that we're creating much of the sense of being overwhelmed by how we think. So we need to create new thoughts and new actions.

Create New Habits of Thought and Action

As you look back on your tracking, however formally or informally you recorded it:

* Did you notice a few things you could change that would get you some much-needed break or rest time?
* Did you find leisure confetti in your day that you could deliberately savor?
* Did you identify any chronophages—time eaters—that interfere with your ability to focus on the most important tasks of the day?

Using what you've learned, it's now time to take back control and make new choices that serve your true priorities. Here is a set of steps that have been shown to support behavior change.

1. *Identify a new choice.* Make it so small that you know you can do it. Fly under your resistance radar. For example, I now put newspapers away in the morning rather than leaving them out. This cuts my print-straying time significantly. You might:

   • End your workday fifteen minutes earlier than usual to put things away and make a few notes for yourself about where to pick up.

- Set up a schedule for checking e-mail or Facebook. Say at 10:30, 12:30, 2:30, and 4:30—just not all the time.

- Try the 45-15 approach and see how it works for you.

- Get up from your desk for lunch and take a fifteen-minute walk.

2. *Test your new choice* a couple of times to see how it feels. Is it doable? Do you like it? Is it small enough? Is it enough of a challenge?

3. *Find a trigger or cue.* Attach your proposed new habit to something you do regularly. This will become your habit trigger. For example, I put away newspapers after I clear the breakfast table. If possible, tack your e-mail schedule to the end of regular meetings. Attach your fifteen-minute walk to the end of your lunch. The regular combination will help enforce your new habit.

4. *Get support.* It is essential to find someone to support you—to cheer you on, cheer you up, and also hold you accountable.

5. *Practice.* Do your new habit every day. Aim to enjoy your new habit and appreciate yourself in the process of doing it.

6. *Know that you will forget.* Understand that you may occasionally forget about your new habit completely. This doesn't mean that you don't want to change. A dip in practice seems to be a regular part of habit change. Notice that you forgot, and remind yourself that recalling and restarting seems to be a pivot point of change.

7. *Keep going again and again.* Be prepared to get back to practice. Keep going. You may lose the thread several times before your habit becomes entrenched. Getting back on the horse is a big part of creating a new habit.

8. *Reward yourself.* Every time you catch yourself doing your new habit, reward yourself liberally. Sing big praises, jump up and down, congratulate yourself, play your favorite song.

The Need for Boundaries

You now have a greater understanding of what your life is like and greater compassion for your role in setting things up the way they are. You may even have identified a few small but potent actions that could lead to significant change in the way you spend your time. Creating stronger boundaries—the focus of the next chapter—and setting limits in every area of life are keys to creating more time for what matters most.

STRENGTHENING BOUNDARIES

B uilding strong boundaries around work of any kind and actively creating a rhythm of deep rest and renewal assist with moving toward a different kind of time. You can't experience the real letting go and deep renewal of true oasis time if you only *casually* put work aside for a certain number of hours every week; the stress of unfinished tasks will just be too much of a distraction. Instead, you need to create a strong boundary around work and accomplishment time so that you can deliberately enter the pleasures of oasis time. Boundaries are key to replenishment.

Boundary setting is a habit we can actively build into our lives. Strong boundaries stem from a mind-set that allows us to say yes and no more clearly and proactively. In our fast and furious world, most people are in a perpetual learning mode around how to set stronger, more distinct boundaries. You can do the hard work of learning where your limits are and then setting them. It's certainly possible to blame someone else for our exhaustion—boss, parents, kids, needy friends, life partners—but that ultimately doesn't help.

My friend Susan, like so many of us, struggles with setting boundaries.

Susan is a middle manager in a large computer company. Her job is complicated; she manages seventeen (yes!) projects while acting as a liaison between many different teams in a diffuse and chaotic work environment. She is warm, friendly, even motherly, and that makes her good at this complex job. Susan also has two teenagers and a half-hour commute. Not surprisingly, she has a difficult time getting enough sleep.

Lately, she's been trying a new plan to improve her slumber so that she will have more energy during the day. Her plan involves becoming stricter about setting limits with her work. She's pretty easygoing and breezy; she's a pleaser. Clear boundaries aren't her thing. But her work and home life are eating her up.

Susan described an average night to me as an example of how she struggles to stick to her plan. She came home late one Tuesday with a strong intention to get at least seven hours of sleep. "I'm so tired, I've just got to go to sleep earlier tonight," she said to herself as she left work later than she had intended. "Tonight, I've got to be in bed, lights out, at ten thirty."

But she came home to a dirty kitchen; her teenagers had eaten dinner and started their homework, leaving the dishes for her. "I've got to make a better agreement with them," she said to herself again, as she did the dishes and cleared off the counters while raging internally at her kids but not saying anything. Then her phone rang. Her brother, who rarely called, was on the line. "We haven't spoken for a while," she said to herself. "I can't keep putting this off." The conversation was not easy, as usual. They discussed a few sensitive issues about their mother's estate.

When they finally got off the phone, Susan thought, "I'm too upset to go to bed. I'll watch TV for a few minutes to relax." She was soon caught up in the show and fell asleep on the couch. Groggy and disheveled, she struggled to bed at three a.m.

Susan had good intentions, but she allowed her desire for more sleep to be overruled by other tasks. Of course, a clean kitchen, a good relationship with her brother, and a cooldown period at the end of the day are all important, but Susan allowed those things to override her need for sleep, which is key to making her life better. We talked about how to set boundaries with tasks that aren't on her critical path to sleep.

Rather than responding to every situation like a pinball, ricocheting haphazardly between issues as they come up, Susan could set boundaries around her time and focus. However, it turns out that it is not easy to set clear boundaries because subtle and complex issues are often at play. Sometimes it takes inner work. As Susan tried to understand why it was so hard to get the sleep she obviously needed, she saw that her urge to please others made it challenging to establish the boundaries she needed. She was afraid of offending people if she said no. She did not want to risk others' anger at her, and she hated feeling rejected. Susan undermined her commitments to herself and her need to maintain her health and well-being. The problem with this approach was that she waited to set boundaries until she herself was quite stressed out and angry, and then she expressed herself in harsh ways that risked her relationships anyway.

Gaining an awareness of your underlying motivations is the first step in learning how to make boundaries that honor your limits without hurting others. Could Susan have called her teens into the kitchen to clean up after themselves? Could she have called her brother back the next morning, when she was feeling more refreshed? Abby Seixas, author of *Finding the Deep River Within,* points out:

> *Making boundaries has to do with saying "no" to what we don't want or don't mean to do, in order to say "yes" to what we do want or do mean to do. . . .*
>
> *We need boundaries in order to slow down, to take time-in, and to stay centered and on course in daily life. Without them, we're in constant "response mode" . . . which is both an unsatisfying and an ineffective way to live.[1]*

Knowing and appreciating our limits will help with setting boundaries. There is so much we want to see and do, so many goals we want to accomplish. Unfortunately, nearly all of us operate in a fast-paced reactive mode, where boundaries are determined by the needs of the moment and by the (perceived) expectations of others. In reactive mode, we lose a sense of ourselves that we can only recover through understanding and accepting our limits.

You need to train yourself to establish physical, mental, emotional, and spiritual boundaries in a world of relentless action. Let's take a look at how you can strengthen those boundaries as part of your efforts to make oasis time happen. Boundaries can be harder to strengthen when you work at home or if your work is giving care to loved ones. But it still can and must be done. Caregivers in particular can wear themselves out and need real replenishment every day.

Physical Boundaries

Physical boundaries help us establish spatial and temporal distance from our work, chores, errands, and all our maintenance tasks. We can turn off our computer, close the door to the office, and return home from work. If our workspace is in our living room, we can cover that space with a beautiful cloth to indicate that it is closed. We can decide to leave our work at work, rather than bringing an important task home and telling ourselves, "I'll get to that after dinner, or after the kids get to bed." We do the same with endless chores. Making a clear separation allows us to get the rejuvenation we need from our labor in the world.

Deciding *when* you will and will not work is another way to establish tangible buffers. Setting temporal boundaries is vital to well-being. Susan had gotten in the habit of staying late at work, then bringing work home and planning to work more after dinner. Her efforts were stopped only by exhaustion. She had to learn to stop sooner than that.

Susan needed to set two physical boundaries to launch herself back into more effective work patterns. First, she chose to stop kidding herself about working at night, and so she no longer brought work home. In fact, she went a step further by consciously choosing to leave the office at six p.m., as well. (This made her anxious, but she adjusted to it.) Second, she decided that she wanted to be in bed with the lights out at eleven o'clock. Turning off lights is setting a physical boundary.

Once she made this decision, she found the TV show she loved most and made plans to watch it at ten o'clock with her younger daughter. This conscious choice enabled her to have the pleasure of watching her show *and* to be in bed and asleep by eleven. After dinner, Susan and her daughter both got into pj's, setting another boundary signifying the end of her workday. She helped her daughter with homework rather than lay out her own work. This ritual became a treat they both looked forward to.

Her daughter focused on getting homework done by ten so she could watch the show with her mom. They both enjoyed the TV cuddle time. At ten thirty, Susan turned off the television (it took some work to build this habit too) and prepared for bed at the same time as her daughter, so that when they said good night, she was ready to head to bed herself. This new set of habits took a while to set up and get used to, but she loved feeling more refreshed the next day. With more sleep, she was better able to focus on getting work done during the day, and she was just happier and easier to be with.

A good night's sleep changed Susan's ability to focus at work, and her whole unproductive cycle began to shift. Improving sleep is a good place to start in creating better physical boundaries, such as between home and work, because fatigue fuels slippery boundaries. These strengthened physical boundaries can be essential in creating oasis time.

Mental Boundaries

As Susan took action to establish physical boundaries with work, she realized she needed to strengthen her mental boundaries. She had to stop thinking about work. She had to get some control over the nagging problems that stayed with her even after she left the office.

Sometimes simply writing down the problem will help resolve it. Susan tried this and found that writing things down helped her get them out of her head. The sheer act of writing can create perspective. Talking about her concerns with someone else also gave Susan a little distance and enabled her to figure out where she needed to set a boundary. When work concerns surged through her mind, Susan called a friend who always asked two questions: What was Susan's contribution to the problem?

What one constructive action could she take to relieve her obsessing? The questions were not accusatory in any way, and Susan knew that her friend completely understood the difficulty of the situation. But those questions helped Susan feel like she had some power over what felt like a hopeless situation and gave her traction on her problem.

After a busy day, everyone's mind needs a break. It's helpful to practice consciously turning to other things that will absorb your attention. Most scientific breakthroughs happen when the researcher is *not* thinking about the problem; much creative problem solving comes when the mind is at rest. We are usually relaxed in the shower, focused only on enjoyment of the water, and that's why it is a great place to happen upon ideas that solve tough problems. ("Shower solutions" are not just folklore!) In contrast, a worried mind is simply not that creative. Ironically, in order to resolve our worries, we often need to let go of them. This skill of releasing worries helps us make the most of oasis time.

Exercise

Do you have a little ticker tape of worry humming in the back of your mind? You can practice setting a boundary with your monkey mind right now.

1. Seize a minute to write down what is bothering you—on your phone or on paper.
   a. What's the problem?
   b. Why is it bothering you?
   c. What are some action steps that could help? Write them down. You don't have to act on them right now.

2. Inhale and exhale a few long, deep breaths and deliberately turn away from your concern for just five minutes by doing something active that absorbs your attention. Get up and move for a couple of minutes. Stretch your body. Make a face. Take another deep breath.

3. Talk to yourself with compassion. Remind yourself that whatever is bothering you now will pass. You will find ways to deal with the situation.

Each of these moves helps you create mental distance from your concerns.

Emotional Boundaries

Finding ways back to serenity when painful emotions hold sway becomes necessary when you, like Susan, cannot let go of anxiety, grief, or anger, even after the incident that triggered the feelings has passed. Setting an emotional boundary begins with accepting the feelings you have.

Susan embarked on a practice called mindful self-compassion, which entails being aware of feelings and responding to them with kindness and understanding. Buddhist teacher Tara Brach, PhD, calls this approach to emotional work RAIN (an acronym of the four steps in the process). As described in her book *True Refuge,* RAIN is a way to be with and work with difficult emotions.

Recognize what is going on.
Allow the experience to be there, just as it is.
Investigate with interest and care.
Nourish with self-compassion.[2]

Susan describes how practicing RAIN has helped her: "I find this so helpful when I am foundering around, upset and unhappy and unfocused. First, I notice that I am upset. Even this isn't easy for me at times. And this is the important initial step of 'recognize.' Then, I allow myself to think and feel whatever it is. No matter how bad it seems to me, it's a storm of emotion passing through me. This is 'allow and accept.'

"After that, when I am ready, I inquire a little bit. What's going on? What am I feeling? Do I have any idea what the trigger was? This is the step called 'investigate.' Then I take a moment to speak kindly and gently to myself like a kind mama: 'There, there, honey. It's okay and you're okay. . . . Whatever you are feeling is fine. What do you need?' I kindly and gently take my attention away from the mean things I am saying about someone else or to myself and offer myself comfort. This is 'nourish with self-compassion.' It is so helpful with the waves of sadness that can arise once I realize how helpless I feel at work."

Susan decided to honor her feelings of fear rather than trying to squash them. She also wanted to understand better what she was so mad about. In her view, her boss was not respectful of her boundaries. He gave her additional tasks without checking to see if she could manage them. In her view, it was all his fault. He was insensitive, he was manipulative, he was selfish. Then she began to talk to herself a little differently. She finally realized that she was giving her boss no indication that she was struggling with overload. When she could see that she had a role in creating her difficult circumstances, she gained a sense of power. She learned how to be more assertive at work and how to let go of the outcomes so that she would have more peace of mind at home.

As Susan gradually set boundaries around emotions generated by her work, she became more available to her daughters. She applied mindful self-compassion to her home life too. Because she began recognizing her contribution to the household upsets, she was less exasperated at home. When she became a calmer mom, she was better able to deal with her daughters' fears and angers and could, in turn, teach them how to calm themselves.

It's easy to focus on the emotional work that *someone else* has to do, but that path is fruitless. It's far more fruitful to explore and heal whatever unresolved wounds in your own psyche have been triggered. Susan stopped railing helplessly about how her boss needed to become more sensitive and how her girls needed to grow up. There was nothing she could do about those things. She realized she needed to be aware of her limits much earlier so that she could set better boundaries and not feel taken advantage of.

It can be a relief to pursue your own emotional work, to take responsibility for your part of a dispute and upset. Others are often not available to do their own emotional work, and you only waste energy wishing they would do it. Many people use oasis time for doing their emotional work. Part of finding enough peace to take oasis time is accepting the immense woundedness of others (and ourselves) and finding small ways to bring more openness, mutual appreciation, and understanding to our relationships.

SPIRITUAL BOUNDARIES

Creating spiritual boundaries with the sources of your nonstop action involves exploring choice and acceptance in life. With better boundaries, you come to deeply understand where you have choice and influence in a situation, and where to let go and accept that what is happening is out of your control.

You can work on ending your struggle and let go of trying to exert your will. You turn your difficulties over to your sense of a higher power or God or reality or whatever source of calm and spiritual sustenance you have. Releasing control to a higher power is an essential step in effective twelve-step programs that address addiction and other chronic, painful issues. You can also draw on your yoga, meditation, or prayer practice to enhance your inner strength.

As Susan learned more about setting limits, she remembered something her mother used to do when Susan was a child. Before going to bed, her mother would finish the dishes, tidy up the house, and then place her hands on her children and say, "Here are my blessing hands. Can you feel the blessing coming through my hands to you? Now it is time to go to sleep."

The idea spoke to Susan, and she tried out her own practice of blessing hands. As she put things away at night, she felt the blessing energy go from her hands into her home. She felt that she was bringing peace to the space. Especially after arguments or struggles with her daughters, she made sure to offer each girl a blessing for a good night's sleep. She felt a sense of spiritual settling as she did this. Serenity entered her home.

For some, entering oasis time is entering a sacred time and space. This feeling helps set a spiritual boundary against the helter-skelter feeling of the week. Oasis time is a chance to encounter the awe and majesty of a time dedicated to the spiritual realm.

This may be what Rabbi Abraham Joshua Heschel means when he calls the Sabbath a "palace in time." If we were ever to approach a king or queen, we would take the encounter seriously. We would dress with care.

We would enter the palace with excitement and awe. We would engage in the appropriate ritual behavior, which would remind us of the honor of entering the royal realm. We can treat our oasis time like royalty, but in this case we are honoring ourselves and the awe-inspiring world in which we dwell. Some people say this is when they feel most sovereign in their own realm.

The ritual and practice of spiritual boundary setting can deepen the experience of the sacred during oasis time. Rituals remind us of the spiritual boundary. Blessings, candles, silence, and ritual washing acknowledge spiritual boundaries that help us turn toward a realm where control and accomplishment fade into the background and awe, connection, joy, song, festivity, and timelessness come into focus.

We set a spiritual boundary when we deliberately remind ourselves that this moment is enough. We are enough. We have done enough. We are steeped in gratitude. We receive blessing. We focus on the river of goodness flowing around us. Can we take a breath? That is enough for now. Does one person love us? That is enough. Can we see? That is an immense blessing. Can we move through space? We are grateful for the ability to move, whether by legs or aided by wheelchair or walker. We can take time right now to recognize that just for this moment, enough is enough.

Strengthening Boundaries in Action

Once we establish our physical, mental, and spiritual boundaries, we need to maintain them. As with so many of the elements that bring us to our oasis time, we need to make a regular practice of our boundaries, turning them into habits. There are tools and strategies that can help us do this.

Make SMART Agreements

Where do the tasks on our lists come from? Many of them arise because we told someone else we would do them. In other words, we made an agreement. When we say yes to a request, we sign away a chunk of time—

that is a commitment we often make without fully understanding what is being asked.

Even a conversation as mundane as "Could you call the electrician?"—"Yes, sure," can invite misunderstanding. Although this conversation ends with an agreement, the person making the request could have meant "some time in the next week," while the person who was asked assumes that the need is urgent and drops everything to make the call. That kind of distraction can throw a day off track, which in turn can cause tempers to flare, all through a misunderstanding.

Clarifying our agreements is part of creating strong boundaries. What are the elements of a good agreement? In brief, it should be SMART.

* **S**pecific. What are the key details of the agreement?

* **M**easurable. What is the scope of the agreement? What are the standards? How will you know when the agreement has been met?

* **A**chievable. Does it seem reasonable within the available time frame and resources?

* **R**elevant. What is the context for the agreement? Why is this task important? Is it a priority right now?

* **T**ime sensitive. What is due when? What kinds of check-ins will you have along the way?

For an agreement to be truly generative, both parties must agree on these elements. In a sense, making a good agreement should look more like a back-and-forth negotiation than a simple request and assent. Know that it often seems easier and faster to say yes than to take another minute or two to hammer out a doable agreement.

We often mindlessly say yes to requests for many good reasons. We want to be helpful, we want to be cooperative, we want to support the team or the family. Yet in our rush to say yes, we can overload ourselves, again causing exhaustion and an inability to execute commitments that we made.

So there are several ways to respond to a request to help shape a SMART agreement. An unqualified yes to the request is rarely one of them.

* "I need clarification."

    Get more information from the requester so you know what you are responding to. Make sure you fully understand the request.

* "I'll check my resources."

    "I'll check and get back to you by [insert date]" gives you a chance to think about what you really can do. Give the person making the request a time when you will get back to her, and make sure you respond promptly. This makes it clear to the other person that you're doing the best that you can without infringing on your boundaries.

* "Here's what I *can* do."

    If you can't fulfill the full request, offer an alternative based on your perception of the other person's needs: "I can't do X, but I can do Y. How will that work for you?"

* "No, I am sorry, I wish I could, but I can't do it."

    If you're not able to completely fulfill the request and there isn't a good compromise, decline clearly and respectfully. The message you send in doing this is "I'd rather turn you down than let you down." Be firm; if that's not an answer the requestor can respect, that's more his issue than yours.

Say No Even When You Feel You're Supposed to Say Yes

Practicing good agreement making is not easy, and we may experience pitfalls and challenges as we learn this skill. Many people feel compelled to say yes and are uncomfortable saying no. The strongest advice in this area is not to make an agreement that you are not positive you can keep. If you are uncertain what your time commitments are, like so many of us, don't say yes to a request until you have checked your calendar to determine whether and when you will be able to honor it. Negotiate until you are certain that you can deliver what you are agreeing to.

Exemplar: Harry Spence's Important Agreement

Harry Spence is known for being highly productive and at the top of his field. Deputy schools chancellor of the New York City Board of Education during the Giuliani administration is only one of several top jobs he has held. He has also been commissioner of the Department of Social Services for the Commonwealth of Massachusetts and the director of the Boston Redevelopment Authority. I found out from him that he is adamant about taking a month off each summer.

When he took the New York City Board of Education position, he met with Chancellor Rudy Crew to discuss the terms of his appointment. The first thing he said was that he took a month off every summer, and he would only take the job if he could continue doing so. "'You will have to defend me,'" I said, "'because I *will* take this month off.' When the time came, I told Rudy Giuliani's people that I was taking a month, and they went crazy. They said that I couldn't leave, that I was needed. How could the schools get along without me?" They pulled out all the stops, but Spence was adamant, and Rudy Crew was fully behind him. He took the month off, and *nothing* terrible happened.

"I learned this from my first job," Spence explains. "I worked so hard that I completely burned out. I gave it my all, and then I realized that I lost all my bounce, I lost my patience, resilience, creativity, imagination. So I realized that I couldn't keep doing this. Part of my job was always to care for myself so that I was as good in the fifth year as in the first. People can't stop thinking about work when they are anxious. It is all about managing anxiety. When I got home from my first job, I was sick to my stomach with anxiety every day. Most people learn to manage their anxiety through taking more action, but I think it is essential to stop to get perspective.

"I needed to take vacation time. Much of my value is to see connections among disparate elements in the life of the organization, and to do that you have to have a clear vision of the organization. If you get caught up in the trees, you can't see the forest, and that is costly. When you pull back and see the whole of the organization, your imagination starts to take in the whole. I have done this for sixteen years. And I am absolutely convinced that everyone should take all the vacation accorded to them.

"I don't work on weekends either. My general rule is that I don't work evenings. I work hard between nine and six, and then I let it go. My rule is that I keep the work within work hours. I need respite every day.

"I would say more broadly—if my work is driven by anxiety, the chances that work is a source of joy are diminished. If I hear someone say that they can't take a day off because they are overwhelmed, I know they will not be able to do good work. High anxiety does not produce new answers. How do we move from anxiety to satisfaction and joy? We need to know that we will be immensely more effective when we do that."

Spence's example shows the interconnected and mutually supportive nature of commitment, negotiation skills, and a healthy work life. Because he was committed to his own time, he was able to negotiate his vacation from a position of clarity. The vacation time enabled him to be a positive, effective force at work, which in turn justified his continued commitment to his time.

Set Good Boundaries through Self-Care

Because of my early work successes, the world of work feels like my emotional home. As a child, I looked for—and received—kudos for good grades. As a young adult, my long hours brought me achievement and recognition. But my determination to get things done can backfire. I find myself pushing too hard, to the point that I'm deeply exhausted and tired of my work altogether. As my perfectionism surfaces, I put more work in, with diminishing results, until I sit down at my desk less optimistic and less confident that I can get things done.

I have often interpreted this feeling of depletion as a need for more stimulation, so I reach for sugar or caffeine. But what I actually need at that moment is a truly replenishing break. In other words, this is a moment for bolstering my boundaries with work through breaks and self-care. Here are a few tips for doing just that.

1. Take at least two breaks each morning and two each afternoon. Fatigue can lead you down unnecessary ratholes. Breaks help keep things in perspective and maintain the quality of your work as high as you want it to be for the rest of the day.

2. Set your goals, then cut back on them. Being ruthlessly realistic about what you can achieve in a day will help you actually do it.

3. Take oasis time in the middle of the week. Consider what activities truly nourish you, and do them. A walk outside, a call to an old friend, a good song, a chapter of a good book, perhaps some qigong. Arrange for a longer lunch on a Wednesday or a good workout on Wednesday evening.

The mind, body, and soul crave nourishment. When you begin to actively practice these techniques, you will be as amazed as I was by the increased focus and productivity, but perhaps more important, the return of that "bounce," as Harry Spence puts it—that irreplaceable vitality and love of life.

Stand Firm in the Face of Boundary Slippage

Rachel Macy Stafford, author of the *New York Times* bestselling book *Hands Free Mama,* is a can-do active mom who took on more and more school-related tasks, volunteering and keeping a high level of order in her house. She describes her own insights around boundary slippage during what she calls her "highly distracted years—when to-do lists took over . . . when the pace of my life was a constant mad dash to a finish line that couldn't be reached . . .when I gripped devices tighter than the hands of my loved ones . . . when I said yes to everything requested of me *outside* the home and said no to the most important activities *inside* the home, like playing, laughing, and making memories."[3]

One day, she realized that she was missing the best thing in life: being with her children as they grew. She wrote a blog post called "How to Miss a Childhood" in which she gave a formula for missing out on the joys of parenthood. The most important steps: Hold on to your phone when you're with your kids, and shoo them away when they interrupt your phone use.

The post hit a nerve and went viral, and Stafford received a request from National Public Radio to interview her at five p.m. on a Friday, right in the middle of the time she had newly committed to her kids. She contemplated breaking that day's agreement with her daughters. After all, the opportunity to be interviewed on NPR might not come again. But in that moment, she realized that she needed to stick with her kids and her commitment to them. When she did, she felt surprisingly triumphant, even though there was no other time to reschedule the NPR interview. Triumphant because she stuck to her newly realized values. Triumphant because she had not missed what mattered most to her.

Make Boundaries That Are Firm and Flexible

Learning how to *maintain* your weekly oasis in time takes further discernment and experimentation. The goal is to create a boundary that is distinct, yet not so rigid that it feels stifling.

We have to be flexible, because life and emergencies and circumstances may come up that take priority. But it's important to have strong enough boundaries that you don't have to evaluate every situation individually and ask, "Is this worth an interruption?" Do you truly need to respond to an e-mail ping, or can you ignore it and trust that someone will call if there's an emergency? Over time, you will understand viscerally that you can let go of the stream of communications and interruptions. Can you block off time on your calendar, even thirty minutes during lunch, to go outside and clear your head so that the afternoon is as filled with truly good work as the morning? Yes, you can.

Boundaries are a dance between yourself and your work, your needs and your desires, you and the world around you. As you embrace the idea of oasis time, you will see that strengthening boundaries is part of the path to that spacious time of sustenance, respite, renewal, and awe that you crave. Once you consciously work on your physical, mental, emotional, and spiritual boundaries, you will find that you can create time for restorative breaks over the course of your days and in your regular rhythm of weekly rest.

You will also discover that crafting your rhythm of rest and renewal entails constant commitment and recommitment. Boundaries tend to be a moving target. Just when you think you have learned to say no, you will say yes to an irresistible request that makes no sense for your schedule. The key is to notice yourself in action and deal responsibly with the anger or frustration that might result. You might get to bed on time for five nights in a row, but on the sixth night, you succumb to the lure of one more e-mail, which leads to hours more at your computer, or one more show, followed by a rough, exhausted workday. But if you own your firm yet flexible boundaries, if you let go of perfectionism and approach your setbacks with self-compassion, if you make a habit of recommitting, you will get to bed on time again on the eleventh night, and you will say no again when you need to.

This is the journey toward oasis time. Little by little, you create more focused time during your week. You make more time for your family and friends because not only do you see how important it is, but you also are getting better at living by your personal creed of doing what matters most to you. Ultimately, you will own your time, you will decide how to spend it, and you will gain the renewal and sustenance you desperately need.

NAVIGATING
YOUR DAYS

Five Key Practices

Once you take stock and start firming up your boundaries, you will also want to manage every day a little better. You'll get to your oasis time through a set of new, small choices that you make every day. These new choices help you be far more effective during the week. You make these choices over and over again, slowly developing them into habits, so that they eventually become the fundamental trusted practices that shape your days and weeks.

What do your workdays look like now? You may have made your day's plan by checking your to-do list, your calendar, and your intuition for any inner promptings and reminders; now you are off and running. But the day rarely goes the way we envision it. Too often, events run their own course, often quite different from your plans, even if you are the most organized person around. Inevitably, things change, and after a few meetings, e-mails, and text messages—or a leaking toilet, tantruming child, or a sick dog—your day looks different than what you planned. This basic scenario holds whether you work in an office, from home, or at a coworking space; it's true whether you work for money or work to care for your children, home, or relatives.

We might imagine that a typical work day unfolds like this: Get started, focus on accomplishing the day's goals, eat lunch, attend a meeting, return to focusing on accomplishing goals, wrap it up. But what really happens is something more like this: focus, interruption, accomplish a bit, change tasks, text message, new task, interruption, irritation, phone call, transition, look for something, low blood sugar, new task, eat, interruption, relational issue, eat, wrap it up, check e-mail, keep going, walk quickly for exercise, try to wrap it up, one more thing, just one more thing, and so on. Does that sound familiar? Part of our work is to keep coming back to what is important.

What if we accept that those deviations are normal? What if, rather than berating ourselves for failing to maintain our focus on accomplishing goals, we apply a little self-compassion? What if, rather than trying to hold ourselves up to impossible standards of perfection, we adopt some strategies that move us from reactivity to proactivity? This chapter provides a set of tools—what I call the Five Key Practices—for navigating your day realistically, flexibly, and in a way that protects both you and your work.

These time-management tips entail making new choices based on our deeply held values to steer the ship through the rough waters of everyday life. Over time, they help us make better choices in the moment and long term. They enable us to strengthen our boundaries, do more of what is most important, and navigate toward our oasis time with courage and determination. The more we integrate these practices into our ways of managing ourselves, the more they improve our capacities and abilities in our work and our lives. They go hand in hand with creating oasis time. They are:

1. Pay Attention to *How* You Work, Not Just What You Do

2. Make Your Trade-Offs Consciously

3. Use Transitions Purposefully

4. Work with a Productivity Buddy

5. Complete and Celebrate

Key Practice 1:
Pay Attention to *How* You Work,
Not Just What You Do

When we name our priorities for the day, we tend to list what we *must* do, but we can also include how we do it. In fact, the ways that we carry out our obligations show a lot about who we are. How we act significantly impacts our productivity, emotional intelligence, and sense of fulfillment. In Stephen Covey's influential book *The Seven Habits of Highly Effective People*, he starts by saying that what makes us effective is being proactive and inner directed. By inner directed, he means guided by our values and character, not by our impulses, moods, and feelings. Covey points out that we don't realize how good it feels to live by cultivating our character strengths such as courage, integrity, patience, and kindness. In fact, the original subtitle of his book was "Restoring the Character Ethic."

Living by our values and, hence, drawing on and developing our strength of character takes place all day long. Challenges to our deeply held values come up frequently and aren't easy to resolve. Do we say what we think in a tough meeting, or do we hold back? If we do say what we think, do we speak in a way that might be heard and well received? Or do we just spout it out and deal with the repercussions? Do we listen carefully to a concern that someone has brought to us, or do we dismiss their problem as a function of their personality defects? Do we check our e-mail or social media every half hour or fifteen minutes, or do we try to figure out what would be a more constructive use of our time?

We want to work in a way that makes us feel good about ourselves as people with ethics and integrity. However, values in action are different from our espoused values, the values that we say we are living by. We can learn a lot from carefully examining the choices we actually make, in real time, day to day. We can say that we value patience or honesty, for example, but when we really look at ourselves we notice that we are quite short with people or hedge the truth much of the day. We want to look back at the day and say, "That was a day *well lived*," not just a day of checking everything off the task list. Still, most of us don't have an equivalent list for our character traits or know how to cultivate them.

Among Benjamin Franklin's considerable accomplishments was the development of a way to put our espoused values into practice. Franklin was a very practical man, and he came up with a practical plan. He described thirteen values or traits that he wanted to live by and then made a chart so that he could keep track of how he exhibited them. His values, which he called virtues, included sincerity, moderation, justice, temperance, and industry, among others. Starting at age twenty, he decided to track his behavior every day because he noticed some mismatches between his actions and his values. We wouldn't work on "virtues" nowadays; the term sounds quaint. Yet, we can follow his lead and work on our character traits.

Franklin's plan included focusing on one of his thirteen character traits each week. Then he cycled through the list four times a year. He said, "I grew convinced that *truth, sincerity,* and *integrity,* in dealings between man and man, were of the utmost importance to the felicity of life; and I formed written resolutions, which still remain in my journal-book, to practice them ever while I lived."[1] He met with a group of friends weekly so that they could pursue an ethical life with support.

I have tried Franklin's method and found it highly rewarding. The big trait that I had to work on, above all others, was order. I valued order, but I couldn't seem to put it into practice. I ran late, lost things regularly, had difficulty opening my mail. I concentrated on improving my skills and my value for order, and through that, I have transformed the way I live in the world. My current list includes order, of course, patience (I have a growing boy), balance, and trust. I also meet with a group and regularly consult several contemporary guides to developing stronger character traits such as *Climbing Jacob's Ladder* by Dr. Alan Morinis.

Everyday Practice: Pay Attention to How You Work

- Make a list of your valued character traits.
- Choose one to cultivate as you set your priorities for the day.
- At the end of the day (or week), identify times when you were feeling pinched or uneasy. Chances are these moments of discomfort occurred when you were not acting in accordance with your values.
- Write down how you want to act in those situations the next time.

KEY PRACTICE 2:
MAKE YOUR TRADE-OFFS CONSCIOUSLY

Part of our work is to keep our priorities in front of us when other things come up. When we are interrupted, or when tasks take longer than expected, we have to adjust and decide what is most important now, given the new circumstances. Some people think multitasking is the answer to changing plans and added priorities, but actually that slows us down further. In fact, the answer is to accept that we can't do it all and *consciously* reprioritize.

If we make these trade-offs haphazardly, we end up in a frantic end-of-day triage: "It's too late to send that e-mail. It's too late to shop and make dinner. I'll bring work home, get takeout, and forget about exercising." Sound familiar? The Yiddish expression "You can't dance at two weddings with one *tuchas* [tush]" captures this dilemma. You have to make a choice.

When we live in a world that values getting as much done as possible, we often aren't aware of the trade-offs we are making until it's too late. We look up and realize that we've eaten take-out food every night for six days (or six weeks), even though we value homemade food. We realize we haven't taken even a short walk for a week, though we know how important daily exercise is for health and productivity. Many of us let go of self-care—sleep, good food, exercise—for the false allure of more productivity. But when you make trade-offs consciously, you have a better chance of doing what's most important over time. Observe what tasks you jettison and be aware of how you procrastinate. Then get savvy about your choices.

Part of making conscious trade-offs is knowing that we will be pulled toward what is easier and quicker. We work better when we remember our tendency to procrastinate on the bigger, harder things. Keep this in mind when you are deciding what to focus on at any given moment. As my client Anjana said to me, "I would much rather clean out my in-box than rework my annual goals. I'm usually moving too fast to think about the big stuff." Now, however, Anjana says that when she needs to, she takes a walk outside her building and sits for a few minutes of meditation. Once she does that, she is ready to tackle the important work of reprioritizing. Otherwise, she is in reactive mode all day long.

We Lean Toward the Easy and Quick Tasks

"Easy and quick"	"Difficult and time-consuming"
Short-term ◄———————	Long-term
Urgent ◄———————	Important
Comfortable ◄———————	Challenging

As you see in the chart above, we often prefer easy and quick actions, but we get real traction in our lives when we steer ourselves toward the right-hand column. Because it's common to slip and slide into quick and easy tasks, many people report that they never have time to do the things that could bring true rewards and growth. To develop the skills to tackle the difficult and time-consuming work, ask these questions.

* What essential tasks have you "not gotten around to" or do you "not have time for"?

* What feels most urgent and compelling? Why does it feel that way?

* Are you blaming someone else for their part in not getting an important thing done? Have you played a role in the situation? What would happen if you didn't cover for them? Or didn't make excuses for yourself?

* What are the consequences of not doing this right now? How important is it really?

When we opt to complete easy and quick tasks, we put off the difficult and time-consuming tasks that are equally if not more important. We all delay things from time to time, and each of us has a familiar procrastination script. For example, you say, 'I'm going to the gym," but instead you come home hungry, eat a snack, turn on the TV "just to check the news," and end up too tired and not in the mood to exercise. You may not be aware of it, but you have just set yourself up to not work out. How you talked to yourself and how you prepared led you to the couch and TV, even though you promised yourself you absolutely would not do exactly that. As psychologists put it, you have "primed" yourself to *not* go to the gym.

But you can also prime yourself to do what you really value, even if you don't feel like it in the moment. You can design and practice a sequence of cues that enable you to do what you most value. For example, if you really want to exercise, bring your workout clothes to work, change there, and eat a banana before you leave so that you aren't too hungry when you get to the gym, yoga class, or the park. Plan your workout in detail so there is no wondering what to do next: "I'll drive to the park and park my car next to the track. Then I'll run around the track six times, do my stretches on the grass in the middle, and pick up a juice as a reward on my way home."

"If-then" statements are another powerful aid: "*If* I can get home, grab an apple, go upstairs, and change into my workout clothes, *then* I can get to the gym." "*If* I feel my cell phone vibrating with a new text message, *then* I can take a breath and stay on task." The goal with heightening awareness of all the trade-offs you make during the day is to develop the habits and practices that help you make the best choices.

Talk yourself through what's difficult. If you are working on a challenging and time-consuming project, keep yourself on task by changing your self-talk from "I'm going so slowly! I'm not making headway!" to "I can do three fifteen-minute sessions, and little by little, I will make headway. Yes, it is difficult right now. But I can do just five minutes if fifteen minutes is too hard. The more I can do now, the more time off I can have later." It's the same with exercising. Talk yourself out of lying on the couch. Say, "I'll run for five minutes if that is all that I can muster. Even a minute of jumping jacks is better than nothing." You will feel so much better.

Everyday Practice: Making Trade-Offs

Three-minute triage. Do this when you have too much to accomplish over the next several hours.

- Note the time.
- List everything you want to get done for the rest of the day.
- Assign a time estimate to each item.
- Ask yourself which items you can delegate, pare down, postpone, or produce with a "good-enough" standard.
- Consider how much time you have. Really. If you are doing a three-minute triage at two p.m., be realistic about how much energy you have left. Consider food and

exercise needs. Factor in meetings and phone calls. Now, how much time do you *really* have remaining?

- Look at your list. What *must* you do on the list? Don't exaggerate and don't engage in wishful thinking. What do you owe other people? By when? What do you need to renegotiate?

- Take into account the three previous steps and produce a list that will get you through the day and get the right work done.

KEY PRACTICE 3:
USE TRANSITIONS PURPOSEFULLY

While we usually think of good time management as managing our tasks and assignments well, much is gained by good transitions. So, good daily timing also entails *managing transitions*—moving from one activity to another. Transitions can be as essential to sustaining ourselves and our work as our activities themselves. Leaving time for transitions acknowledges the reality of the need to stop one activity and start another.

First of all, you need an accurate sense of how long your transitions take so you can factor them into your plans for the day. How many days include back-to-back activities? One way to get better time estimates for transitions is to pick a transition you make frequently and time it. If you are setting out for a meeting, how long will it take to get there? Ten minutes? Fifteen? Make a guess before you leave. When you arrive, calculate the exact travel time. How accurate was your estimate? Pay attention to whether you simply move from one activity to the next. Make sure to plan for transition time in your schedule or try to add in other activities as you go along.

When you plan a series of phone calls, it might seem that scheduling them from 10:00 to 10:30, 10:30 to 11:00, and 11:00 to 12:00 is realistic. But think again: You haven't scheduled a minute to summarize the most recent call, run to the bathroom, or stretch your legs.

Moving from one thing to the next also gives us the opportunity to check in with how we are doing. It allows us to ask ourselves, Where are we? Where are we going? What do we need next? It doesn't take long to check this internal dashboard, but it does require attention. Many of us lose focus and momentum during a transition when a well-earned break slides into a distraction. But if you tune in when you are in transition, you will get the signals you need to sustain yourself all day long. You'll be much more effective, and you will feel much better.

Your Navigation Dashboard

Think of yourself like a pilot who has an instrument panel that signals the altitude of the plane, fuel levels, distance traveled, and how far there is to go. While the body doesn't have a literal instrument panel, you can be more aware of what I call your "self-regulation dashboard" to keep flying on schedule and in a safe way. Our internal meters are tuned to our mental, physical, emotional, and spiritual states; when we check our personal instrument panel, we note how we are doing—and then we use that information to correct our course as necessary.[2]

Here are some of the questions I periodically ask myself to check my dashboard.

* **Mentally:** Am I awake? Focused? Distracted?

* **Emotionally:** Am I calm? Upset? What's upsetting me? Am I angry? Sad? Hurt?

* **Physically:** How are my energy levels? Do I need water? (The answer is almost always yes.) Food? Activity? Rest? A hug? Am I moving or thinking too fast or too slowly? We often need to adjust our pace and have a range of paces. I'm working on moderato, myself.

* **Spiritually:** Am I in tune with my purpose? My intuition? Am I inspired or deflated? Am I behaving ethically?

It looks like a long list, but in practice, it is a brief scan of your condition. If you ask these questions during a transition, you can use the answers to quickly meet your needs so you are ready to dive into your next activity. Perhaps you take a pause to refocus yourself, make a short phone call to process your feelings with a friend, grab a glass of water or an apple for some energy, or even do a two-minute triage to ensure your next activity is aligned with your purpose. Taking this kind of break when you're at a point of transition helps you stay on course without burning out.

We have a collective habit of trying to do more than is possible in any given day. We try to catch up by squeezing our transition time, but reducing transition time doesn't help us move faster; *au contraire*, it often slows us down. So instead, try being realistic and focused about your transitions. You may even find yourself using them as tiny bits of oasis time. When I am able to move through my days at my best, my mantra for transitions is:

* Receive

* Relax

* Refocus

Receive the blessing and celebrate any accomplishment. *Relax* my mind and body. *Refocus* now on what is coming next.

Everyday Practice: Check Your Self-Regulation Dashboard

Create three questions that will serve as your personal self-regulation dashboard. Mine might be:

- Do I need to have a drink of water?
- Do I need to stand up and stretch for a minute?
- What does my intuition say about how to get ready for what is next?

These three things are important to me and make a real difference in my sense of well-being.

Similar dashboard check-in questions include:

- Am I focused or distracted?
- How does my body feel?
- What kind of help do I need?

What might your three self-regulation check-in questions be? List them, then make a practice of checking them at your transition points.

KEY PRACTICE 4:
WORK WITH A PRODUCTIVITY BUDDY

Talking through your work challenges with another person can give you the accountability and support you need for high productivity. In addition to listening and giving advice, your buddy provides a fundamental point of connection, so you are not alone with your challenges and successes.

A productivity buddy is a friend, colleague, or coach who helps you stay focused, helps you get unstuck, and gives you feedback—or the courage to get the feedback you need. No matter what your work is or where it takes place, a productivity buddy can help you stay on track and give you support when you go off course. We do so much better when there is someone in the trenches with us, on our side.

Without accountability, I can lose hours to e-mail or the Internet, even though I know full well that I have better ways to spend that time. When I am in a funky state, in a bit of a fog, dodging something important, or just experiencing low energy, I find it invaluable to check in with my buddy by text or phone.

In his book *Mojo,* Marshall Goldsmith, one of the nation's top coaches, describes how important his accountability partnership is. "Every day, no matter where either of us is in the world, we try to connect on the phone and ask each other our key questions about our health, work, and personal relationships. The results were astonishing. After the first eighteen months of adhering to this ritual, Jim and I both weighed exactly what we wanted to weigh, exercised more, got more done, and I was nicer to my wife."[3]

A productivity phone call with your buddy should last three to six minutes, no more. It is not a social exchange but a chance to talk through your next steps with support. Sometimes just naming my quandary to a good listener can help. All of a sudden, my fog can lift. Such a phone check-in might sound like this edited example:

BUDDY: What do you want to get done in the next hour or two?

ME: I have three things hanging over me. I'm not sure which to focus on. I have to send an evaluation to my client, and I have to plan the workshop on productive conversations, but I really need to edit my blog post and make progress on it today. I'm avoiding the editing. I'm afraid I don't have time to polish it the way I want to.

BUDDY: How much time do you think you need for the evaluation and the budget? And what's the minimum you can do on the evaluation and the budget to get them off your desk? [She knows I'm a perfectionist.]

ME: I can spend one hour finishing the evaluation. It doesn't need to be perfect. Then I'll take a break. Next, I'll spend fifteen minutes editing the blog post. That doesn't need to be perfect either. Actually, I'll *start* with the outline while I'm fresh. I can block all interruptions for the next hour. Then, I will take a break and reevaluate. Thank you so much. So what are your goals for the next hour or two?

BUDDY: I have a report due to the head of HR at the end of the week, and I want to spend my first hour on that. I am going to spend thirty minutes collecting data and thirty minutes drafting the first three paragraphs. I've been avoiding the data collection, but it won't be hard once I start. I'll text you that I have gotten started.

ME: I'll look forward to getting your text in about fifteen minutes. How does that sound?

Now we each have someone to be accountable to for the next hour or two. Our buddy check-in allows for a shame-free conversation about the next steps to our goals.

Your buddy may be a coworker, a supervisor, or a friend. You can touch base with a buddy via phone, text, or chat. Regular check-ins allow you to uncover patterns in your behavior by tracking your productivity

Everyday Practice: Productivity Buddy Check-In

Find a friend or colleague who will try daily check-ins, either during the day or after work. Allow two or three minutes for each person. It doesn't have to be long-term.

- Set your timer for three minutes.
- Ask your buddy what he or she would like to focus on.
- Remind him or her to set a clear goal for the next amount of time.
- Now your buddy will ask you what you want to focus on.
- Identify your goals for the next period of time.
- Check in again by phone or text to describe what you have done in this set period of time.

Was that helpful? If yes and you are both available, do it again. Alternatively, text your immediate task goals to your buddy with a commitment to finish them by a certain time. Be sure to let your buddy know how you are progressing.

week after week. You can ask deeper questions. You can stay focused when all you really want to do is surf the Web. You can even hold each other accountable for the quality of your life. When things are hard, you can ask each other, "What's my role in this? How is it that I find myself in this situation again?" Having a buddy can make you hyperaware of your procrastination patterns, and being accountable to another person who is watching you closely is the fastest way to truly commit to better habits.

KEY PRACTICE 5: COMPLETE THE DAY
AND CELEBRATE ACCOMPLISHMENTS

How often do we go to bed beating ourselves up about the things we didn't do, tasks we didn't complete, calls we didn't get to, and goals we didn't reach? That negativity can become a habit of thought, generating a lot of tension in our bodies. After a while, we face a self-perpetuating situation: We get used to assuming that we can't get ahead or get on top of our lists.

Imagine, instead, ending each day by celebrating the things that you did accomplish. This practice establishes a self-perpetuating habit of feeling good about work, which allows us to face each new day with a sense of excitement rather than dread, which in turn could help us get more done.

"Completing" means bringing your day's work to a clear end point, so you know you are done. I like to use the phrase "shutdown complete," which I've borrowed from computer science professor and work expert Cal Newport, PhD.[4] It means this work is *over.* You have cleared the decks, you have a good sense of where your vital tools are, you know what you have done, you have a feeling of completion, and you have made notes on what's coming up next. You put things away. You locate your keys or tools. You pack your gym bag.

Part of completing is celebrating what we have been able to do. It's important to celebrate *whatever* accomplishments we have made, whether they match our expectations or not. Why? We often focus on (1) what's next and (2) what we didn't do. This viewpoint tends to leave us feeling empty. In contrast, focusing on what you have accomplished gives you permission to break the pattern of results scarcity.

Even small tasks deserve acknowledgment. Teresa Amabile, PhD, of Harvard Business School has done extensive research into what leads to success. In her book *The Progress Principle*, she shows how small daily wins in the pursuit of meaningful goals lead to work satisfaction. She says, "Our participants' thoughts, feelings, and drives fared better when successes, *even small ones*, were celebrated and then analyzed for knowledge gained."[5]

So acknowledge yourself both for task accomplishment and character-building actions: Did you overcome a fear in order to accomplish a goal? Did you persist in the face of distractions, even just once? Were you courteous when you wanted to bite off someone's head? Perhaps you had a difficult conversation with someone, but you kept your temper and were actually productive in the end. Or you were able to do something particularly helpful or effective. Perhaps you accomplished a task you had been delaying. Or perhaps you did something you really didn't want to do, and you did it moderately cheerfully (or at least not-so-grumpily). All of these are accomplishments and deserve an internal nod, a moment of personal celebration.

Keep an eye on all those tasks you completed that weren't on your original to-do list. Often we think certain jobs don't count because they are related to kids or the house or they're personal errands. But they do count! I have a friend who creates a list of all the things she did during the day that weren't on her original list, then she crosses them off the new list with a flourish and gives herself that glow of accomplishment.

Accomplishment celebrations can take place all day. From a stress and productivity perspective, things go better when you offer yourself a stream of pats on the back as soon as you complete your tasks. Researchers at the University of California, Berkeley, found that the more congratulatory touch, the greater the success of basketball teams. The more "fist bumps, high-fives, chest bumps, leaping shoulder bumps, chest punches, head slaps, head grabs, low fives, high tens, half hugs, and team huddles" that team members shared during the whole game, the better they did.[6] Try this with yourself and others. Celebrate all day long, during the whole "game"—although I tried the head slaps and head grabs with a few people, and that didn't go over so well.

Reward yourself even if you accomplish something imperfectly. No, scratch that. Reward yourself *especially* if you accomplish something imperfectly. Sometimes what keeps us running nonstop is a fruitless yet compelling quest for a perfection that doesn't exist. Many of us need to appreciate ourselves for our mistakes as well as our successes.

Everyday Practice: Celebrate the Small Win

Give yourself a nod of acknowledgment whenever you finish anything. This leads to a stream of inner talk that sounds like, "Yup, that's done, managed to respond well to that request, got right back to them, did a good job with this task; yes, that's off my plate, good response to that message, handled that interruption well . . ."

When you're getting ready at the end of the day:

- Review today's accomplishments and identify a few wins. If there are things you didn't get to, ask why not. What can you learn from your response? Put those tasks on tomorrow's list.

- Declutter your desk or workspace; put things away.

- Make lists of errands (e.g., grocery store, pharmacy, farmers' market) and double-check: Is tomorrow the right day for each errand? Can you consolidate? Can you delegate?

- Review tomorrow's calendar and make a plan for the day, including key action items. Send any necessary reminder e-mails.

- Check meal plans. What's for lunch? Dinner? Who's doing food prep and shopping?

The Five Key Practices Lead to Oasis Time

If managing our days and our weeks so we can find the time we need to rejuvenate, restore, and sustain ourselves brings us to oasis time, we can see the Five Key Practices as standing at the heart of oasis time, as being its very essence. (1) Oasis time embodies expressing our values and character strengths. (2) Choosing to embrace oasis time entails making a challenging but powerful trade-off, letting go of the everyday world's siren call in favor of our time of rest. (3) As we saw in previous chapters, managing transitions well is key to entering and emerging from oasis time. (4) Enjoying our community and buddies is one of the most restorative things we can do during oasis time. (5) Finally, oasis time can be the greatest celebration we have—of ourselves, our connections and communities, and life itself. If we turn the Five Key Practices into habits, we can have all this and so much more.

12

BEYOND A HAVEN, AN INCUBATOR

O ur oasis time offers a chance not only for rest and renewal but also for transformation. This is the unexpected benefit of taking regular time off: The nurturing haven you create each week can become an incubator to support the kind of growth you need to face your greatest challenges. Oasis time, with its uniquely nurturing setting, provides the perfect conditions to prepare us for deeper engagement in life.

People often assume that happiness comes from ease and affluence. In fact, the pursuit of security through wealth and possessions might actually be undermining our well-being.[1] Experience shows that once basic income needs are met, true happiness derives from meaningful action and having a sense of belonging to something greater than the individual self. Oasis time can orient you toward these goals.

Three types of oasis time experiences can lead to long-term trans-formation: (1) experiencing awe, (2) developing emotional resilience, and (3) connecting deeply with friends and neighbors for a higher purpose.

Through awe, we turn toward the ineffable, gain perspective, and regain our imagination. Awe opens us up to humility and the sense of vulnerability that helps bind us to others.[2] This openness can lead to a need and willingness to engage our difficult emotions. As we engage our full emotional life, we enhance our stability and vitality and can reach out more easily to others—thus creating strong relationships in service of the greater good, not just sociable connections. We learn how much we are capable of in community. And through accessing our tribe, we increase our sense of belonging, an essential experience for thriving.

These elements of life—awe, emotional resilience, connectedness—enrich the spiritual soil in which we grow. When that soil is rich, loose, and tilled, there is space for roots to expand. If our soil is rocky, packed, and parched, nothing can thrive.

Nourished by Awe

But just what is awe? In her TED talk, comedian Jill Shargaa asks, "How many times have you used the word *awesome* today? Once, twice, seventeen times?" As she points out, we call so many things awesome that we have lost track of true awe. Awe is defined by *Webster's New World Dictionary* as "Fear mingled with admiration or reverence; a feeling produced by something majestic; sublime." Allowing ourselves to experience awe makes us feel better in so many ways. Awe slows down time, gives us perspective, opens us to others, and relieves us of the trap of our endless preoccupation with ourselves. University of California professors Paul Piff and Dacher Keltner note that "awe is the ultimate 'collective' emotion, for it motivates people to do things that enhance the greater good. . . . [A]we helps bind us to others, motivating us to act in collaborative ways that enable strong groups and cohesive communities."[3]

The experience of awe is far more available than many of us realize. We can cultivate it by priming ourselves to this transformational experience. When we slow down for oasis time, we could retreat to the familiar—to read a book, perhaps, or chat with a neighbor—but a slight shift in awareness allows us to cultivate awe and a sense of the sacred. In his book

The Blue Zones, Dan Buettner observed how in Sardinia, a place of extended longevity, one shepherd would "stop to take a long look over the emerald green plateaus below. He'd seen that same sweeping view daily for almost 80 years, yet still took time every day to appreciate it."[4] Buettner suggests that the shepherd's appreciation of his magnificent landscape was one of the factors that helped him live much longer than most people. We too can cultivate awe every day. We don't have to wait for astonishing sunsets or magnetizing views; we can find awe in the flow of water as we do the dishes or in the moment that our highly active child manages to fall asleep.

When Ari was ten or so, he became more self-aware. There was a brief period of time when he would exclaim, "Mom! How is it that we are talking to each other? How do we do this? It's amazing!" And then the wonder faded. But every once in a while, I remember those moments, and I too am astonished by our capacity for speaking and listening. (How *do* we do that?) As Rabbi Abraham Joshua Heschel said:

> Our goal should be to live life in radical amazement . . . get up in the morning and look at the world in a way that takes nothing for granted. Everything is phenomenal; everything is incredible; never treat life casually. *To be spiritual is to be amazed.*[5]

Recently, I went into Ari's room to share our morning gratitude prayer. I said, maybe a little too earnestly, "When we say this prayer, we look out of the window and notice . . ." With a teenager's bluntness, he interrupted me: "Holy crap, it's so bright!" And he rolled over in bed and pulled the blankets over his head. He's right; it is bright out there. So bright that sometimes we too want to pull the blankets over our heads. But we still have to get up and keep going, despite our demons and denials. We are here for such a brief moment. Each week, our oasis in time can give us practice in celebrating the kind of astonishment that creates a welcome reprieve from the mundane of the everyday.

Feeling awe raises our life to another level.

I slow down, just in this moment of writing; I really see the bright sun-light streaming into the living room. I experience the joy of witnessing our amazing world. I notice the tall tree with the spindly branches that shoot up and out. What is that tree? Suddenly, and only because I have paused to really look, I see the wind blowing the leaves. The light plays on the leaves: so many shades of green, also dappled with gold. Fireworks of greens and golds outside my window, in this moment. In that short breath of time, I receive the immense blessing of this particular moment and the stunning world around me.

Simply being alive is a miracle, and oasis time lets us heed that. Consider the biblical story of the burning bush. Moses the shepherd came across a bush that was on fire but not burning up. "Moses said, 'I must turn aside to look at this marvelous sight: why doesn't the bush burn up?'"[6] Moses stopped for the miracle instead of passing it by. If he had been in a rush, he might not have detected this odd, extraordinary sight, because in the midst of an ordinary life, it's easy to miss the miracles right in front of us. But then a voice called to him from the burning bush. "Do not come closer. Remove your sandals from your feet, for the place on which you stand is holy ground."[7] This is the ultimate call to awe, to amazement. Notice that right here, right now, we are witnessing a miracle; whatever it might be, this time and place is sacred. Wake up, says the voice. Stop and be aware.

From time to time, we must remove our "sandals" or our shoes—those casings that enable us to travel far, move fast, and live in ways that are out of touch with nature. We can only move so quickly because we are out of contact with the ground of being, the source of our vitality, the earth. When we first remove our shoes, our feet are tender and sensitive to the sticks and leaves on the ground; like roaming barefoot, our deeper connection to the world can take getting used to, and we have to move more slowly and look where we are going or we will get hurt. But let's go spiritually barefoot for a while so that we can remember where we are.

We are on our precious planet. We need to make time for Gaia, our living Mother Earth, and learn how to live in harmony with her vast treasures.

Oasis time is an occasion to stop and notice that we are on sacred ground. We see miracles every day, but we may not recognize them as such, as Thich Nhat Hahn, the Buddhist priest and Nobel Peace Prize nominee, describes.

> People usually consider walking on water or in thin air a miracle. But I think the real miracle is not to walk either on water or in thin air, but to walk on earth. Every day we are engaged in a miracle which we don't even recognize: a blue sky, white clouds, green leaves, the black, curious eyes of a child—our own two eyes. All is a miracle.[8]

Recognizing everyday miracles and being nourished by awe are essential. Rabbi Heschel wisely observes:

> As civilization advances, the sense of wonder declines. Such decline is an alarming symptom of our state of mind. Mankind will not perish for want of information, but only for want of appreciation.[9]

STRENGTHENED BY EMOTIONAL RESILIENCE

Awe leads to greater openness and vulnerability, especially to the river of our inner life. When we learn to accept the wide range of feelings integral to our makeup, we become stronger and better able to move through those emotions. Living a full, emotional life is part of coming home to ourselves. Mostly we want to be happy and make our contribution, but true happiness derives from the joys of and capacity for a rich emotional life. As we slow down and open, we might be surprised by unexpected difficult feelings. Trust that the inner pain or instability can heal and that a full range of emotions is a sign of health and resilience.

Too often, we check out from the full, rich life of our feelings by operating in a trance of busyness: Somehow, many of us got the idea that being productive entails putting our feelings aside. We hustle about in constant motion, crossing things off our to-do lists as we go, and sometimes using our productivity to flee from our genuine heart and soul. As seductive as it is to get things done, our achievements may mask an inability to be present in our lives. When people slow down, they may discover that their inner world is a rocky landscape or that they feel bleak or lonely.

"In our moments of speeding around, we are not living in our body. We're homeless, we are not perceiving our belonging to life," says Buddhist teacher Tara Brach.[10] While we are speeding about, Brach notes, we might notice that we generate a lot of judgmental thoughts—about ourselves, others, and our situations. If we can release our judgments, we come closer to the real truth of self and world. Buddhism teaches us to sit still while thoughts and feelings rise and fall. Slowly we begin to recognize our patterns of emotional reactivity and become able to stay ahead of them. We start to see what triggers us to feel overwhelmed, scared, or sad; stillness allows us to experience and release those emotions rather than fear or dread them. We no longer get quite so caught up in the tangle of our reactivity. We are less often at the mercy of the natural flow of emotion. Instead, emotion becomes energy in motion—it becomes a resource for us.

Sometimes we are fleeing from difficult emotions, but sometimes we don't have access to positive feelings—and we don't even realize that those uplifting emotions are missing. For instance, in the spring of my junior year in college, I traveled to West Africa on a research project sponsored by my professor at Columbia. When I got off the plane in Abidjan, the capital of Ivory Coast, I was hit by an intense, moist heat. The air was thick and hot in the early morning, and the tarmac felt soft.

After meeting each other at the hotel, we members of the research project arrived at our destination late one afternoon. We traveled to a tiny village of the Abron people, about two hundred and fifty miles north of Abidjan. When we arrived, the head woman of the village thrust a chicken into my hands. It was a wonderful gift, and the villagers were surprised that I didn't know how to pluck a chicken.

Life was slow. Mornings were silent. After eating simple food, we headed out for a day of work—but not work as I had known it. Several morning hours of gardening in the fields were followed by a long, peaceful midday rest until the strength of the sun faded. Then it was time to collect water or prepare another simple meal for dinner. Since there was no electricity in the village, sundown meant getting ready to sleep. I slept long hours there. I gradually adapted to the heat. The villagers were very friendly, and, with the help of palm wine, there was much singing and dancing in the cool of the evenings.

The village was small. Soon I had met everyone. After several days, I experienced some unfamiliar feelings: A lifting in my heart. A sense of ease in my body. A quiet in my mind. "What is this?" I wondered. I slowly realized that it was happiness, a sense of lightness and well-being that remained with me throughout the trip and accompanied me back home, until it slowly faded and disappeared.

I was in that village for only a couple of weeks, but in that time I tasted something I would not encounter again until I visited another foreign land and moved abroad for several years: I learned what it was like to feel happiness and contentment. Up to that point, I had known a life of substantial achievement for a young person: the president of my high school student government, an environmental activist and youth leader, a National Merit Scholar finalist, a youth committee member for a governor of Massachusetts, a student at an Ivy League college. But there, in Africa, a rich and keen happiness arose unbidden in a very different world. I didn't know that I had felt so pressured and burdened by my achievement-oriented life until I went so far away.

We have all experienced that desire for a deeper, more profound sense of peace and happiness. For many of us, when we feel that yearning, we respond by eating or shopping or making another plan. But we don't need food or stimulation; we need stillness and awe, perhaps, or gratitude and genial company. We may want to alleviate an ache with a possession, but when we consume instead of connect, we miss the subtle cues that teach us the slow, unfamiliar route to truly sate our needs with connection and awe. Barbara Brown Taylor describes the situation this way in her book *The Practice of Saying No.*

Most of us move fast enough during the week to outrun [our feel-
ings], but if you slow down for a day, then all kinds of alarming
things can happen. You can start crying without having the slightest
idea why. You can start remembering what you loved about people
who died before you were ten, along with things you did when you
were eighteen that still send involuntary shivers up your back. . . .
You discover that you are far less hungry than you thought you were,
or at least less for groceries than for the bread no one can buy.[11]

And the fears that can emerge when slowing down can yield to joys,
as author Dominique Browning pointed out, after she lost her job.

As I stop struggling so with fear and simply accept the slow tempo of
my days, all those inner resources start kicking in—those soul-saving
habits of playfulness, most of all: reading, thinking, listening, feeling
my body move through the world, noticing the small beauty in every
single day. I watch the worms, watch the hawks, watch the fox, watch
the rabbits. . . . I find room in my life again for love of the world, and
give myself over to joy. What a surprise![12]

All of our feelings are a valuable part of ourselves and a natural part
of a rich human life. We need to take a little time each week to stop trying
to make ourselves feel okay or happy or competent and to allow ourselves
the wide spectrum of our experiences. While we might think that we'd
prefer to be happy all of the time, that stance can make us brittle and cau-
tious. Instead, we need a little time to experience our inner world, to see
what unwanted flotsam and jetsam of life surface—the fears, the anxiet-
ies, the wishes for revenge, the grief, and the unconsidered dreams that
tend to get pushed down as we rush about.

Sustained by Belonging

When we are running fast through life, we can build up so much momentum that our identity is in the speed. There is something rewarding and

thrilling in that just-barely-keeping-up feeling. But our nonstop pursuit of doing and productivity may mask the sense of emptiness and loneliness that many of us feel. We forget who we are and what we value.

In his blockbuster bestseller *Tribe,* Sebastian Junger points to the troubling amount of loneliness and disconnectedness that has emerged in our highly affluent society. Often, neighbors don't know one another because they don't need one another; individual affluence precludes the need to share and seek neighborly help. By contrast, stripped of the protective illusion of ease and affluence, we can rediscover the natural web of connectedness that is genuinely life affirming.

Junger notes that it can be surprising how related, right, and strong people feel in times of collective adversity. He describes the work of US Army Captain Charles Fritz, who wanted to know why social scientists find that mental illness declines and communal service increases during hard times, during both war and natural disasters. Fritz postulated that "modern society has gravely disrupted the social bonds that have always characterized the human experience and that disasters thrust people back into a more ancient, organic way of relating."[13] When we grasp the power of communal cooperation for something better, we can lead life with greater satisfaction. You can't get enough of what you don't need. But when you get what you *do* need, it can lift your life up to new levels.

Not too long ago, new neighbors moved in across the street from our house. I invited them for dinner. It was a spontaneous gesture of welcome, the obvious right thing to do: "Please join us!" As the time drew closer, though, I regretted my generous impulse and was kicking myself because I had so much else to do. At the last minute, I managed to cobble together an easy dinner, and when our guests arrived, they were bearing wine, fruit, and goodwill. Within minutes, the conversation flowed easily. My to-do list faded from my mind. My husband and I loved the conviviality. Our new neighbors were fantastic with Ari. By the end of the evening, we all did dishes together and it felt like we were on our way to becoming friends. We are back and forth often now, with joy in the easy connectedness.

Humans are designed to face challenges together. We positively thrive on collaboration. In natural disasters, people reach out to one another to help. We are wired to assist each other, even to sacrifice greatly and put ourselves aside, and that gives us a deep sense of connection and well-being. I've noticed this collaborative spirit here on my block. We live close to the Hayward Fault in the San Francisco Bay Area, meaning we are in an earthquake-prone neighborhood. Earthquake preparedness is part of the local zeitgeist.

Part of being prepared is knowing your neighbors. We've talked about what we each could contribute in a crisis. Our neighbor across the street is a nurse. Next door is a very handy guy. Our house has a double-reinforced basement designed to be secure in an earthquake. We need to be ready to assist each other, and it helps to know one another before disaster hits. Therefore, we not only know who lives in the houses nearby, but we chat and occasionally celebrate special moments. This is in stark contrast to our old town, where a friendly smile on our street was met with a stare that said, "Do I know you?"

Clearly, one side effect of the busyness of today's world is diminished expectations of each other. People want connectedness, but trying to shoehorn it in doesn't always work. One beautiful afternoon several summers ago, my husband and I invited longtime friends to meet us at our old neighborhood pool. We had been looking forward to seeing them and had made yummy summer food to share. They arrived about an hour late, full of apologies—they had been to an art exhibition that morning, and it took more time than anticipated to see the artwork, and then they hit traffic en route to our house.

We all swam, then took our food to a picnic table. Sated and soaking in the sun, David and I thought we would now enjoy a slow summer afternoon of catching up, sharing stories, and perhaps strolling around the neighborhood, or watching the kids playing in the pool. Suddenly our guests started packing up. "We're off to the farmers' market," they said cheerfully. "We wish we could stay, but we told some friends we would meet them there. Yes, we are running a bit late, but that's okay; they'll understand. Come along, kids, we've got to hurry now."

And they left.

Haven't we all packed our weekends full of activities? I certainly have. But when you rush from activity to activity, you don't give your relationships and communities the care and attention they need to thrive. You skim the surface. You miss the profound connections, relationships, and the magic of spontaneous depth that you get to experience only when you wade into it deep enough. While that thrill of doing it all and being the busiest of all can provide a temporary rush, eventually you will hit a moment where sheer momentum cannot compensate for the fact that you are running on empty and that friends may not be there when you need them.

By running through our lives and never slowing down, we run the risk of not truly living them. A focus on external forces—personal and professional demands, the constant pings of phones or watches to let us know that we've received another message—can prevent us from nurturing the inner knowledge we need in order to navigate the challenges we will inevitably face. By leaving little time in our lives to nurture deep, sustaining relationships, we may find that all the professional and material success is nowhere near as sweet.

If you take away one thing from this book, I hope it is this: Stay connected with people. Don't rush so quickly through life that you miss out on profound friendship and community. Don't let your connections fray because you want to cross one more item off of your list. Because then, when you need comfort or support from a friend, it may not be there. Your friends don't show up when you need them or the friendship can't hold your pain or grief. Remember that the real "stuff" of life is the laughter and the tears with our fellow travelers, the ones physically far away and the ones right up close. Oasis time is the moment to find and connect with our tribe. We need to belong.

In a culture that values busyness over stillness and action over reflection, making time for rest and renewal can feel risky. After all, who wants to fall behind when everyone else seems to be surging ahead toward greater success and fulfillment?

But why can't we have both? Why can't we be astoundingly productive and still deeply value having a social life and lots of time together? Why can't we savor the joys of work *and* the joys of stopping and unwinding? Of course, we can have both, and that is why oasis time is so important.

In the end, the good news is that we can make choices each day to build the future we want. We can choose to rest and renew our energy so that we face the challenges of our world energized and with healthy perspective. We can elect to use technology well without becoming slaves to it. We can consciously set aside time for friends instead of reluctantly scheduling them in like another chore to accomplish. We can cultivate a strong, spiritual, internal self that allows us to feel control when facing the buffeting winds of the outside world.

It's now time to turn to the day that we have set apart for freedom. This is a day to be with ourselves, to be with others face-to-face in congenial timelessness, in a shared experience of awe and reverence on a day in which, as Rabbi Heschel points out, we can stop struggling.

> *A day in which we stop worshipping the idols of technical civilization, a day on which we use no money, a day of armistice in the economic struggle with our fellow men and the forces of nature—is there any institution that holds out a greater hope for man's progress than the Sabbath?*
>
> *The solution of mankind's most vexing problem will not be found in renouncing technical civilization, but in attaining some degree of independence of it.*[14]

We cannot protect ourselves from hardship, but we can return to our island of tranquility and connection once a week, and in so doing become resourceful enough to rise to our challenges and stand up with vigor and vitality to the—at times—overwhelming forces of life. As you continue learning how to create oasis time, it becomes an essential part of your life. Week by week, you'll turn to your oasis time with relief. When you keep choosing to rest, to savor, to connect more with others, and to let go of the relentless quest for more, you create ballast and stability for the treacherous waters ahead. You'll be the captain of your ship, which you can navigate more surely to your true home.

Appendix A

{ **QUICK START FOR A SLOW TIME** }

re you ready for oasis time? Here are some suggestions for making your early oasis experiments successful.

Get curious. Put your experimental mindset on. Whatever happens, this is going to be interesting.

Block off the time. Schedule your beginning and ending. Put it in your calendar.

Describe your vision. What would you like your oasis time to be? Personal downtime? Social time? Family time? Nature time? Arts, crafts, or music time? Sports time?

Plan to do something really different. Choose something that is not about achievement in any way—perhaps something that you have wanted to do for a really long time but never quite got to. Or try something you would never do—you just haven't had the time.*

Write the activity you choose in your calendar. Sleep, walk, shoot hoops, sit on the porch, make art, make cookies, read a novel, play with a child, play with an animal, do absolutely nothing.

Do what you need to do to get ready. Get food in the kitchen. Make plans with people.

Unplug. Figure out where to put your phone, computer, and tablet so you aren't tempted to get on a screen. Let people know how to contact you—or not.

Slow down. Slow your movements. Savor your experience.

Live your oasis time. Experience life in the present moment. What happens for you? What do you notice as the time unfolds? Meet with your oasis time buddy, if you have one. Go to sleep if you are tired. Sit by water or green grass or trees if you are wired. Calm down. Be grateful.

End with a flourish. Sing a song. Receive the blessings of your rest time. Pull your cover off your computer or phone with a grand gesture.

Debrief. What did you like? Not like? What did you learn? Take some notes. Talk to a friend about your experience.

Do it again next week. Change it up based on what you learned.

---

* Preferably choose something that doesn't involve a screen. But, in fact, some people never watch movies, and in that case, a movie or a couple of episodes of a series feels like just what they need. Just remember, though, the research is in: Watching screens doesn't restore us much.

Appendix B

OASIS TIME
MINI-GUIDE

Oasis time takes preparation. But it's best to keep it simple! Simple preparation makes your oasis time truly replenishing. Here is some guidance as you get ready—choose any or all of these suggestions as a means to generate a fulfilling oasis time. For each, I've included an action and an accompanying thought to make your oasis time real.

I know this looks like a recipe with a lot of ingredients. It is a little daunting, but you'll soon see that the ingredients are easy to put together. So give it a shot and you will have a great time. Think of this mini-guide as your crib sheet. Print out a copy and keep it with you as you move through your oasis time (marilynpaul.com).

Prepare mind, heart, and spirit

Action	Thought
Reflect for 2 minutes every day.	*Every day, I imagine how good my weekly renewal time will be. I deserve to be brimming with vitality and joy.*
Make a plan for soul and spiritual time, both shared and individual.	*I plan ahead and write oasis time in my calendar. I ensure time and space for my practices for soul renewal.*

Arrange for delicious food

Action	Thought
Buy food.	*I buy good ingredients or prepared food in advance of my oasis time so that I can happily nourish my body easily.*
Serve food.	*I (cook and) serve wonderful food in a beautiful way so that I (and we) can truly enjoy a feast during our time off.*

Set up nourishing, renewing activities

Action	Thought
Set up social time.	*I make sure that I have friends and family to spend nourishing time with. I find others to join with in lifting our spirits and renewing our souls.*
Arrange time in nature. Look for nearby spots that might offer water, land, forests, mountains, or gardens.	*I find a place in nature that I love. I allow being in nature to deeply renew me and connect me with the beautiful world that we are a part of.*
Set up self-care time.	*I make sure to take good care of myself. I plan a nap, a bath, a good read, or whatever refreshes me.*

Plan activities for your children or other dependents

Action	Thought
Set up care for your dependents. If possible, arrange for screen-free activities that they can enjoy.	*I need my own space within our oasis. My children or parents will be fine without me for several hours. I find activities for my children that add to their enjoyment of oasis time and allow me to be refreshed. Then we all come back together in a more present and loving way.*
For older children, ensure that they have engaging activities.	*I am a much better parent or caregiver when I am refreshed and have taken good care of myself.*

Prepare your space

Action	Thought
Straighten up.	*I create space by putting things away. I make room for rest, for growth, for peace, and for guests by creating beauty and order in my home.*
Clean the house and self.	*I prepare for my oasis time by cleaning away the dirt and grime of the week. I shower off the weekly accumulations of worry and difficulty. Even a little bit of cleaning helps.*

Close up shop

Action	Thought
Put work away.	*I consciously put my work away in preparation for oasis time, knowing it will go much more smoothly when I return.*
Take notes.	*I take notes on where I am when I stop so that it's easier to start again when I get back to work.*
Alert people that you are in a no-work zone.	*I let people know that I am not available for work calls or any work or school conversations, phone calls, or e-mails during this time.*

Create a festive atmosphere

Action	Thought
Put on special clothes that remind you that you are entering renewal time.	*I put on clothes that make me feel connected to the specialness and beauty of oasis time.*
Put on relaxing, energizing, or evocative music. Print out song sheets if you want to sing together.	*Music reminds me to be joyful and let go. I love singing with other people.*

Enter oasis time

Action	Thought
Set up what you need for an oasis time start ritual.	*I perform a ritual that helps me feel that I have entered my renewal zone. I am now entering sacred time and space for renewal of my heart and soul.*
Consciously shed your worries.	*I trust that, for now, I have everything I need, and I can refresh my mind and heart by turning toward the ineffable. If needed, I write down what is bothering me. I let go of resentments and grudges during oasis time.*
Enter a space of joy.	*I light candles, make music, dance, sing, or go outside. This helps me find an inner place of joy.*

Immerse in oasis time

Action	Thought
Unplug.	*I refrain from using my devices. When I get bored or feel I need connection or stimulation, I seek out people in person, I walk, I read, I explore the actual world.*
Slow down.	*I move slowly so I can pay attention to what matters. I am mindful of the beauties and joys of my life.*
Let go of achieving.	*Every time I think of something urgent to do, or when work or family worries arise, I either write the thought down or ignore it.*

End your oasis time

Action	Thought
Draw the restoration time to a close.	*I am ready to reenter the world of action. I maintain my sense of peace and joy.*
Return to the world of action with energy.	*I start with activities that bring me joy as I reenter my week.*

Appendix C

REMEMBER THE SABBATH—A CHRISTIAN VIEW

A church in Hartford, Connecticut, is experimenting with ways to bring contemporary Christian living and worship alive for its congregants. One of the ways is to bring more of a Sabbath into their lives. Erica Thompson is an associate minister at the Asylum Hill Congregational Church, a bustling, vibrant church that proposes the Simple 7 of Christian life. Those practices are: Sunday Worship, Scripture Reading, Seeking God in Prayer, Service, Stewardship, Spiritual Friendship, and Sabbath. She explains that these principles are "simple, sacred ways to grow in faith and love." Erica told me that they had started with the Simple 6, and then a congregant said, "Wait, we have forgotten Sabbath." So, now there are seven practices.

The following passages are adapted from the Asylum Hill Congregational Church website. You can visit the site at ahcc.org/about-ahcc/what-we-believe/simple-7 for more information.

Most of us know what it takes to be physically healthy: eat a nutritious diet, drink plenty of water, exercise, get enough sleep, visit your doctor, reduce stress, laugh often. We might not do all of those every day, but we at least know how to live a healthy life. What about our spiritual lives? What promotes spiritual health and vitality? Are we as clear about that as we are about our physical lives? Yet, our spiritual needs are just as important—maybe even more so. After all, our bodies are temporary; the soul is eternal.

From the very beginning, Christians have turned to seven basic practices to nurture the soul and deepen our eternal journey with God.

These Simple 7 practices are not a spiritual scorecard or a way to become a "super Christian," whatever that is. The Simple 7 are simply ways to help us grow in faith and love as disciples of Jesus. They are food and exercise for the soul.

One of the Simple 7 Is the Practice of Sabbath

God blessed the seventh day, because on that day, God rested from work, all the creating God had done.—Genesis 2:2

In our work-crazy, on-the-go, device-dependent, highly distracted lives, we have lost the important balance of work and rest. In a world where the universal mantra is "I'm so busy," practicing the Sabbath is downright countercultural!

Even though we are routinely exhausted, we carry our busyness like a trophy. The busier we are, the more important we must be. The commandment to "Remember the Sabbath" is not only a command to stop and smell the roses but also a nudge to take a step outside ourselves and appreciate the bigger picture. The world does not depend on us. We are not as important or as necessary as we might think. In the Judeo-Christian tradition, no one is more important than God—and even God took a day off.

Practicing Sabbath means we deliberately set aside time to unplug, relax, reflect on our blessings, and do as little as possible so God can do as much as possible with us.

For some, Sabbath-keeping will mean taking several hours, or up to a full day, off doing as little work (including housework) as possible. For others, it will mean injecting 5 to 10 minutes of silence into every day. Start small and build up each week. God is waiting to take a breather with you!

SEVEN SIMPLE WAYS TO "KEEP THE SABBATH"

1. Check e-mail only at set times during your day and live free of it the rest of the day.

2. Learn to say no to things that fill your schedule and leave little time for rest and renewal.

3. Always eat lunch and always eat dinner, sitting down, perhaps with a tablecloth or cloth napkin you keep in your desk drawer.

4. Make a list of things you would do if only you had the time. Do one a week.

5. Write a letter to an old friend, clean a corner of your home, or take time to prepare a special meal with friends or family.

6. Look at an old photo album. Turn the pages slowly. Linger over each picture.

7. Whenever the phone rings or the clock dings, take two slow breaths.

Appendix D

$$\left\{\begin{array}{c}\text{ADDITIONAL}\\\text{RESOURCES}-\text{BOOKS}\end{array}\right\}$$

These are some of the books that I consulted as I wrote *An Oasis in Time.*

COMMUNITY, FAMILY, AND CONNECTION

Steiner-Adair, Catherine. *The Big Disconnect: Protecting Childhood and Family Relationships in the Digital Age.* New York: Harper, 2013

Banks, Amy, and Leigh Ann Hirschman. *Wired to Connect: The Surprising Link between Brain Science and Strong, Healthy Relationships.* New York: Penguin, 2015.

Jackson, Maggie. *What's Happening to Home? Balancing Work, Life, and Refuge in the Information Age.* Notre Dame, IN: Sorin Books, 2002.

Junger, Sebastian. *Tribe: On Homecoming and Belonging.* New York: Twelve, 2016.

Lipkin, Lisa. *Bringing the Story Home: The Complete Guide to Storytelling for Parents.* New York: W. W. Norton & Company, Inc., 2000.

McKnight, John, and Peter Block. *The Abundant Community: Awakening the Power of Families and Neighborhoods.* San Francisco, CA: Berrett-Koehler Publishers, 2010.

Nelson, Shasta. *Frientimacy: How to Deepen Friendships for Lifelong Health and Happiness*. Berkeley, CA: Seal Press, 2016.

Palmer, Parker J. *A Hidden Wholeness: The Journey toward an Undivided Life*. San Francisco, CA: Jossey-Bass, 2004.

Turkle, Sherry. *Reclaiming Conversation: The Power of Talk in a Digital Age*. New York: Penguin, 2015.

Weinstein, Miriam. *The Surprising Power of Family Meals: How Eating Together Makes Us Smarter, Stronger, Healthier, and Happier*. Hanover, NH: Steerforth Press, 2005.

Consumer Culture

Graaf, John De, David Wann, and Thomas H. Naylor. *Affluenza: How Overconsumption Is Killing Us—And How We Can Fight Back*. 3rd ed. San Francisco, CA: Berrett-Koehler Publishers, 2014.

Kasser, Tim. *The High Price of Materialism*. Cambridge, MA: MIT Press, 2002.

Schor, Juliet B. *The Overspent American: Upscaling, Downshifting, and the New Consumer*. New York: Basic Books, 1998.

Slater, Philip E. *The Pursuit of Loneliness: American Culture at the Breaking Point*. Boston: Beacon Press, 1970.

Twist, Lynn. *The Soul of Money: Reclaiming the Wealth of Our Inner Resources*. New York: W. W. Norton & Company, Inc., 2013.

Creativity

Cameron, Julia. *The Artist's Way: A Spiritual Path to Higher Creativity*. New York: Jeremy P. Tarcher/Putnam, 1992.

Dinwiddie, Melissa. *The Creative Sandbox Way: Your Path to a Full-Color Life*. Mountain View, CA: Pluralite Press, 2016.

Gilbert, Elizabeth. *Big Magic: Creative Living beyond Fear*. New York: Penguin, 2015.

Environment and Nature

Francis, Pope. *On Care for Our Common Home (Laudato Si')*. Huntington, IN: Our Sunday Visitor, 2015.

Klein, Naomi. *This Changes Everything: Capitalism vs. the Climate*. New York: Simon & Schuster, 2014.

Louv, Richard. *Last Child in the Woods: Saving Our Children from Nature-Deficit Disorder*. Vol. 2. Chapel Hill, NC: Algonquin Books of Chapel Hill, 2008.

McKibben, Bill. *The Comforting Whirlwind: God, Job, and the Scale of Creation*. Cambridge, MA: Cowley Publications, 2005.

Facing Death

Albom, Mitch. *Tuesdays with Morrie: An Old Man, a Young Man, and Life's Greatest Lesson.* New York: Doubleday, 1997.

Butler, Katy. *Knocking on Heaven's Door: The Path to a Better Way of Death.* New York: Scribner, 2013.

Gawande, Atul. *Being Mortal: Medicine and What Matters in the End.* New York: Metropolitan Books, 2014.

O'Kelly, Eugene. *Chasing Daylight: How My Forthcoming Death Transformed My Life.* New York: McGraw-Hill, 2008.

Pausch, Randy. *The Last Lecture.* New York: Hyperion, 2008.

Health, Well-Being, and Personal Growth

Brach, Tara. *True Refuge: Finding Peace and Freedom in Your Own Awakened Heart.* New York: Bantam Books, 2012.

Brown, Brené. *Rising Strong: The Reckoning. The Rumble. The Revolution.* New York: Spiegel & Grau, 2015.

Hillis-Jaffe, Janette. *Everyday Healing: Stand Up, Take Charge, and Get Your Health Back ... One Day at a Time.* Pompton, NJ: New Page Books, 2015.

Neff, Kristin. *Self-Compassion: Stop Beating Yourself Up and Leave Insecurity Behind.* New York: William Morrow, 2011.

Rubin, Gretchen. *Better Than Before: What I Learned about Making and Breaking Habits—to Sleep More, Quit Sugar, Procrastinate Less, and Generally Build a Happier Life.* New York: Broadway Books, 2015.

Seixas, Abby. *Finding the Deep River Within: A Woman's Guide to Recovering Balance and Meaning in Everyday Life.* San Francisco: Jossey-Bass, 2006.

Overwhelm

Gallagher, Winifred. *Rapt: Attention and the Focused Life.* New York: Penguin Press, 2009.

Hallowell, Edward M. *CrazyBusy: Overstretched, Overbooked, and about to Snap!* New York: Ballantine Books, 2006.

Jackson, Maggie. *Distracted: The Erosion of Attention and the Coming Dark Age.* Amherst, NY: Prometheus Books, 2008.

Jones, Kirk Byron. *Addicted to Hurry: Spiritual Strategies for Slowing Down.* Valley Forge, PA: Judson Press, 2003.

Schulte, Brigid. *Overwhelmed: How to Work, Love, and Play When No One Has the Time.* New York: Farrar, Straus, and Giroux, 2014.

Stafford, Rachel Macy. *Hands Free Life: 9 Habits for Overcoming Distraction, Living Better & Loving More.* Grand Rapids, MI: Zondervan, 2015.

Philosophy

Aurelius, Marcus. *Meditations*. Translated by Maxwell Staniforth. New York: Penguin Books, 1964.

Gellert, Michael. *The Way of the Small: Why Less Is Truly More*. Lake Worth, FL: Nicolas-Hays, 2008.

Haidt, Jonathan. *The Happiness Hypothesis: Finding Modern Truth in Ancient Wisdom*. New York: Basic Books, 2006.

Irvine, William Braxton. *A Guide to the Good Life: The Ancient Art of Stoic Joy*. Oxford: Oxford University Press, 2009.

Lenoir, Frédéric. *Happiness: A Philosopher's Guide*. Translated by Andrew Brown. New York: Melville House, 2015.

Philosophy of Time

Easwaran, Eknath. *Take Your Time: How to Find Patience, Peace & Meaning*. 2nd ed. Tomales, CA: Nilgiri Press, 2006.

Eberle, Gary. *Sacred Time and the Search for Meaning*. Boston: Shambhala Publications, 2003.

Graaf, John De, ed. *Take Back Your Time: Fighting Overwork and Time Poverty in America*. San Francisco: Berrett-Koehler, 2003.

Honoré, Carl. *In Praise of Slowness: How a Worldwide Movement Is Challenging the Cult of Speed*. San Francisco: HarperSanFrancisco, 2004.

McEwen, Christian. *World Enough & Time: On Creativity and Slowing Down*. Peterborough, NH: Bauhan, 2011.

Powers, William. *Hamlet's Blackberry: A Practical Philosophy for Building a Good Life in the Digital Age*. New York: HarperCollins, 2010.

Schor, Juliet B. *The Overworked American: The Unexpected Decline of Leisure*. New York: Basic Books, 1991.

Productivity

Loehr, James E., and Tony Schwartz. *The Power of Full Engagement: Managing Energy, Not Time, Is the Key to High Performance and Personal Renewal*. New York: Free Press, 2003.

McKeown, Greg. *Essentialism: The Disciplined Pursuit of Less*. New York: Crown Business, 2012.

Newport, Cal. *Deep Work: Rules for Focused Success in a Distracted World*. New York: Grand Central Publishing, 2016.

Tracy, Brian. *Eat That Frog! 21 Great Ways to Stop Procrastinating and Get More Done in Less Time*. San Francisco: Berrett-Koehler Publishers, 2007.

Sabbath and Shabbat

Berry, Wendell. *Sabbaths.* New York: North Point Press, 1987.

Brueggeman, Walter. *Sabbath as Resistance: Saying No to the Culture of Now.* Louisville, Kentucky: Westminster John Knox Press, 2014.

Buchanan, Mark. *The Rest of God: Restoring Your Soul by Restoring Sabbath.* Grand Rapids, Michigan: Thomas Nelson, 2006.

Heschel, Abraham Joshua. *The Sabbath: Its Meaning for Modern Man.* New York: Farrar, Straus and Young, 1951.

Lieberman, Joseph. *The Gift of Rest: Rediscovering the Beauty of the Sabbath.* New York: Howard Books, 2011.

McKibben, MaryAnn Dana. *Sabbath in the Suburbs: A Family's Experiment with Holy Time.* Atlanta: Chalice Press, 2012.

Muller, Wayne. Sabbath: *Finding Rest, Renewal, and Delight in Our Busy Lives.* New York: Bantam Books, 2000.

Schley, Sara. *Secrets of the Seventh Day: How Everyone Can Find Renewal through the Wisdom and Practices of the Sabbath.* Ashland, Oregon: White Cloud Press, 2013.

Shulevitz, Judith. *The Sabbath World: Glimpses of a Different Order of Time.* New York: Random House, 2010.

Zion, Noam. *A Day Apart: Shabbat at Home.* Jerusalem, Israel: Shalom Hartman Institute, 2004.

Social Action

Alexander, Michelle. *The New Jim Crow: Mass Incarceration in the Age of Colorblindness.* New York: The New Press, 2012.

Braun, Adam, and Carlye Adler. *The Promise of a Pencil: How an Ordinary Person Can Create Extraordinary Change.* New York: Simon & Schuster, 2014.

Coates, Ta-Nehisi. *Between the World and Me.* New York: Spiegel & Grau, 2015.

Glassman, Bernard, and Rick Fields. *Instructions to the Cook: A Zen Master's Lessons in Living a Life That Matters.* New York: Bell Tower, 1996.

Jaffe, David. *Changing the World from the Inside Out: A Jewish Approach to Personal and Social Change.* Boulder, Colorado: Trumpeter Books, 2016.

Kristof, Nicholas D., and Sheryl WuDunn. *A Path Appears: Transforming Lives, Creating Opportunity.* New York: Random House, 2014.

Stroh, David Peter. *Systems Thinking for Social Change: A Practical Guide to Solving Complex Problems, Avoiding Unintended Consequences, and Achieving Lasting Results.* White River Junction, Vermont: Chelsea Green Publishing, 2015.

Appendix E

{

ADDITIONAL
RESOURCES

}

Web Sites

A Network for Grateful Living ANGeL: http://www.gratefulness.org

ANGeL provides online resources for experiencing gratitude and an active international community for sharing and discussing such experiences.

Carl Honoré: http://www.carlhonore.com/

Carl Honoré is the author of *In Praise of Slow,* which catalyzed the slow movement. His website offers online video, audio, courses, and more for embracing slowness.

Center for a New American Dream: http://www.newdream.org

The Center for a New American Dream seeks to improve human well-being by shifting the ways we consume.

The Family Dinner Project: http://thefamilydinnerproject.org

This site is an excellent source of recipes, conversation ideas, and inspiration for family dinners.

Greater Good: http://greatergood.berkeley.edu/

The Greater Good provides scientific, evidence-based solutions for improving individual and collective happiness and compassion.

The New Road Map Foundation http://financialintegrity.org

This is an outstanding site for helping to get your finances in line with your values.

Reboot. http://www.rebooters.net.

The sponsor of National Day of Unplugging. Get a free cell phone sleeping bag.

Resurgence Slow Sunday: http://www.resurgence.org/take-part/slow-sunday.html

Slow Sunday is a secular effort to reclaim Sunday as a day of rest, reflection, and connection with family and neighbors through community events.

Sabbath Manifesto: http://www.sabbathmanifesto.org/

Principles and discussion for slowing down and unplugging on your day of rest. There is a great little video called "How do you unplug?" under the tab "National Day of Unplugging."

Share Save Spend: http://www.sharesavespend.com

Share Save Spend offers tools, resources, and an online virtual video library (Money Sanity U) all designed to prepare people for a lifetime of financial opportunities and responsibilities.

Slow Movement: http://www.slowmovement.com/

The Slow Movement website provides extensive examples and resources for slowing down and connecting to food, place, and—most importantly—life.

Take Back Your Time: https://www.takebackyourtime.org/

Take Back Your Time aims to eliminate the epidemic of overworking and improve quality of life for working people.

Apps

30/30: This app helps you plan your day.

Friday: This app turns off your phone on Friday nights.

Unplugged: This app helps you put down your phone.

Endnotes

Introduction

1 Laura Ingalls Wilder, *Little House in the Big Woods* (New York: HarperCollins, 2004).

2 Oliver Sacks, "Sabbath," *New York Times*, Aug. 14, 2015, SR1.

3 Elizabeth Gilbert, entry on her Facebook page, May 20, 2016.

Chapter 1

1 Paul J. Rosch, "The Quandary of Job Stress Compensation," *Health and Stress*, vol. 3 (March 2001), 2–3. While some consider the methods used to derive the $300 cost of stress controversial, Rosch considers this figure to be a very conservative estimate and critics have not proposed an alternative figure nor an alternative estimative process.

2 "The State of American Vacation 2016: How Vacation Became a Casualty of Our Work Culture," Project: Time Off (2016). projecttimeoff.com/sites/default/files/PTO_SoAV%20Report_FINAL.pdf.

3 Sonia van Gilder Cooke, "Bon Voyage!: Why Europe's Vacation-Loving Ways May Make Economic Sense," *Time* (March 19, 2012). http://content.time.com/time/world/article/0,8599,2109263,00.html.

4 Gallup, Inc. "In U.S., 40% Get Less Than Recommended Amount of Sleep," Gallup.com (Dec. 19, 2013). www.gallup.com/poll/166553/less-recommended-amount-sleep.aspx.

5 Sara Martin, "'Our Health at Risk': APA's Latest Survey Finds That Many Americans Don't Understand How Stress Can Undermine Their Health," American Psychological Association's *Monitor on Psychology*, vol. 43, no. 3 (March 2012), 18. www.apa.org/monitor/2012/03/stress.aspx.

6 "Stress," American Diabetes Association, 2016. www.diabetes.org/living-with-diabetes/complications/mental-health/stress.html.

7 Cari Romm, "Americans Are Getting Worse at Taking Sleeping Pills," TheAtlantic.com, Aug. 12, 2014, http://www.theatlantic.com/health/archive/2014/08/americans-are-getting-worse-at-taking-sleeping-pills/375935/.

8 MCM Research, *WTAG Binge-Drinking Research, Rep. Wine Intelligence*, Sept. 2004. www.sirc.org/publik/binge_drinking.pdf.

9   Rebecca C. Thurston, PhD, and Laura D. Kubzansky, PhD, MPH, "Women, Loneliness, and Incident Coronary Heart Disease," *Psychosomatic Medicine*, vol. 71, no. 8 (October 2009), 836-42.

10 Mary K. Alvord, PhD, et al, "Understanding Chronic Stress," APA Help Center, American Psychological Association, Nov. 2016. www.apa.org/helpcenter/understanding-chronic-stress.aspx.

11 *The Common Sense Census: Media Use by Tweens and Teens*, report of the Common Sense Media Inc., 2015. www.commonsensemedia.org/sites/default/files/uploads/research/census_researchreport.pdf.

12 Sherry Turkle, *Reclaiming Conversation: The Power of Talk in a Digital Age* (New York: Penguin, 2015).

13 Interview with Tanya Schevitz, Oct. 2015.

14 Emily Feinstein, lead researcher on a Center for Addiction and Substance Abuse at Columbia University (CASAColumbia) project concerning family meals. Founded by Joseph Califano, CASAColumbia is a research organization dedicated to assessing the impact of all substance abuse in all sectors of society. One of their main initiatives is CASAColumbia Family Day, supported by the US president and by the governors of all fifty states.

15 Amy Banks with Leigh Ann Hirschman, *Wired to Connect: The Surprising Link between Brain Science and Strong, Healthy Relationships* (New York: TarcherPerigee, 2015).

16 Thomas Merton, *Conjectures of a Guilty Bystander* (New York: Image Classics, 1968).

17 Mark Buchanan, *The Rest of God: Restoring Your Soul by Restoring Sabbath* (Nashville: Thomas Nelson, 2011).

18 Tony Schwartz, "What I Learned on My Vacation," *The New York Times*, Sept. 5, 2014. http://dealbook.nytimes.com/2014/09/05/what-i-learned-on-my-vacation/?_r=0.

19 Dave Schrader, "Recovering the Rhythms of Rest," The Leadership Circle, Oct. 2014.

20 Renuka Rayasam, "The End of the Inbox: Companies That Banned Email," *BBC Capital* (March 25, 2015). http://www.bbc.com/capital/story/20150324-the-companies-that-banned-email.

21 From interview, Wednesday, November 25, 2015.

22 Senator Joseph Lieberman, with David Klinghoffer, *The Gift of Rest: Rediscovering the Beauty of the Sabbath* (New York: Howard Books, 2011), 208.

23 David Rock et al, "The Healthy Mind Platter," *The NeuroLeadership Journal*, vol. 4 (2012), 1–23.

24 William Powers, *Hamlet's BlackBerry: Building a Good Life in the Digital Age* (New York: Harper, 2010), 229.

25 Mark Bittman, "I Need a Virtual Break. No, Really," *New York Times*, Mar. 2, 2008.

26 "Author One-on-One: Arianna Huffington and Mark Hyman," Amazon.com, https://www.amazon.com/Thrive-Redefining-Success-Creating-Well-Being /dp/0804140863.

27 Powers, *Hamlet's BlackBerry*, 231.

CHAPTER 2

1 Eviatar Zerubavel, *The Seven Day Circle: The History and Meaning of the Week* (Chicago: University of Chicago Press, 1989).

2 The Quran, A*l-Jumu'ah*, 62:9, Yusuf Ali.

3 The Quran, A*l-Jumu'ah*, 62:11, Yusuf Ali.

4 Aisha Stacey, "Friday—The Best Day of the Week," IslamReligion.com, Oct. 18, 2010, http://www.islamreligion.com/articles/10170/friday-best-day -of-week/.

5 Eviatar Zerubavel, *The Seven Day Circle: The History and Meaning of the Week* (Chicago: University of Chicago Press, 1989).

6 Noam Zion, personal communication with the author, May 2014.

7 Gary Eberle, *Sacred Time and the Search for Meaning* (Boulder, CO: Shambhala, 2003).

8 R. R. Hinman, *The Blue Laws of New Haven County, Usually Called Blue Laws of Connecticut; Quaker Laws of Plymouth and Massachusetts . . . First Record of Connecticut* (Hartford, CT: Case, Tiffany & Co., 1838).

9 Ibid.

10 Ibid.

11 Judith Shulevitz, *The Sabbath World: Glimpses of a Different Order of Time* (New York: Random House, 2010), 47.

12 Judith Shulevitch, "Remember the Sabbath," Forward.com, Mar. 31, 2010.

13 Benjamin Kline Hunnicutt, *Free Time: The Forgotten American Dream* (Philadelphia: Temple University Press, 2013).

14 Abraham Joshua Heschel, *The Sabbath: Its Meaning for Modern Man* (New York: Farrar, Strauss, Giroux, 1951).

15 Aristotle, *Nicomachean Ethics X* (1176b30).

16 Ibid.

17 *Tanakh: A New Translation of the Holy Scriptures according to the Traditional Hebrew Text* (Philadelphia: The Jewish Publication Society, 1985), 4.

18 *Tanakh: A New Translation of the Holy Scriptures according to the Traditional Hebrew Text* (Philadelphia: The Jewish Publication Society, 1985), 115–16.

19 Philip Slater, *The Pursuit of Loneliness: American Culture at the Breaking Point* (Boston: Beacon Press, 1970).

20 Bill McKibben, *The Comforting Whirlwind: God, Job, and the Scale of Creation* (Cambridge, MA: Cowley Publications, 2005), 66.

21 Pope Francis, *Laudato Si: On Care for Our Common Home*, May 24, 2015, paragraph 237.

22 Hunnicutt, *Free Time*.

23 Babylonian Talmud Tractate Shabbat, 25.

24 From Yalkut Ve'Etchanan suggested to me in a personal communication from scholar Noam Zion, May 2014.

25 Josef Pieper, "Leisure and Its Threefold Opposition" in *Josef Pieper: An Anthology* (San Francisco: Ignatius Press, 1989).

26 Ibid.

27 Ibid.

CHAPTER 3

1 Sonja Haller, "Top 15 Things I Learned from 52 Sabbaths," *52 Sabbaths*, Aug. 29, 2015, http://www.sonjahaller.com/top-15-things-i-learned-from-52 -sabbaths/.

2 Liu Yi Lin, Jaime E. Sidani, Ariel Shensa, Ana Radovic, Elizabeth Miller, Jason B. Colditz, Beth L. Hoffman, Leila M. Giles, and Brian A. Primack. "Association Between Social Media Use and Depression Among U.S. Young Adults," *Depression and Anxiety* 33, no. 4 (Jan. 19, 2016), 323–31.

3 Stephen Marche, "Is Facebook Making Us Lonely?," *Atlantic*, May 2012.

4 John Schumaker, "The Demoralized Mind," *New Internationalist*, April 2016.

5 Robert Waldinger, "What Makes a Good Life? Lessons from the Longest Study on Happiness," TED.com, December 2015, https://www.ted.com/talks /robert_waldinger_what_makes_a_good_life_lessons_from_the_long.

6 Cayte Bosler, "Make Time for Awe," *Atlantic*, Dec. 2013.

7 William Irvine, *A Guide to the Good Life: The Ancient Art of Stoic Joy* (New York: Oxford University Press, 2009); Zelig Pliskin, *Gateway to Happiness* (Jerusalem: Aish HaTorah Publications, 1983).

8 Brigid Schulte, *Overwhelmed: Work, Love, and Play When No One Has the Time* (New York: Farrar, Strause, Giroux, 2014).

9 John Darley and Daniel Batson, " 'From Jerusalem to Jericho': A Study of Situational and Dispositional Variables in Helping Behavior," *Journal of Personality and Social Psychology* 27, no. 1 (1973), 107.

10 See, for example, the teachings of Rebbe Nachman of Breslo.

11 Seth Godin, *What Matters Now*, Lulu.com (Triibes Press, 2009).

12 From Tim Ferris's blog, "Why You Need a Deloading Phase in Life," March 29, 2016.

13 Stuart L. Brown and Christopher C. Vaughan, *Play: How It Shapes the Brain, Opens the Imagination, and Invigorates the Soul* (New York: Avery, 2009), 5.

14 Mihaly Csikszentmihaly, *Flow: The Psychology of Optimal Experience* (New York: Harper & Row, 1990).

CHAPTER 4

1 Jiddu Krishnamurti, *The Flame of Attention* (San Francisco: Harper & Row, 1983).

2 Arianna Huffington, *Thrive: The Third Metric to Redefining Success and Creating a Life of Well-Being, Wisdom, and Wonder* (New York: Harmony Books, 2015), 1.

3 Erin Callan, "Is There Life after Work?," *New York Times*, Mar. 9, 2013.

4 Erin Callan Montella, *Full Circle: A Memoir of Leaning in Too Far and the Journey Back* (Vancouver, BC: Triple M Press, 2016).

5 Pico Iyer, *The Art of Stillness: Adventures in Going Nowhere* (New York: TED Books/Simon & Schuster, 2014).

6 Stephen Grosz, *The Examined Life: How We Lose and Find Ourselves* (New York: W. W. Norton, 2013), 123.

7 David Roberts, "Reboot or Die Trying," *Outside*, October 2014.

8 Eugene O'Kelly, *Chasing Daylight: How My Forthcoming Death Transformed My Life* (New York: McGraw-Hill, 2008).

9 Ibid.

10 Ibid.

11 Bronnie Ware, "Regrets of the Dying", Nov. 19, 2009, http://bronnieware.com/regrets-of-the-dying/.

12 Brian Tracy, *No Excuses! The Power of Self-Discipline* (New York: MJF Books, 2012).

13 Dale Carnegie, *How to Stop Worrying and Start Living* (New York: Simon & Schuster, 1948).

14 Schulte, *Overwhelmed*, 19.

CHAPTER 5

1 Sara Schley, *Secrets of the Seventh Day: How Everyone Can Find Renewal through the Wisdom and Practices of the Sabbath* (Ashland, OR: White Cloud, 2013).

2 Dean Ornish, *Dr. Dean Ornish's Program for Reversing Heart Disease: The Only System Scientifically Proven to Reverse Heart Disease without Drugs or Surgery* (New York: Ivy Books, 1995).

3 Bill Burnett and Dave Evans, *Designing Your Life: How to Build a Well-Lived Joyful Life* (New York: Alfred A. Knopf, 2016), 199.

4 Tiffany Shlain, Technology Shabbats, http://www.moxieinstitute.org/technology_shabbats.

5 Benyamin Lichtenstein, interview with the author, Jan. 2014.

6 Powers, *Hamlet's BlackBerry*.

7 Brené Brown, *The Gifts of Imperfection: Let Go of Who You Think You're Supposed to Be and Embrace Who You Are* (Center City, MN: Hazelden, 2010).

8   Ibid., 102.

9   MaryAnn McKibben-Dana, *Sabbath in the Suburbs: A Family's Experiment with Holy Time* (St. Louis, MO: Chalice Press, 2012).

CHAPTER 6

1   Erin Bried, *How to Build a Fire and Other Handy Things Your Grandfather Knew* (New York: Ballantine Books, 2010), 251–52.

2   Chögyam Trungpa, *Shambhala: The Sacred Path of the Warrior,* reissue ed. (Boulder, CO: Shambhala, 2007).

3   Lynn Twist, *The Soul of Money: Reclaiming the Wealth of Our Inner Resources* (New York: W. W. Norton, 2003), 43.

4   Rev. Dr. Martin Luther King Jr., *I Have a Dream: Writings and Speeches That Changed the World,* edited by James M. Washington (New York: HarperOne, 1986), 172.

5   Interview with Orit Kent, December 2016.

6   Bruce Feiler, "This Life: The Stories That Bind Us," *New York Times,* Mar. 15, 2013.

7   Jerry Mander, *In the Absence of the Sacred: The Failure of Technology and the Survival of the Indian Nations* (San Francisco: Sierra Books, 1991).

8   See contemporaryjewishlearning.com/conversationstarters. Also see thefamilydinnerproject/conversationstarters.

9   Turkle, *Reclaiming Conversation.*

CHAPTER 7

1   Interview with Shasta Nelson, Nov. 2015.

2   Interview with Ronny Perlman, May 2014.

3   Interview with Odin Zackman, April 2015.

4   Interview with Brigid, Feb. 2016.

5   Interview with Jeffrey, March 2016.

6   Sara Schley, *Secrets of the Seventh Day: How Everyone Can Find Renewal through the Wisdom and Practices of the Sabbath* (Ashland, OR: White Cloud Press, 2014).

7   Thich Nhat Hanh and Lilian Cheung, *Savor: Mindful Eating, Mindful Life* (New York: HarperOne, 2010).

8   Percy Bysshe Shelley, "Ozymandias," in *The Top Five Hundred Poems,* edited by William Harmon (New York: Columbia University Press, 1992), 495.

9   Gary Eberle, *Sacred Time and the Search for Meaning.*

CHAPTER 8

1   Ray Williams, "Workaholism and the Myth of Hard Work," *Psychology Today.* March 15, 2012. psychologytoday.com/blog/wired-success/201203/workaholism-and-the-myth-hard-work>.

2　*The Workaholics Anonymous Book of Recovery,* 1st edition (2005), 11–15. http://www.workaholics-anonymous.org/literature/book-of-recovery. Reprinted with the permission of Workaholics Anonymous World Services Organization. Copyrighted material may not be reproduced in any form without the written permission of the WAWSO.

3　Sonja Haller, *52 Sabbaths.*

4　Richard Louv, *Last Child in the Woods: Saving Our Children from Nature-Deficit Disorder* (Chapel Hill, NC: Algonquin of Chapel Hill, 2006), 64.

5　Interview with Jesse Sachs, Sept. 2016.

6　Mirabai Bush, interviewed by Krista Tippett, *On Being with Krista Tippett,* podcast audio, July 16, 2015.

7　Quote from Rev. Dr. Kirk Byron Jones. Interview December 11, 2015.

8　Robert Kegan and Lisa Lahey, *Immunity to Change: How to Overcome It and Unlock the Potential in Yourself and Your Organization* (Boston: Harvard Business Press, 2009).

9　Interview with Lisa Lahey, Nov. 2015.

10　McKibben-Dana, *Sabbath in the Suburbs.*

11　Kegan and Lahey, *Immunity to Change.*

CHAPTER 9

1　Julia Gifford, "The Secret of the 10% Most Productive People? Breaking!" Blog post. Desktime, August 20, 2014. blog.desktime.com/2014/08/20/the-secret-of-the-10-most-productive-people-breaking/>.

2　Schulte, *Overwhelmed,* 8–20.

3　Katherine Ellison, *Buzz: A Year of Paying Attention* (New York: Voice, 2010).

CHAPTER 10

1　Abby Seixas, *Finding the Deep River Within: A Woman's Guide to Recovering Balance and Meaning in Everyday Life* (San Francisco: Jossey-Bass, 2006).

2　Tara Brach, *True Refuge: Finding Peace and Freedom in Your Own Awakened Heart* (New York: Bantam, 2013).

3　Rachel May Stafford, "Vow to Breathe," *Hands Free Mama,* Jan. 7, 2014, http://www.handsfreemama.com/2014/01/07/vow-to-breathe/.

CHAPTER 11

1　Benjamin Franklin, *The Autobiography of Benjamin Franklin,* edited by Frank Woodworth Pine (New York: Henry Holt and Company, 1922).

2　I learned this metaphor from Rabbi David Lappin, consultant and spiritual teacher.

3　Marshall Goldsmith with Mark Reiter, *Mojo: How to Get It, How to Keep It, How to Get It Back if You Lose It* (New York: Hyperion, 2009), 179–80.

4   Cal Newport, *Deep Work: Rules for Focused Success in a Distracted World* (New York: Grand Central Publishing, 2016).

5   Teresa Amabile and Steven Kramer, *The Progress Principle: Using Small Wins to Ignite Joy, Engagement, and Creativity at Work* (Boston: Harvard Business Review Press, 2011).

6   Michael W. Kraus, Cassy Huang, and Dacher Keltner, "Tactile Communication, Cooperation, and Performance: An Ethological Study of the NBA," *Emotion* 10, vol. 5 (Oct. 2010): 745–49.

CHAPTER 12

1   Tim Kasser, *The High Price of Materialism* (Cambridge, MA: MIT Press, 2002), 9.

2   Paul Piff and Dacher Keltner, "Why Do We Experience Awe?" *New York Times*, May 22, 2015, http://www.nytimes.com/2015/05/24/opinion/sunday/why-do-we-experience-awe.html.

3   Ibid.

4   Dan Buettner, *The Blue Zones: Lessons for Living Longer from the People Who've Lived the Longest* (Washington, DC: National Geographic, 2008).

5   Abraham Joshua Heschel, *God in Search of Man: A Philosophy of Judaism* (New York: Farrar, Strauss, Giroux, 1976).

6   *Tanakh: A New Translation of the Holy Scriptures according to the Traditional Hebrew Text* (Philadelphia: Jewish Publication Society, 1985), 87.

7   Ibid.

8   Thich Nhat Hanh, *Miracle of Mindfulness: An Introduction to the Practice of Meditation* (New York: Beacon Press, 1978).

9   Heschel, *God in Search of Man*, 46.

10 Brach, *True Refuge*.

11 Barbara Brown Taylor, *The Practice of Saying No* (New York: HarperOne, 2012).

12 Dominique Browning, "Losing It," *New York Times Magazine* (March 25, 2010).

13 Sebastian Junger, *Tribe: On Homecoming and Belonging* (New York: Twelve, 2016), 52.

14 Heschel, *The Sabbath*, 28.

Acknowledgments

I began learning about Shabbat when Rabbi Mark Margolius introduced me to a havurah, a Shabbat group at Yale. He started me on this path.

Heartfelt thanks to Rabbi Jim Ponet and Elana Ponet for teaching me how to keep Shabbat and becoming such good friends in the process. They helped me receive this great gift of the Jewish spiritual tradition and discover how to wrestle with it, love it, and live it. And so much appreciation to our friends in Jerusalem whom we shared Shabbat with—Judith and Jeff Green, Susan and Yedidya Fraiman, Avner and Sara Haramati, cousins Carolyn and Jonathan Kornbluth, Jay and Randi Rothman, Deena Rosenfeld and Jeff Friedman, Danny and Hana Matt, Danny Paller and Rachel Freilich, cousin Ronny Perlman and Sonia (of blessed memory), and Robin Twite.

I first called Jane von Mehren, who had been my editor at Penguin Books, hoping for some editorial support for a pamphlet about learning to keep Shabbat. Instead she said, "I think this could be a book." She helped me write the proposal and then brought the book to market as my literary agent. Thank you so much, Jane, for making this happen!

When my editor Leah Miller bought the book for Rodale, I felt as if I had fallen in with a group of fellow travelers. Thank you so much to Leah for guiding the book as it grew to be what it is today. Her sensitivity and creativity show up in every chapter. And the Rodale team was 100 percent behind the book. A big thank you to publisher Gail Gonzales and much gratitude to Jackie Cirelli, Angie Giammarino, and Suzee Skwiot. Anna Cooperberg was practically holding my hand by the end. Thanks to Aly Mostel for her genuine interest and support for the book. And another big thank you to Editorial Director Jennifer Levesque for stepping in as the book was completed.

When I approached creativity consultant Donna Zerner of Portland, Oregon, for assistance, she was immensely supportive and helped me shape the initial vision for the book. Ilene Prusher of Jerusalem read several drafts of the proposal. Becca Steinitz of Arlington, Massachusetts, is a brilliant and compassionate editor who totally got the book, and she is the one who made it readable. Her gifted edits show up on every page.

Benyamin Lichtenstein read many drafts of the book, always offering helpful feedback with savvy and enthusiasm. Russ Eisenstat, who was a key supporter of my first book, was consistent and persistent in his support for this one as well. Thank you!

Deep thanks to the following people who took time out of their busy lives to speak with me about the book: Alan Abbey, Lesley Alderman, Noah Alper, Tova Averbuch, Aya Baron, Dr. Jeremy Benstein, Dror Bondi, Shirley Burdick, Christine Carter, Cidney Carver, Kristin Cobble, Melissa Dinwiddie, Rabbi Tamar Elad-Appelbaum, Judy Feierstein, James Flaherty, Amy Fox, Professor Victor Friedman, Rabbi Ruth Gan Kagan, Professor Emily Hunter, Yacub ibn Yusuf, Professor Tim Kasser, Orit Kent, Alenka Kuhelj, Tim Lawrence, Mark Leach, Judah Levenson, Professor Benyamin Lichtenstein, Lilit Marcus, Rabbi Natan Margalit, Rabbi Marc Margolius, Rabbi Dahlia Marx, Ruth Mason, Evan McGonagil, Rabbi Jessica Minnen, Ali Nazar, Professor Cal Newport, Yoav Peck, Morten Primdahl, Dr. Michael Rich, Deena Rosenfeld, Professor Jay Rothman, Randi Rothman, Jesse Sachs, Rev. Kathryn Schreiber, Brigid Schulte, Jay Schultz, Tony Schwartz, Rabbi Alex Shandrovsky, Tanya Shevitz, Tiffany Shlain, Rabbi Susan Silverman, Harry Spence, Rachel Macy Stafford, Doug Stone, Jeffrey Sweet, Casper Ter Tuile, Rev Emily Thompson, Renee Trudeau, Ayelet Waldman, Joey Waldman, Rabbi Sara Zacharia, and Noam Zion.

Many friends also provided listening ears and moral support during the years of working on the book. Thank you, Karen Erickson, Maxine Freedman, Amy Goldfarb, Michele Gravelle, Pam Hoffman, Jo Hannah Katz, Pam Kogut, Grady McGonigal, Amy Metzenbaum, Nancy Norton, Beth Sandweiss, Abby Seixas, Tom Taylor, Joel Yanowitz, and Ronit and David Ziv-Kreger,

Many thanks to Yossi Abramowitz, Amy Goldfarb, Pam Kogut, Benyamin Lichtenstein, Amy Metzenbaum, Greg Nelson, Shasta Nelson, Ronny Perlman, Jesse Sachs, Austin Salzwedel, Susan Silverman, Harry Spence, Casper Ter Tuile, Brigid Williams, and Odin Zackman for allowing me to use their stories.

A big thank you to Noam Zion for sharing his extensive knowledge about Shabbat resources. Thank you to Lisa Lahey for helping me frame her work on immunity to change for an oasis in time. Sheila Heen gave encouragement, and Rabbi Marc Baker always made me feel like I was on the right track. Thank you to Rabbi Menachem Creditor for offering unstinting inspiration as the going got tough.

My author support group is made up of dear friends Rabbi David Jaffe and Janette Hillis-Jaffe and my husband David Peter Stroh. Thank you so much for your support, amazing listening, and all the wisdom that you share in so many ways.

Rusty Shelton and Shelby Janner of Zilker Media came on board to bring their brilliant PR support. Jared Wood of Berkeley, California, provided top-notch editing and web design support. And Ben Norton gave consistently helpful social media support.

Many thanks and much love to my brother, David Paul, who met me weekly as a study partner at the Lindgren Cafe in Berkeley, helping me muster the energy and focus to keep going when writing was hard. Gratitude to Tina Saadi for helping out in so many ways.

Betsy Cohen Kallus provided invaluable friendship and support. Many thanks to her, Menachem and Yochanan for so many amazing Shabbat meals in Jerusalem. Patricia Sanders was ever available with deep empathy, loving friendship, and pointed coaching.

What can I say to my beloved family? Thank you for being there for me all the way. Ari, you are so much fun, and you have found a multitude of ways to make our oasis in time work for you. And David, you continue to be my constant support, reading draft after draft of this book, listening to many versions of so many ideas, sharing our oases in time, and being my life learning partner. I am so blessed!

Index

A

Abramowitz, Yosef, 17
Accepting tool, 144
Accomplishments, 75, 194, 206–8
Accountability, 203–6
Addicted to Hurry (Jones), 150
Addictions, 141–46, 171
Alan (physician), 4–5
Alcohol abuse, with stress, 8
Alper, Noah, 15
Amabile, Teresa, 207
Amen, Daniel, 85–86
American Diabetes Association, 8
American Institute of Stress, 5
American Psychological Association, 7, 9
Artistic oasis in time, 126–27
Asking tool, 144
Attention paid to work, 193
    with balance, 196
    challenges of, 194
    with character traits, 195
    with honesty, 195
    with order, 195
    with patience, 195
    with trust, 196
    with truth, sincerity, and integrity, 195
    values relating to, 194–95
Awareness, 62–63, 75, 134–35
Awe
    definition of, 211
    experience of, 210, 211–14
    Heschel on, 212, 214
    humility and, 211
    nourished by, 211–14

B

Back to Earth program, 149–50
Balancing tool, 144
Banks, Amy, 11
Barbara (lawyer), 5–6, 7
Begin and end, of oasis time, 38, 44, 120
    cues for, 104
    example of, 101
    plan for, 100–101
    rituals with, 42–43, 102–4

Belonging, 217–20
Big why, 58
    awareness relating to, 62–63, 75
    costs relating to, 61 62
    fatigue spiral relating to, 63–65, 68
    personal reasons for, 59–60
    purpose, for change relating to, 61
Bittman, Mark, 16
Blue laws, 25–26, 27
Blue Zones, The (Buettner), 212
Boundaries
    choices with, 174
    dance of, 190–91
    habit of, 175
    slippage of, 189–91
    of Susan, 175, 178–83
Boundaries, strengthening of, 175–77
    in action, 184–91
    emotional, 181–82
    mental, 179–80
    physical, 178–79
    by saying no, 186 87
    with SMART agreements, 184–86
    spiritual, 183–84
Boundary setting
    motivations for, 177–78
    through self-care, 188–89
    struggle with, 175–78
Brach, Tara, 181, 215
Brainstorm, 89–90, 119
Breaks
    commitment to, 84, 86
    from daily life, 14, 15, 16, 21
    midweek, 125
    need for, 5–6, 36, 57, 155, 161, 162
    oasis time with, 95, 99, 138, 143, 145
    replenishment with, 169, 172, 180, 188, 191
    rest with, 18, 79
    rhythm with, 20, 51
    sneaking in, 164–65, 167, 168
    tips for, 189
    from work week, 24, 32–33, 38, 136

Brown, Brené, 90–92
Brown, Steve, 90–92
Brown, Stuart, 55
Browning, Dominique, 217
Buchanan, Mark, 12
Buddhist practice
    emotional reactivity relating to, 215
    uposatha as, 23
Buddy. *See also* Productivity buddy
    for oasis design craft support, 83–85
    for Sabbath, 41, 83, 84, 107, 166
Buettner, Dan, 8–9, 212
Burnett, Bill, 85
Burnout costs, 11–13
Bush, Mirabai, 150
Busting Your Corporate Idol (Marcus), 156
Busyness, 75, 214, 219, 220
Buzz (Ellison), 166

C

Callan, Erin, crisis of, 66
Carnegie, Dale, 74
Casting Lots (Silverman), 129
Change, immunity to, 150–53
Chaplin, Charlie, 3–4
Chasing Daylight (O'Kelly), 70
Choices
    with actions, 169–72
    about addictions, 171
    with boundaries, 174
    change mind, 169
    of new habits, 172–74, 192
    power of, 172
    with responsibilities, 170
Christian Sabbath, 23–24
Chronic illness, with stress, 7
Chronic stress, 7, 9
"Circle Day" of rest, 124–25
Claxton, Guy, 147
Climbing Jacob's Ladder (Morinis), 196
Cognitive restructuring, 73–74
Commitments, 87–88, 151, 153–57
Community. *See also* Food and community
    connectedness with, 220
    oasis design craft support of, 84–85
Competing commitments, 151
    big assumption relating to, 154–57
    core motivations for, 153–54
    unearthing of, 153–57
Complete and celebrate accomplishments,
    194, 206–8
Connectedness
    belonging and, 217–20
    with community, 220
    disconnectedness relating to, 218
    experiences of, 210, 211, 217–20
    external forces and, 220

of food and community, 128
    with friendships, 220
    loneliness relating to, 218
    missing of, 220
    of modern society, 218
    with neighbors, 218–19
    resource books for, 241–42
Contemporary Sabbath, 34–35
Conversational skills, 116–18
Costs
    of big why, 61–62
    of burnout, 11–13
    health, of stress, 7–9
    of technology, 9–11
Covey, Stephen, 194
Craft support, for oasis design, 81,
    83–86
    buddy for, 83–85
    from community, 84–85
    Schley on, 83
Crew, Rudy, 187
Crises, 58
    of Callan, 66
    of Huffington, 65–66
    with illness, 67–68
    of Iyer, 66–67
Csikszentmihaly, Mihaly, 56
Culture
    consumer, 242
    of productivity, 5, 7, 74–75

D

Death, 58, 243
    illness and, 71–73
    learning from, 69–72
    Perfect Moments relating to, 71–72
    regrets with, 73
    sacred time relating to, 70
DeskTime software, 161
Diabetes, 8, 9
Diamond Cutter, The, 124
Digital technology, 9–11
Disconnectedness, 146, 218
Disconnect to connect, with oasis time, 38,
    100, 120
    examples of, 106–7
    with others, 44–46
    plan to connect, 106–7
    plan to unplug, 104–6
    preparation for, 104–6
    with something greater, 46–47
Downshifting weekly
    benefits of, 13–17
    companies with policies of, 14
    Sabbath relating to, 15
    types of, 15
Downtime benefits, 7

E

Earthquake preparedness, 219
Eat, Move, Sleep (Rath), 161–62
Eat, Pray, Love (Gilbert), 52
Eberle, Gary, 139
Edlund, Matthew, 53
Ellison, Katherine, 166–67, 169
Emotional boundaries, 181–82
Emotional resilience
  contentment with, 216
  experiences of, 210–11, 214–17
  happiness with, 210, 214, 216
  joy with, 217
  natural flow with, 215
  peace with, 216
  reactivity with, 215
Energy, 61, 63
  of Goodman, 14
  limited, 67–68, 148
  oasis time and, 40
  positive, 18, 64
  renewal of, 20, 28, 40, 42, 43, 44, 48, 55
  Schwartz on, 12–13
  take stock of, 161
Evans, Dave, 85
Everyday Healing (Hillis-Jaffe), 109
Examined Life, The (Grosz), 67
Experiences. *See* Oasis time experiences
Experiment, with oasis design, 81, 92–95
  middle ground with, 93
  rules replaced with discernment, 93–95

F

Fatigue spiral
  acknowledgment of, 63
  consequences of, 64
  renewal cycle for, 64, 68
  sleep and, 64–65
52 Sabbaths (Haller), 43, 146–47
Finding the Deep River Within (Seixas), 177
Five Key Practices
  complete and celebrate, 194, 206–8
  make trade-offs consciously, 193, 196–200
  pay attention to how you work, 193, 194–96
  use transitions purposefully, 194, 200–203
  work with productivity buddy, 194, 203–6
Flame of Attention, The (Krishnamurti), 63
Food and community. *See also* Meals
  ample dessert, 129–30
  with Betsy, 128–29
  connections of, 128
  for oasis time, 128–30
  potluck lunch, 129
  with Schley, 129–30
  shared brunch, 128–29
Francis (pope), 31
Frankfurter, Felix, 26
Frankl, Viktor, 169–70
Franklin, Benjamin, 195
Fritz, Charles, 218
Full Circle (Callan), 66

G

Gaia (Mother Earth), 214
Gateways. *See* Oasis time gateways
Gifts of Imperfection, The (Brown, B.), 91
Gilbert, Elizabeth, 52
Gilday, Cindy, 118
Goldsmith, Marshall, 204
Goodman, Tamir, 14
Good Samaritan experiment, 48
Grosz, Stephen, 67

H

Haller, Sonja, 43, 146–47
Hallowell, Edward, 45
Hamlet's BlackBerry (Powers), 15–16, 88–89
Hands Free Mama (Stafford), 189
Hanson, Rick, 46–47
Happiness, 210, 214, 216
Havdalah, as end of Shabbat, 138
Health costs, of stress, 7–9
"Healthy Mind Platter" (Rock and Siegel), 15
Heschel, Abraham Joshua, 53
  on awe, 212, 214
  books by, 82, 127
  on palace of time, 15, 19, 183
  on Shabbat, 15, 19, 27–28, 221
Higher Progress, 27, 31
Hillis-Jaffe, Janette, 109
How the Way We Talk Can Change the Way We Work (Kegan and Lahey), 151
How to Stop Worrying and Start Living (Carnegie), 74
Huffington, Arianna, 16
  crisis of, 66–67
Hunnicutt, Benjamin Kline, 27
Hyman, Mark, 85–86

I

Ideas generated, for oasis design, 81
  brainstorm, 89–90, 119
  joy and meaning with, 90–92
Illness, 7
  crisis of, 67–68
  death and, 70–72
  with lack of time off, 18–19

Inner strength, cultivation of, 81
   with belief, 87–88
   with commitment, 87–88
   with courage and determination, 89
   with grit, 86–87
   self-efficacy relating to, 87
   with tenacity, 88–89
Insomnia, with stress, 8
Intelligence in the Flesh (Claxton), 147
In the Absence of Sacred (Mander), 118
It Can't Be True, 135
Iyer, Pico, crisis of, 66–67

J

James (musician), 6–7
Jeffrey (graduate student)
   Catholic wife of, 127
   God relationship with, 127–28
   as Quaker, 127
   Sabbath observance of, 127–28
Jewish Sabbath. *See* Shabbat
Jones, Kirk Byron, 150
Journal, 163
Joy and meaning, 90–92, 217
Al-Jumu'ah as Muslim observation, of
      Sabbath, 24
Junger, Sebastian, 218

K

Kegan, Robert, 151, 156–57
Keltner, Dacher, 211
Kent, Orit, 117
Krishnamurti, Jiddu, 63, 125

L

Lahey, Lisa Laskow, 151, 153, 156–57
Lamott, Anne, 47
Last Child in the Woods (Louv), 148–49
Laudato Si: On care for Our Common Home,
    31
Laws, for Sabbath, 25–26, 27
Layla (interior designer), 6, 7
Leisure, 31
   activities for, 3
   Pieper on, 32–33, 34
   Sabbath for, 32
Leisure as the Basis of Culture (Pieper),
    32–33
Leisure confetti, 163, 169
Let go of achieving, with oasis time
   to play, 38, 51, 55–56, 115–16
   preparation for, 113–15
   to reflect, 38, 51, 54–55, 116–19
   to rest, 38, 51, 53–54, 115, 210
   tools for, 115
Lichtenstein, Benyamin, 87

Lieberman, Joseph, 15
Loehr, Jim, 56–57
Loneliness, 8, 218
Long-term stress, 9
Louv, Richard, 148–49

M

Management
   for purposeful transitions, 200
   of stress behavior, 9
Mander, Jerry, 118
Marcus, Greg, 156
McKibben, Bill, 31
McKibben-Dana, MaryAnn, 95, 151–52
Meals
   advanced planning for, 108–9
   cooperative cleanup with, 111–13
   easy food for, 109
   food prep for, 110–11
   gracious guest for, 111–12
   herbs with, 110
   hosting of, 108–13
   late-night snack, 133–34
   Shabbat dinner, 40, 82, 83, 107,
    109
   tidy home with, 112–13
Meditation, 17–18, 74, 145
Mental boundaries, 179–80
Merton, Thomas, 12
Minnen, Jessica, 107
Modern Times, 3–4
Mojo (Goldsmith), 204
Morinis, Alan, 196
Moses, burning bush and, 213
Motivations
   for boundary setting, 177–78
   for competing commitments, 153–54

N

Natural rhythms
   breath relating to, 148
   of core self, 148
   disconnection with, 146
   of our bodies, 146, 147
   out of touch with, 146–50
Navigation, of days, 192–93. *See also* Five
    Key Practices
   for oasis time, 208–9
Navigation dashboard, 201–3
Needs
   for breaks, 5–6, 36, 57, 155, 161, 162
   for oasis time, 19–21, 31
   unmet, 81–83
Nelson, Shasta
   Greg as husband of, 122
   guiding values of, 122

Sabbath activities and, 122–23
Seventh-day Adventist tradition of,
    122
Nhat Hanh, Thich, 135, 214
No Excuses! (Tracy), 73
Nurturing haven, 210
Nurturing tool, 144–45

O

Oasis, design of
  craft support for, 81, 83–86
  experiment with, 81, 92–95
  ideas generated for, 81, 89–92
  imagination with, 79–80
  inner strength cultivated, 81, 86–89
  practice developed for, 81, 95–97
  for Sara, 80–81
  say yes with, 82–83
  unmet needs relating to, 81–83
Oasis time, 34, 36
  breaks with, 95, 99, 138, 143, 145
  decluttering for, 113
  energy and, 40
  navigation practices for, 208–9
  need for, 19–21, 31
  obstacles to, 157
  preparation for, 104–6, 113–15, 119–20
  renewal with, 37, 210
  with Sabbath, 37
  solidifying resolve for, 75–76
  for transformation, 210
  weekly time off and, 19–21
  of Zackman, 124–25
Oasis time, living it, 121
  in afternoon, 136–37
  artistic oasis in time, 126–27
  beginning of, 132
  in evenings, 132–33
  with family reading, 135
  food and community, 128–30
  island in storm, 124–25
  letting go of work temptations, 136
  in mornings, 134
  ours, 130–38
  with outdoor time, 137–38
  pockets emptied, 131–32
  real day off, 123–24
  remembering what really matters,
    122–23
  with stories, 137–38
  storm before calm, 130–31
  taste of heaven, 127–28
  unexpected oasis moments, 138–40
  unwinding with, 133
  waking up with awareness and gratitude,
    134–35

Oasis time, traction for
  big why, 58, 59–65, 68, 75
  catalyst, of personal crisis, 58
  way of living, 58
Oasis time experiences
  awe, 210, 211–14
  connectedness, 210, 211, 217–20
  emotional resilience, 210, 214–17
Oasis time experiments
  block off time, 223
  debrief, 224
  describe your vision, 223
  do it again next week, 224
  end with flourish, 224
  get curious, 223
  get ready, 224
  live oasis time, 224
  plan something different, 224
  slow down, 224
  unplug, 224
  write chosen activity on calendar, 224
Oasis time gateways, 57, 80. *See also* Begin
    and end, of oasis time; Disconnect to
    connect, with oasis time; Let go of
    achieving, with oasis time; Slow
    down, to savor oasis time
  plan for, 99–100
  protect and prepare, 37, 38–42, 98–99
Oasis time mini-guide
  close up shop, 227
  delicious food arrangement, 226
  festive atmosphere creation, 227
  guidance for, 225
  nourishing, renewing activities set up,
    226
  oasis time, end, 228
  oasis time, entering of, 228
  oasis time, immerse in, 228
  plan activities, for children and
    dependents, 226
  prepare mind, heart, and spirit, 226
  prepare your space, 227
Oasis time reflection, 38, 51, 54–55
  for children, 118–19
  conversational skills for, 117–19
  with family stories, 118–19
  with meaningful conversations, 116–18
O'Kelly, Eugene, 69–71
Ornish, Dean, 85
Overdrive, living in
  burnout costs, 11–13
  health costs, of stress, 7–9
  technology costs, 9–11
  working too hard, 4–7
Overwhelmed (Schulte), 48, 163
Oz, Mehmet, 85–86

P

Palace of time, 15, 19, 183
Panigrosso, Marissa, 67
Perfect Moments, 70–71
Perlman, Ronny
  on Friday afternoons, 123
  as peace activist, 123, 124
  as refugee, 123
  as retiree, 123
  on Saturdays, 123–24
  in Tel Aviv, 123
Physical boundaries, 178–79
Pieper, Josef, 32–33, 34
Piff, Paul, 211
Plan
  to connect, 106–7
  for meals, 108–9
  for purposeful transitions, 200–201
  to unplug, 104–6
Plan, for oasis time, 40–41. See also Begin
    and end, of oasis time
  with gateways, 99–100
  rituals for, 102–4
Play
  with oasis time, 38, 51, 55–56, 115–16
  as Workaholics Anonymous tool, 143–44
Playing tool, 143–44
Plisken, Zelig (rabbi), 47
Positive energy, 18, 64
Power, of choices, 172
Power of Rest, The (Edlund), 53
Powers, William, 15–16, 20, 88–89
Practice development, for oasis design, 81
  cultivation relating to, 96–97
  oasis "muscles" built for, 95–96
Practice of Saying No, The (Taylor), 216–17
Preparation, for oasis time, 104–6, 113–15,
    119–20. See also Protect and
    prepare, for oasis time
Primdahl, Morten, 14
Proactivity, 169–72
Productivity
  culture of, 5, 7, 74–75
  reactivity to, 193
Productivity buddy, 194
  for accountability, 203–6
  check-in with, 205
  for partnership, 204
Progress Principle, The (Amabile), 207
Protect and prepare, for oasis time, 37,
    38–42, 98–99
  make a plan, 40–41, 99–104
  say no, 39–40
  seek validation and reinforcement, 41
  start small, 40
  why relating to, 39
Pursuit of Loneliness, The (Slater), 30

R

RAIN, 181
Rath, Tom, 161–62
Reactivity, productivity to, 193
Reclaiming Conversation (Turkle), 10
Religious tradition, of Sabbath, 22
Renewal
  cycle, for fatigue spiral, 64, 68
  of energy, 20, 28, 40, 42, 43, 44, 48, 55
  with oasis time, 37, 210
Resource books
  on community, family, and connection,
    241–42
  on consumer culture, 242
  on creativity, 242
  on environment and nature, 242
  on facing death, 243
  on health, well-being, and personal
    growth, 243
  on overwhelm, 243
  on philosophy, 244
  on philosophy of time, 244
  on productivity, 244
  on Sabbath and Shabbat, 245
  on social action, 245
Resources
  Apps, 248
  Websites, 247
Rest
  beliefs, 73–75
  with breaks, 18, 79
  "Circle Day" of, 124–25
  freedom and, with Jewish Sabbath,
    28–30
  with oasis time, 38, 51, 53–54, 115, 210
  rhythm of, 68, 162
  "Restoring the Character Ethic," 194
Rhythm. See also Natural rhythms
  with breaks, 20, 51
  if rest, 68, 162
Rituals, 42–43, 83, 102–4
Roberts, David, 68–69
Rock, David, 15
Rollman, Dan, 34–35, 105
Rudd, Melanie, 46

S

Sabbath. See also Shabbat
  buddy for, 41, 83, 84, 107, 166
  commentary on, 32
  contemporary, 34–35
  Iyer on, 67
  al-Jumu'ah as Muslim observation, 24
  laws relating to, 25–26
  for leisure, 32
  in Middle Ages, 25
  oasis time with, 37

purpose of, 27–30
reconsideration of, 35
religious tradition of, 22
ritual with, 83
stopping work for, 27–30, 34–35
uposatha, as Buddhist practice, 23
weekly time off for, 17–20
Sabbath, Christian view of, 23–24
  with contemporary Christian living and
    worship, 229
  with Simple 7, 229–38
Sabbath, The (Heschel), 82
Sabbath in the Suburbs (McKibben-Dana),
  95, 152
Sabbath Manifesto, 34–35, 105
Sabbath World, The (Shulevitz), 26
Sachs, Jesse, 149–50
Sacred, sense of, 211
Sacred time, 24, 25, 36, 69, 213
Sacred Time and the Search for Meaning
  (Eberle), 139
Savor (Nhat Hanh), 135
Saying no, 39–40, 186–87
Saying yes, 82–83
Schevitz, Tanya, 10
Schley, Sara, 83, 129–30
Schrader, Dave, 13
Schulte, Brigid, 48, 75, 163, 169
Schwartz, Tony, 12–13
Secrets of the Seventh Day (Schley), 83
Seixas, Abby, 177
Self-care, with boundary setting,
  188–89
Seven Habits of Highly Effective People
  (Covey), 194
Shabbat, 32
  Havdalah as end of, 138
  as Hebrew word for Sabbath, 22, 29
  Heschel on, 15, 19, 27–28, 221
  meals for, 40, 82, 83, 107, 109
  observance of, 25, 87, 93–94, 96, 97, 107,
    123, 130
  rest and freedom with, 28–30
Shargaa, Jill, 211
Shelley, Percy Bysshe, 139
Shlain, Tiffany, 43, 86
Shoe removal, 213
Shulevitz, Judith, 26
Siegel, Daniel, 15
Silva, Jason, 46
Silverman, Susan, 129
Simple 7
  for disciples of Jesus, 238
  Sabbath, 229, 239–40
  Scripture Reading, 229
  Seeking God in Prayer, 229
  Service, 229

Spiritual Friendship, 229
Stewardship, 229
Sunday Worship, 229
Slater, Philip, 30
Sleep, fatigue spiral and, 64–65
Sleep-deprived, 6
Slow down, to savor oasis time, 38, 120
  activities for, 107–8
  Adam and, 49
  "Good Samaritan" experiment relating
    to, 48
  hosting meals relating to, 108–13
  for new mothers, 50–51
  racing mind relating to, 47–48
SMART agreements, 184–86
Soul of Money, The (Twist), 116
Spence, Harry, agreement of, 187–88
Spiritual boundaries, 183–84
Stafford, Rachel Macy, 189–90
Stress
  chronic, 7, 9
  health costs of, 7–9
  long-term, 9
  management behavior for, 9
  symptoms of, 8
Stress, causes of, 5
  alcohol abuse as, 8
  chronic illness as, 7
  insomnia as, 8
Susan (friend)
  boundary setting of, 175
  emotional boundaries of, 181–82
  focus ability of, 179
  lack of sleep of, 176
  mental boundaries of, 179–81
  physical boundaries of, 178–79
  spiritual boundaries of, 183
  stress of, 177
  teenagers of, 176–77

T

Take stock
  of breaks, 161–62
  of energy, 161
  of focusing patterns, 168–69
Take stock, of time, 161–62
  with ATracker, 165
  with hourly check-in, 166
  with Hours, 165
  with journal, 163
  by listing all commitments,
    166–67
  tools for, 164–67
  by tracking every fifteen minutes,
    164–65
  by tracking unfolding activities, 165
Taylor, Barbara Brown, 216–17

Technology
    alternatives to, 105
    costs of, 9–11
    digital, 9–11
    downside of, 9–10
Technology Shabbat (Shlain), 43, 86
Ter Kuile, Casper, 82–83
Thinker, The, 54
Thompson, Erica, 229
Time. *See also* Oasis time; Take stock, of
        time; Weekly time off
    assessment of, 201
    palace of, 15, 19, 183
    sacred, 24, 25, 36, 69, 213
    speeded-up, 3
    tracking, 164–65
    vacation, 5–6
Tools. *See also* Workaholics Anonymous
        tools
    for oasis time, 115
    for take stock, of time, 164–67
Tracking time, 164–65
Tracy, Brian, 74
Trade-offs made consciously, 193
    easy and quick actions relating to, 197–98
    with focus, 197
    with if-then statements, 198–99, 200
    priming relating to, 198, 200
    priorities relating to, 196
    procrastination relating to, 197
    with reprioritizing, 197
    with self-talking, 199
    with three-minute triage, 199
Transitions purposeful use, 194
    with management, 200
    with navigation dashboard, 201–3
    with planning, 200–201
    with time assessment, 201
Tribe (Junger), 218
True Refuge (Brach), 181
Turkle, Sherry, 10
Twist, Lynne, 116

U

Underscheduling tool, 143
Unmet needs, 81–83
Uposatha, as Buddhist practice, 23

V

Vacation time, 5–6
Vaillant, George, 45–46
Values, 122, 194–95
Vanderkam, Laura, 161

W

Waldinger, Robert, 45–46
Ware, Bronnie, 72
Weekly time off
    illness with lack of, 18–19
    meditation relating to, 17–18
    oasis time as, 19–21
    Sabbath relating to, 17–20
*What the Most Successful People Do on the
        Weekend* (Vanderkam), 161
Williams, Brigid
    as Boston architect, 126
    painting activity of, 126
    weekend oasis time of, 126–27
Wired to Connect (Banks), 11
Work. *See also* Attention paid to work
    as addiction, 141–46
    with productivity buddy, 194, 203–6
    rest beliefs and, 73–75
    rest rhythm and, 68, 162
    temptations relating to, 136
Work, stopping of
    dictators relating to, 30–31
    history of, 22–27
    for leisure, 31–33
    for Sabbath, 27–30, 34–35
Workaholic, 141–42, 145
Workaholics Anonymous tools, 146
    accepting, 144
    asking, 144
    balancing, 144
    meditation, 145
    nurturing, 144–45
    playing, 143–44
    underscheduling, 143
Workdays, 192–93
Working too hard
    Alan, 4–5, 7
    Barbara, 5–6, 7
    James, 6–7
    Layla, 6, 7
Work week breaks, 24, 32–33, 38, 136

Z

Zackman, Odin
    demanding job of, 124–25
    FOMO of, 125
    Wednesday oasis time of, 124–25
Zion, Noam, 24
Ziv-Kreger, Ronit, 119